CALL ME
'YOUR LADYSHIP'

The Secret History of a Rhondda Girl

Catherine Osborn

All paper used in the printing of this book has been made from
wood grown in managed, sustainable forests.

ISBN: 978-1-78003-865-0

Printed and published in the UK

Author Essentials Ltd
4 The Courtyard
South Street
Falmer
BN1 9PQ

A catalogue record of this book is available from
the British Library

Cover design by Jacqueline Abromeit

ACKNOWLEDGMENTS

A heartfelt thanks to members of the Life Story class at the U3A in Hampstead for their support and encouragement. Also, a very special thanks to Caroline Natzler of the City Literary Institute for her help in getting my book into shape.

Also by Catherine Osborn

For children:

Behind The Attic Door

The Image Of Jonathan Plum And Other Stories

The Monster Of Hagstone Hall

For adults:

Tales Of Mischief And Menace

INTRODUCTION

The idea of a life story started during a session with a psychotherapist. Difficult questions confronted me, like: why have I made such a muddle of my life? What, if anything, have I achieved? Have I reached a mid-life crisis but in old age?

So, in an effort to make sense of the muddle, I began my life story, joining a class at the U3A to help achieve this task, and obtaining much encouragement in the process.

This then is in part a psychological study of growth and change over the years both in myself and in the society that helped shape me – a story of then and now.

Catherine Osborn
May 2013

CONTENTS

Continued…

PART 4
Heartaches, Homes And Helpers 1966–1974

PART 5
Love, Marriage, Death ~

SCENES FROM A WELSH CHILDHOOD

1935–1950

THEN AND NOW

CHAPTER ONE

JOURNEY BACK TO CHILDHOOD

(November 2011)

"So, you feel you've achieved nothing?"

Her voice is cool, matter of fact, with a hint of German in the clipped tones. She sits there, facing me, notebook on lap, waiting for me to speak.

I feel my face grow hot as I fiddle with my handkerchief, crumpling it, tugging at the corners, thinking, I've already talked too much. I came because I can't damn well sleep. But what do I do? Give her my life history, whinge on about living alone, with the constant fear of *dying* alone. What a wimp! All I need are a few sleeping pills.

I stick the hankie into my bag and snap it shut. Accept it, I tell myself. The world is full of ageing widows in the same boat. Join the club.

She looks at me quizzically a moment, strokes her chin and says softly, "You don't seem to have done so badly. You pulled yourself out of poverty, in spite of obstacles, got yourself through university, took up a worthwhile career, even married a man with a knighthood."

"No merit on my part," I say. "*He* was the one with the knighthood. I merely married him."

"Still, it must have been interesting."

There is a pause while I consider this. My first marriage wasn't without its perks, I suppose, what with invitations to St James's, chats with cabinet ministers, meeting the Queen...

"It was a mistake," I mumble, "He was a good man, but I married him on the rebound. I didn't love him."

1

"And he died. Of course he was so much older than you."
Her voice is non-judgmental.

Another pause – a longer one this time. My eye strays to
the clock on the wall. Half past ten. Another half hour to go.
But perhaps I'll leave early. Make some excuse. I should never
have come in the first place. If I haven't solved my problems
at my age, I might as well give up.

She scribbles something in her notebook, a shaft of grey-
brown hair falling onto her forehead. She flicks it back and
smiles. "You've mentioned death a lot today. Have you always
been preoccupied with thoughts of death?"

"Perhaps."

"How old were you when these thoughts first began? Do
you remember?"

"Three, I think."

She raises her eyebrows, but soon her face settles into its
former state of repose. "Tell me what happened. Can you take
yourself back to that time and be that child again?"

Right. Here we go. All problems stem from childhood,
upbringing. How come I get stuck with a Freudian analyst? If
she starts blathering on about *denial* or *repression*, I shall throw
up.

However… I'd best cooperate. I've *paid* enough.

I do as she says. Close my eyes and let the years roll back.
Back to a day in1938. I'm called *Shirley* then, not *Catherine* and
I'm three, living in a Welsh mining valley, and standing in my
grandmother's garden.

The garden was at the back of the house, the grass so long it
reached my waist. I remember its cool and wispy feel against
my legs as I ran about in it.

I liked it better than the garden next door. There the grass
was short. Mr Lloyd kept cutting it and planting flowers. They
grew in a tidy border round the garden but you couldn't run
about in it, as you could in ours.

Gran was too old to cut the grass or plant flowers. It didn't matter. We had lots of dandelions and daisies, so you could make daisy-chains. Cousin Joan showed me how to do it.

At the bottom of the garden, there were pretty red flowers all in a tangle together. Gran called them *tea-roses*. And at the top end stood my favourite flower. It came right up to my chin and had big yellow petals which hung down and had a pattern on them. "It's a tiger-lily," Gran said. We didn't know where it came from but I hoped it would stay. It was my special friend.

I stood close to Tiger-Lily, touching its velvety petals ever so gently so I didn't hurt them.

Then I heard Gran call me from the kitchen. "Shirley!"

I said goodbye to Tiger-Lily and ran into the back-yard, up the steps and into the kitchen. Gran was standing there in her flowery apron waiting for me. I saw tears in her eyes. She took my hand and we went together into the front room.

"Grandpa's ready now," she said, "ready for you to say 'goodbye'."

She picked me up and carried me towards a kind of shelf at the back of the room. On the shelf was a long wooden box with shiny handles.

Gran held me over it so I could see Grandpa lying inside. A gauzy thing like the veil on Mam's hat covered his face. Gran drew it aside to show me how nice and peaceful he looked.

"He's on the way to Heaven now," she said.

"He'll be happy there, won't he, Gran?"

"Oh yes. Everyone's happy in Heaven."

She put me down, and I ran back into the garden to talk to Tiger-lily.

"Grandpa's dead," I said, "and I've cried loads, me and Gran together – on the rocking-chair. I hope Gran doesn't go off to Heaven, even though Heaven's so nice. I want her to stay with me. Forever." I kissed Tiger-Lily's petals. "I want

3

you to stay too, Tiger-Lily. You're my friend, my special friend."

I stop reminiscing, my mind jumping forward to the present. I smile to myself. Friendship with a flower! How quaint is that?

The psychotherapist looks up from her notes. "Wasn't it scary seeing your grandpa in his coffin?"

"Not at all. It seemed quite natural." I sigh. "It's not death that scares me. It's *dying*. Alone. Grandpa wasn't alone."

She takes her glasses off, polishes them, and waits for me to continue.

I stay silent.

She gazes at me through her polished glasses and asks, "Were you lonely being an only child?"

"I was a bit, until the evacuees came. I used to whine to Gran, 'I haven't got anyone to play with'. I'd pester her then to play Snap or Ludo with me. She often did."

"Tell me more about Gran. Was it she, mainly, who brought you up?"

"Yes. Her name was Margaret Ann, but everyone called her Maggie. She was short, stocky, a typical old lady of those days, grey hair in a bun, black dress…"

I pause, letting my mind drift back, this time to 1942 (wartime) when I'm nearly seven. It's Monday and I'm with my grandmother in the back room…

Gran sat on the rocking-chair, the wooden rockers going 'creak, creak', as she rocked backwards and forwards. She had taken her piny off and wore the black dress that smelt of cough-sweets. A hair-pin stuck out from her bun. Her eyes were closed.

"Thank God for a good rest," she said. "I'm tired out." Yawning, she leaned back further in the chair.

She'd been washing clothes out in the backyard. That's why she was tired. Then, it started raining so she'd brought them in to dry, hanging them on the clothesline above the firegrate: stays, petticoats, my yellow dress…

Every Monday in school holidays, I liked to plonk down on the step in the backyard and watch as she bent over the tub full of froth and bubbles. It was fun to see her thumping all those clothes that swished about in the water. She did it with a big wooden thing called a dolly. She scrubbed the clothes first on a board with shiny grooves. It stood against the inside of the tub. Gran called it a wash-board.

"Let me have a go with the dolly, Gran," I'd plead. But her answer was always, "Time enough for that, *Cariad*."

Her eyes still shut, and her hands red from wringing out the clothes, she went on rocking. I wanted to climb on her lap. It felt soft and comfy there. I liked it when she cuddled me and told me stories.

I stood, watching her for a while, staring at the brown spots on her face and the wrinkles around her mouth. Then I thought, she's had her rest now. I'll get on her lap.

I did, nestling against the folds of her dress smelling of cough-sweets. "Tell me a story, Gran."

Gran opened her eyes. They were light-blue, and the white bits, yellowy, almost as yellowy as her skin. "Can't get much rest with you around, can I?" she said. She tut-tutted and shook her head. But then she smiled, and I knew it was okay.

"What sort of story do you want then, *Bach*?"

"Tell me about Grandpa. About how you met him, and got married."

She clicked her tongue. "I've told you that story ten times, if I've told you once."

"Tell me again."

"Oh, all right then." And so Gran told me once more the story of her and Grandpa.

"I was a widow when I met him," she began. "My first husband, Jack Williams, died of consumption, see, and left me with two little children, your Uncle Tom and your Auntie

5

Blod. He didn't have any money to leave us, so I had to go out sewing. But they were hard times and there wasn't much work to be had. Even when there was, the money was so poor that me and the little ones often went hungry."

She stopped and I saw her eyes get watery.

"Then Grandpa comes," I reminded her.

"Yes. Tom Stephens, your grandpa, wanted me to be his best girl. But I wasn't sure."

"Was it because they called him Tom the Terror?"

"No, no. And it wasn't the miners calling him that. It was them at the top. He went to jail, see, love, during the riots when miners went on strike for a decent wage. To the big-nobs him and his friends were 'trouble-makers'. But they only wanted to keep the roofs over their heads and have food in their bellies."

She paused again, her lips tightening.

I grew impatient for the next part. "Now tell me about him asking to marry you."

Gran looked at me, sternly. "Who's telling this story, me or you?" She got up. "D'you want a glass of pop and a biscuit?" She stepped into the pantry at the far side of the room.

Soon, we were sitting together on the rocking-chair again, sipping drinks and eating biscuits. In between, Gran carried on with her story.

"Well, I didn't exactly love your grandpa, but I got fond of him, just the same. One day I asked him in for a cup of tea. While we were there, little Tom, your uncle, started to cry. 'When are we going to eat, Mam?' he asked. 'We haven't eaten all day, and me and Blod are starving.'

"Well, I had nothing in the house, not even a loaf. Jobs had been scarce, see, and I was too proud to ask for help. But I couldn't bear to see the little ones cry. And it wasn't long before I was crying too.

"The next thing was, your grandpa had jumped up and was out of the front door without a word. In half an hour he was

6

back again, with a load of shopping – bread, meat, potatoes…"

"That was kind of Grandpa, wasn't it?"

"It was. And I never forgot it. Soon afterwards he asked me to marry him. I said, 'Now look, Tom *bach*, I must be honest. I don't love you. But I do *like* you. You're kind, and good to my children. If you can marry me, knowing that, I'll be your wife. The children need a father.' So I married him."

I felt tears come to my eyes. I didn't know why. This was the *happy* part of the story.

Gran got up to rinse the dishes in the sink. Then she sat down again.

"He was a good husband and father," she went on. "And when little Sydna, your mother, came along, he didn't favour her above the others. He treated them all the same. And they all loved him."

"I loved him too. I said goodbye to him in his coffin, didn't I?"

Gran sighed. "Yes, *Cariad*. So you did."

I still felt sad. I didn't want to grow up. Grown-ups couldn't play. They worked all the time. I said to Gran "I don't want to go out sewing when I'm big, and not have enough money to buy food."

She stroked my hair. "Things are better now, love. I got a pension coming in. Twelve shillings a week. And your mam's not bad off. Factory work pays better than going out sewing."

I wrinkled my nose. "Mam makes bombs."

Gran shook her head. "No, *Cariad*. But she does work at the factory. She's got to. Cos of the war."

I frowned. "Bombs are horrible. I don't want to work in a bomb factory." Gran put her arms round me. "The war will be over, I hope, before you're grown up."

"I don't want to work at all," I said, "except I wouldn't mind washing clothes and thumping them about with a dolly, like you do. But playing is better."

An idea came to me. "Let's play Snap," Gran heaved another sigh. She didn't want to, I could tell. But then she smiled and I knew it was okay. She said, "All right, little pest. Get the Snap cards out."

I clapped my hands. I was happy again. Then I ran to the drawer to find the snap cards.

"Your grandmother had a hard life."

The psychotherapist looks at me, two thoughtful little lines starting up between her eyebrows.

"Yes. It put me off growing up. When I reached my sixteenth birthday, I cried at losing my childhood. In my mind's eye, I could see life as a long grey road stretching before me: of boring, monotonous work, with everything I earned going to pay bills, of never-ending household chores and bringing up children. I didn't know how I'd stand it."

She glances at the clock on the wall. Eleven thirty.

Time to go.

"Perhaps we'll talk about that next time?"

I nod and make my way to reception, my mind in a whirl. Do I feel chastened after all that rambling about my childhood? Relieved at getting it out of my system? Talking helps I suppose. Lightens the spirit. It also lightens the purse. And if talking is all therapy's about, I might as well have a heart-to-heart with a friend. Or write it all down. Cheaper.

Still, mustn't be closed-minded. She *is* a professional. And there are some things you can't talk about to friends.

But I'm full of doubts as I pay my fee and make another appointment.

CHAPTER TWO

SUCH A PLAIN LITTLE GIRL

Now my hour's up, I'm on the way to London Bridge Station. I don't need to queue for a ticket. I have my Freedom Pass – one of the perks of old age.

I feel quite light-headed after my session with the therapist. I remember her name now. Frieda. One of the worse problems of growing old is forgetting names – names of people, names of places, names of things... It's all to do with losing so many brain cells and getting the wires tangled. I'm probably well on the way to Alzheimer's.

I hop on the train. Crowded. Just my luck. Before long, I feel someone tap my shoulder. It's a young woman offering me her seat. "Thank you," I say, "How kind!" I decide there and then that losing your brain cells isn't the only problem of ageing. It's looking decrepit enough to be offered a seat.

Funny how the aging process often adds to a man's charms, making him look more distinguished, more a person of substance. Perhaps that's why you see so many elderly male presenters on television. Women presenters, on the other hand, disappear from view. They're no longer easy on the eye, no longer sexy. For when nature vandalises a woman's face, it turns it into a kind of prune, full of pits and wrinkles. Kind people call them character lines. All I can say is, they're welcome to mine.

Not that looks are everything. But they're quite a lot. I worked that one out from an early age...

I was not a pretty child. Anyone could see that. Most of all, myself. Even as an infant, I was aware of the homeliness of my looks: round face, small, skinny body, staring eyes. This awareness began after overhearing the chance remark of a neighbour. I was six at the time.

"The clock's stopped," Gran said that morning, with a sigh. She heaved her plump body out of the armchair. "Go over the road to Lou, that's a good girl, and ask if she's got the right time."

I skipped over, dodging the kids playing hop-scotch nearby and the two boys playing whip-and-top in the middle of the road. Nothing to alarm us: no sign of a car or bus to send everyone dashing for the pavement. And Mr Hooper's horse with its cartload of groceries had already clip-clopped past.

I carried on skipping as Lou came to the door. "Please have you got the right time?" I chanted.

She smiled. "Just a minute."

She went inside. A moment later, I heard her father ask, "Who's that?"

"Only Shirley," came the answer. "You know, that *plain* little girl from over the road."

I frowned and stopped skipping.

When I got home, the first thing I did was stand on a chair in the front room and inspect myself in the looking-glass above the chimney-piece. I saw there a round, freckly face, straight, no-nonsense hair, and light-blue anxious eyes staring back at me.

"Of course you're not plain," Gran said, when I told her what I'd heard. She pursed her lips, snatched two brass candlesticks from the chimneypiece and started polishing them with a vengeance. She followed this up with an assault on the brass spittoons lying near the fender. "Plain indeed," she growled. "That Lou needs a good pair of glasses."

I wasn't convinced. Lou's words stuck in my mind. If only I were pretty like Anne Gard, I thought, that girl in my class with the dark curls, or Jenny Watts who looked like an angel! I frowned. Perhaps that's why they were always chosen for things, because they were pretty. I'd never be chosen for anything. I was too plain.

When I was seven, well after the war had begun, the evacuees came. There were three of them staying with us: Joy, Marion and Jean.

Jean was my age, and Gran would run up dresses for us on her sewing-machine, both exactly the same.

"Are you twins?" the Watkins girls from the end of the street asked one day as we made our way to school.

"Who's the prettiest?" Marjorie asked her sister, scanning us carefully.

"That one," her sister replied, pointing to Jean.

Marjorie nodded. "Yes, the other one's a funny-looking kid," she said. They both tittered.

I could feel tears prickling my eyes but I brushed them back and stuck out my tongue instead.

I don't care, I told myself. And I didn't for much of the time. I was too busy impressing everyone with my drawings of beautiful princesses and fairy queens.

"Draw me a princess, please," little girls begged. And I did. I lost some of my shyness and soon decided that looks weren't everything.

But later, when I reached ten, I had Mr Cording as my teacher. Mr Cording was a well-built man in early middle age, with a passion for maths and pretty little girls. If you were a budding mathematician, he loved you. If you were useless at maths but had a pretty face, he forgave you. If you were useless *and* plain, God help you. I came into the third category.

My stupidity in maths was made worse by the fact that I always sat at the back, well away from the formidable Mr Cording. From there I was unable to see the blackboard and, since I was too proud to wear my glasses, having been made a figure of fun by the other children the first time I wore them, I was reduced to copying from the child next to me.

Before long, I was utterly lost as well as inattentive. Mr Cording would shout, "Wake up, you silly cake!" At the same time, he would throw a piece of chalk or a board-rubber at me. At other times, he would seize me by the shoulder, drag me to the front of the class and twirl me round several times before flinging me into one of the front desks, usually next to someone as stupid or plain as myself.

I couldn't help feeling that, if I weren't such an ugly duckling, he'd treat me with more respect.

Baker Street. This is where I change and get the Bakerloo line. I awake from my reverie with a sigh. Am I still that child, I ask myself? Still allowing those few crappy experiences to convince me that I'm nothing? Damn Mr Cording. He'd be sued nowadays for treating a child like that. And damn Lou Channing and Marjorie Watkins too, for making me feel such an ugly duckling. You're perfectly okay, I tell myself as I step on the train for Regents Park. You didn't grow into a swan exactly, but you're not bad – for your age. So quit grumbling and thank your lucky stars for your health, your strength and your few remaining brain cells. As for your crumbling looks, if the worse comes to the worse, you can always change your religion and hide yourself under a burka.

CHAPTER THREE

A FREUDIAN PERSONALITY

I've been thinking about Frieda and what we're going to discuss at my next session. She expects me to stick at this therapy lark for at least a year. I'll give it a go, but how helpful can it be, droning on about your life history? Hope she's not one of those who puts everything down to nurture and nothing to nature.

I've come to the conclusion though that she isn't necessarily a Freudian analyst. I'm told that most psychotherapists these days are 'eclectic' and pick and choose from a variety of theories.

I'm glad about that. I've never much cared for Sigmund Freud. He saw psychoanalytic theory as a science but, in my opinion, his Oedipus Complex, interpretation of dreams and so on are speculative rather than evidence-based. His whole system, I feel, is rather like religion, dependent on faith.

Not that I would have thrown all his ideas into the waste basket. His personality types seem reasonable enough, even though the terms he used, such as oral type and anal type sound faintly obscene. Of course, most people are a mixture of both, but I've seen the out and out oral personality many times. A good example is my cousin, Joan, who drinks and smokes all day and never thinks of tomorrow. As for the anal type, I suspect Freud would have found me, as a child, an anal personality par excellence.

(1941–1946)

Even as an infant, I had a habit of postponing gratification. If someone gave me a currant bun, I would pick out the currants, eat the stodgy bun first, and wait till the very end before delighting my taste buds with a mouthful of currants.

13

Then there was my saving and hoarding: If an aunt gave me a penny, I didn't rush to the sweet shop and buy a quarter of sweets. I waited till I could afford a whole pound. Even then, I didn't eat them. I saved them. At home my cupboard bulged with boxes, tins, jars – each filled with bulls' eyes, pennies, or brightly coloured marbles – all gloated over daily and joyfully counted, like some miser's treasure.

It was this passion for collecting that got me into trouble. I was only six at the time but will always remember that humiliating day. It started with my interest in collecting handkerchiefs. From small beginnings my collection grew, for I was quick to seize an opportunity when it arose. And school was a productive source, providing endless chances for expanding my collection.

Each day some child would trot into our class, hold up a crumpled handkerchief and chant, "Has anybody lost this hanky?"

"I have," I'd say. "Pink with daisies? Yes, that's mine."

In two weeks a dozen handkerchiefs were added to my collection. There they were in a tidy pile, flowered, spotted, bordered with elephants – cotton, silk, linen. The pleasure of it. Counting them up, folding them neatly into a brown cardboard box.

Then one morning, held out before us all, a fine pictorial piece: Father Christmas, all rosy cheeks and beard, smiling from the middle, sprigs of holly at each corner. "It's mine," I said, eyeing it greedily. I popped it in my pocket. Fifteen now, I thought.

But then came a reckoning of a different kind. Into the classroom that afternoon stepped an urchin from another class. With quivering mouth, face stained with tears, she sobbed, "I've lost my hanky." She wiped her eyes with a grubby hand, "my best one too. With Father Christmas on it."

My teacher, stern-faced, rose, looked hard at me, a grim and dreadful look to make me crumble. "Hold up that handkerchief," she said, "You know the one."

I held it up, eyes staring at the floor.

"Is this yours, Claire?" she asked the child. "I thought so. Take it then and wipe your eyes. And now…" She turned to me. "Stand on that chair. For some time I've wondered how a child could lose so many handkerchiefs. But she didn't lose them, did she? They weren't hers to lose. So tell me, why have you been taking other people's handkerchiefs?"

I gulped, bit my lip, still staring at the floor. No words would come. I hated handkerchiefs. At last, in whispered tones I said, "I was trying to get to twenty."

I stopped collecting handkerchiefs – I learn fast. But I didn't give up collecting altogether. A year or so later, I developed a mania for collecting photographs of film stars. I got the idea from Cousin Joan who already had a collection. Joan had a strong maternal instinct from an early age and though only four years older than I, treated me as her little girl to be taken under her wing. She made out a list of film stars such as Judy Garland, Bill Boyd, and Veronica Lake and gave me their studio addresses, together with a sample letter for me to copy and send to them.

Over the next few months, I wrote to about fifty film stars. It was the same letter each time and went like this: *As you are my favourite film star, I would be much obliged if you would send me an autographed photograph of yourself – yours sincerely…* I put only a penny stamp on the envelopes even if they went all the way to Hollywood. Goodness knows how they got there, or how I received so many replies. But the arrival of those sepia-tinted photos thrilled me no end. I loved to run my fingers over their glossy surfaces as well as gaze awestruck at the beauty of the actors.

By the age of ten, my interest in film stars was overtaken by my craze for books, and I exchanged my collection of photos for two Enid Blyton books with a girl called Elma Goodenough.

My interest in books had gone on for some time. I loved nothing better than escaping to my bedroom with a copy of *Wind in the Willows* or *Treasure Island*.

One day, gazing longingly at the books in a shop window, I spied one I'd been wanting for weeks: *The Mystery of the Spiteful Letters*. I vowed I'd put away every penny until I'd saved enough money to buy it.

Having lots of relatives helped. If I met an aunt or uncle in the street or one came on a visit, I'd be sure to get a penny or even a sixpence. Soon, there was enough money in my collection to buy that special book.

In great excitement I opened up my money-tin to add the last penny. A moment later I dropped it with a howl of dismay. There were only a few coins left, a paltry one shilling and four pence. The rest had disappeared. I counted it again and again. There was no mistake. Most of my money had gone.

I ran to my mother. "What's happened to all my money?" I wailed.

She gave an awkward shrug. "I don't know. Perhaps mice have got at it.

"Mice!" I echoed. "Mice can't eat coins. Anyway, my tin had a lid on it."

I boiled with rage. She or Gran must have taken it, I thought, probably to pay bills.

I was more careful after that and began to store my money in matchboxes which I squirreled away under carpets, behind picture frames, inside toys. Even then they sometimes found it.

Dipping into a child's savings might seem a rotten way for adults to behave. But it was poverty and admitting to poverty that drove them to it. And there was a lot of it around in the thirties and forties in the valley where I spent my childhood.

It taught me one thing: never get into debt; always keep something aside for emergencies. So in spite of early frustrations,

I didn't give up saving, or turn into one of Freud's oral personalities. I'm still careful – not mean exactly. I do fork out around three per cent of my income on good causes, such as Crisis and the RSPCA. I can't say it gives me a warm glow, that satisfying feeling of what a nice, kind person I am. I do it out of duty and to ease my conscience.

On the other hand, I seldom go to the theatre these days – I balk at the price of seats – and I'm still an old meanie when it comes to spending money on fancy restaurants, mobile calls and taxis. To be perfectly honest, if it wasn't for the Freedom Pass, I'd probably become a recluse.

I keep forgetting that it's no longer necessary to pinch and scrape the way I do. But old habits die hard. I am trying to change. Excessive thrift is not an attractive trait. It's not that sensible either. After all, you're dead an awful long time and, as the old cliché goes, you can't take it with you.

CHAPTER FOUR

GROWING UP IN A MINING VALLEY

(Wednesday morning, November 2011)

I had a bad night again last night. Woke at three and couldn't get back to sleep. Kept going over events in my childhood. Then thinking about Frieda, wondering what the hell I'm doing seeing a therapist, eclectic or not.

This morning my eyes are sore. They usually are after a sleepless night. Too bad. I'm off to the U3A anyway. Sore eyes are not going to stop me.

The U3A stands for University of the Third Age. It's for the over-sixties and it's a splendid organisation – a bit like school, but without the exams.

Today, it's the Current Affairs class. This is where we sort out the problems of the country, and if we're feeling extra creative, the problems of the world. My guess is that this particular morning, we'll be discussing the protest going on outside St Paul's. I can't say I like the idea of people camping in tents in the middle of London. But I'm all for the reform of capitalism if that's what they want. The sort that causes such a wide gap between rich and poor can't be just.

Reflections on poverty and wealth take me back to my childhood again. And as I sip my coffee in this comfortable flat in London W1, I can't help pondering on the poverty that surrounded me in the thirties and forties when I was a girl.

I grew up in a mining valley in South Wales. Most of the men there were miners, including my uncle Theo who lived the other side of the Rhondda River, in Penygraig. You could see him and his fellow-workers plodding home from the pits each day, lunch boxes under their arms, faces black with coal dust.

Once home, my uncle would fling off his dirty clothes and step straight into the tub of water that my Aunt Blod had prepared for him in the kitchen. My aunt, like most married women in those days didn't go out to work, so she was free to carry out this task.

"It's a flaming slog though boiling all this water," she once told me as she struggled to lift a full pan from the coal fire to the tub. "You need the muscles of Popeye for the job."

But it had to be done. Few miners' houses had hot water taps, let alone bathrooms. And it would be years before the pits provided showers.

Fires were needed winter and summer for boiling water, heating irons or making toast. You toasted bread by holding a slice in front of the fire with a toasting-fork till it browned. You roasted meat or baked cake in the black-leaded ovens at each side of the fire grate. Only the better-off could afford the modern gas or electric cookers.

Uncle Theo got paid on Fridays. Like most miners, he handed over the whole pay packet to his wife who gave him a portion for pocket money. She spent the rest mainly on food and paying bills. Uncle Theo spent most of his share at the *Dog and Muffler*.

Not far from my uncle's home, on our side of the river, lay the district of *Trealaw*. I lived there with my mother and grandmother in a stone-walled, terraced house with a small garden at the back, the same as all the other houses in the street.

Few people *owned* their houses. They paid rent. The rent man called on Saturday mornings. Gran used to dread his coming, for sometimes she couldn't pay him.

On such days she and Mam sent me, still an infant, to open the door while they hid, silent and motionless, in the back room. "They're out," I'd say.

It felt uncomfortable telling a fib, but at that age I did as I was told.

There seemed no end to money worries. Once, my grandmother, reduced to tears, said, "I've got to go to the Big House. There's nothing else for it."

The Big House belonged to the Parish. You went there if you were too poor to cope. Gran saw it as a terrible disgrace to seek help at the Big House. "You feel like a beggar," she sobbed, "and the way they look at you there you might as well *be* one."

After Grandpa died, we lived mainly off Gran's pension. My mother, a single parent, didn't work until part way through the war when she *had* to. She suffered from a disorder known then as *neurasthenia*. This meant she was often fearful, tired or depressed. She feared loud noises in particular. During thunderstorms she would pace backwards and forwards, hands clapped over her ears, her whole body trembling.

We might have been poor but plenty in the Valley were in the same boat. Some were worse off than we were. A woman at the end of our street who had six children and looked like a gypsy, went from door to door one day, begging. "Please help. Our Bryn needs shoes bad, so he can go to school. And I'm skint."

Then there was old Mr Lipman who trudged from street to street, carrying panes of glass on his back for mending windows. No one knew where he lived or if anyone took care of him. To the kids of the area, he was an eccentric old tramp. They often followed him, singing out, "Lipman, Lipman, silly old Lipman." And he would play right into their hands by turning on them from time to time and shaking his fist. This made them shriek with laughter as they ran off. I felt sorry for him. He looked so tired and sad. I hoped people would give him work, mending their windows.

We were a community of extended families. Siblings, cousins, aunts and uncles often lived within a stone's throw of each other.

My Uncle Tom and Auntie Ivy though, decided to move to Cardiff. Gran gave a sniff, half of pride, half displeasure at the news. "He's off to live with the lah-de-dahs," she said, putting on a posh voice and sticking out her chest. "That's Ivy's doing. She's such a biggety madam."

Auntie Blod snorted. "That Cardiff lot makes me flaming sick. They laugh at us round here. Call us *People-of-the-Hills*. Damn cheek!"

I bristled with indignation. People of the Hills? They weren't *hills*. They were *mountains*.

I could see one of them from our back room window. It rose like a humpy giant from across the river, lines of terraced houses stretched over its belly. In the sunlight, it gleamed with masses of colours – greens, golds, purples, a joy to see, and no gloomy pit works that side to spoil the view.

I was aware that many children in our area, though hardly rich, were better off than I was. Some had birthday parties and received gifts of bikes or wrist watches. Such luxuries were beyond the means of Gran and Mam. I didn't much care. I was happy with a bar of chocolate or a skipping-rope. I was a great skipper. I could skip the whole length of Ynyscynon Road, past Herbert's the draper, and Hooper's the greengrocer till, reaching the post office at the far end, I would turn and skip back again, even faster than before.

What I enjoyed most cost nothing at all. I decided early on that when I grew up I would become an acrobat and join a circus. Practising acrobatics was free and I practised every day in the school playground, doing splits, cartwheels, even walking upside down in a Chinese bend. Other kids would gather round to watch. I enjoyed the attention and became a regular little show-off.

The children I really envied were those who went to Miss Shirley's dancing school. Each year Miss Shirley produced a pantomime which my mother took me to as a special treat. I gazed in awe at the children in their pretty dresses, singing, dancing, acting, tumbling, and instantly became stage struck.

"Please, *please* Gran, let me join the dancing school," I pleaded.

"No. It's common," Gran replied, nose in the air.

I suspect the real reason was that she and Mam couldn't afford the weekly fee of two shillings.

To compensate, I gathered together some of the kids of our street so we could put on our own show. I, of course, played the lead, being the Queen as well as the acrobat. Most of the others acted as chorus. We had a couple of rehearsals – I even wrote a programme – but then some of the cast dropped out. We never managed to put on the show, even though Mrs Jacobs, living opposite, had promised the use of her backyard as a theatre. I gave a shrug of resignation. Why worry? There'd be other chances. Perhaps one day I'd perform on the *real* stage. The idea set off a string of fantasies: me behind the footlights, bowing to a clapping, cheering audience; adoring fans queuing up for my autograph...

As you might guess, few people in this working class area voted conservative in the general election. The two main candidates were Labour and Communist.

My Uncle Theo and Aunt Blodwen raved about communism. Once, my aunt stuck a photograph of Stalin in front of me and said, "Just look at that face. Isn't it the face of a saint?"

They lived with their two daughters, Mair and Joan, in a crumbling old house where cockroaches invaded the basement each night. My uncle had no ambition to better himself. Taking the scholarship exam as a boy, he'd won second place in the whole county for admission to the top grammar school. He refused to go.

"I'd sooner be with my butties in the elementary school," he said.

Later in life, his cousins emigrated to America. One became a Hollywood film actor, the other, an opera singer.

Theo, the one with the brains, stayed put and worked in the pit.

As a young child I accepted the poverty of my family and our neighbourhood. Wasn't it the same everywhere? It was my reading that convinced me that it wasn't. There were people, I discovered, who didn't have to scrape their way through life as we did – people who lived in comfortable houses, sometimes with servants to tend them. I began to feel that I, my family and the whole neighbourhood were stuck at the very bottom of the social and economic edifice. It wasn't a happy feeling, and I determined that one day I, at least, would climb out of it.

(Wednesday afternoon, November 2011)

It's lunchtime. I've been to the Current Affairs class and now I'm back home, pondering again over poverty and wealth and our discussion at the Current Affairs class.

It was lively as usual with plenty of comments about the rebels outside St Pauls. Someone complained that they were a lot of hypocrites. "What right have they to grumble about the faults of capitalism when so many of them are well off members of the middle class?" she asked.

I jumped up at that point to get my spoke in. "Why is it hypocritical for a middle class person to want a fairer, more equal society?" I demanded. "It's to his credit that he has the imagination to empathise with those worse off than himself."

The class ended at that point. Just as well perhaps.

CHAPTER FIVE

THE TRIALS OF OLD AGE
AND THE PAINS OF CHILDHOOD

I'm not doing too badly for an old crumbly. I can still run up the escalator at Warren Street station, though I confess I'm puffing a bit by the time I reach the top. And I can still do press-ups and turn the odd back-somersault, not that I'm keen to do either on a regular basis. I've kept my waistline too, and, hurrah, I don't yet have a dowager's hump. Better still, my hearing's intact and I haven't gone blind. But how long will this happy state of affairs last?

I'm thinking of my old friend, Eileen, stuck in a Care Home in Richmond. As a young woman she was full of life, a lover of nature, and a frequent visitor to theatres and art galleries. Now, immobile and too weak to hold a book, she watches TV all day, and her only social contacts are her daughter and myself. She sometimes says, "I'm getting tired of this life. I want out." She has been in this state for years following a hip replacement that didn't quite work.

I mustn't let that happen to me. I can't think of anything worse than existing like a vegetable year after year, not knowing what day it is because each day is the same.

Not that old age is necessarily tragic, painful or even boring. If, like me, you're in good health, not too poor, and still have your faculties, it can be an interesting time, giving you more freedom than you've ever had before. Even being retired and living alone has advantages: There's the freedom to get up when you please, go to bed when you please, come and go when you please. You've escaped the nine to five daily grind.

All in all, so long as I don't ponder on difficult subjects like 'the future', I think I prefer life as an oldie, to life in my teens or thirties. Even as a youngster in the 1940s I can remember having to put up with things I'd not have to put up with now.

One of those things was the pressure to consume food I disliked. "Eat your peas," grown-ups nagged. "Think of the starving people of China." I couldn't see how laying into my peas would help the starving people of China. I refused to do it anyway. Whatever punishment I got as a consequence seemed the lesser of two evils.

Then there was the time I had to gulp down a spoonful of cod-liver-oil-with-malt each day. Gran would stand one side of me holding out the spoon. Mam would stand the other, holding a bucket for me to be sick in afterwards. "Come on now, there's a good girl. It's just like toffee," my grandmother would coax. I did my best, but nearly always this dreaded session ended with my being sick in the bucket.

As for school lunches, they were torture to me. If I discovered beforehand that it was going to be something particularly loathsome with tapioca pudding or semolina to follow, I'd hide away and give it a miss, feeling weak with hunger the whole afternoon that followed.

When I reached the top class of the junior school, I and several others were chosen to be dinner monitors. This meant we had to serve the other children before eating ourselves. Sometimes we served semolina pudding. I had a very sensitive nose then and loathed even the smell of semolina. Because of this, I would stretch out my arms as far in front of me as I could while holding a plate of semolina pudding in each hand to carry to the tables.

Not looking properly where I was going, I soon came a cropper. Stepping into a patch of something slimy like treacle, I slipped. Both plates shot out of my hand and smashed into pieces on the floor, dripping semolina everywhere. I can recall no more dinner-monitor duties following this calamity.

Apart from the food problem, there was my cousin Mair to put up with. It would be hard to imagine two sisters so different from each other as my cousins Joan and Mair. Joan was plump, dark-haired and brown-eyed like her father and, by nature, warm, caring and sociable. Mair was blue-eyed, skinny and fair, like her mother and, as a kid, spiky, bitchy, unpredictable and *dangerous*.

I spent a lot of time with my cousins and their parents. They lived near my infant school, higher up the valley, so I was able to lunch with them each day. I adored my aunt and uncle and my cousin Joan. They were good natured and easy-going, and never made me eat what I didn't like. Adoring Mair was another matter. She teased me unmercifully, pulling ugly faces whenever she caught me staring at her; chasing me with handfuls of wet tealeaves, knowing they repelled me, and putting a worm down my neck as soon as she learned I hated worms.

One of the worse things she did was to hold my head under the water at the local swimming pool until I almost drowned. I shall never forget the horror of that day, and my desperate struggle to breathe again. Don't let anyone convince you that death by drowning is an easy option if you want to kill yourself. There's nothing easy about it. I was nearly fifteen before I learned to swim. What held me back was the fear that I wouldn't be able to keep my head above the water.

This brings me to another thing that caused me pain as a child: the sight of so many deaths of animals. I never got used to this, despite its frequency. Nearly every day you saw a cat or dog lying in the gutter or at the side of the pavement, its insides spilling out, having been run over by a bus or car. Yet there was little traffic on the roads. Was it that there were too many animals running around unsupervised by their owners? There appeared to be no rules about keeping dogs on leads.

As for unwanted kittens or puppies, I can remember no visits to vets for humane despatch – maybe there were none in my area or not enough money around to pay the fees. In most cases, the luckless youngsters were drowned in a tub. If you were too tender-hearted to drown them yourself and you happened to live in our street, you popped them over to Ada, a large, softly spoken woman who lived in a house opposite ours, and was prepared to drown all unwanted kittens.

So far as I know she made no charge for this service but did it out of the goodness of her heart. "It's the kindest thing to do," she used to say with a gentle smile. But then, she probably hadn't had a cruel little cousin, half-drowning her one day.

There was also the slaughter-house in the road below us, at the bottom of the valley. I couldn't bear to imagine what might be going on inside. I never heard any animal screams, thank goodness. Maybe this was because I covered my ears each time I passed the place. And I never *walked* past. I *ran*.

Experiences such as these have taught me to hate bullying and to empathise, not only with those at the bottom of the social order, but with non-human animals too.

I suppose, even if we had magical childhoods, we can all remember things that frightened or dismayed us.

For me, as for many children, there was fear of the dark, not helped by my addiction to horror films and to the radio series *An Appointment with Fear*. I crept into bed each night, still hearing the sepulchral tones of Valentine Dyall, my head crammed full of ghosts and zombies, my nerves on edge as I waited with dread for the shadows in my room to assume the shapes of monsters.

At school, there were hates and fears too, like my fear of maths and loathing of domestic science (I'm one of those who really *did* go searching for elbow grease when asked to use it). Another hate was swimming lessons on brisk May mornings in the freezing water of an open-air pool. Once, an irate instructor ordered me out. He couldn't seem to understand why I was shivering so much.

But my early life wasn't all gloom and doom. The nice thing about being the age I am now is that I'm not forced into doing what I don't want to do such as eating peas or immersing myself in cold water. I have some measure of choice. At least, until Nature intervenes and takes it away.

CHAPTER SIX

THE PLEASURES OF CHILDHOOD

My early life, what I remember of it, was for the most part, pleasant rather than painful. Even the war, to an infant like me, seemed more exciting than tragic.

Around 1942 evacuees arrived from shell-racked London, bringing colour and interest to the valley. They settled in well with the locals, though a few grumbled that some cockney youngsters were infested with nits or, worse, that they taught the local children to swear. "I had to smack my Vernon for using the f-word," Mrs Watkins whispered to Gran. "It's those Londoners. *They're* the culprits."

We had no complaints about *our* evacuees. I, for one, was thrilled to have Jean, a girl my own age to play with. Poor Marion, though, was so home-sick, she didn't stay long. She used to moan over and over, "I want to go home." When she wasn't around I'd try and mimic her cockney accent. This seemed to amuse Gran who sometimes got me to entertain the neighbours with my 'imitations'.

With the coming of the evacuees, our school often got overcrowded. We sometimes sat, squashed up, three to a desk, our classroom divided into two, and only a screen to separate them. In each section a different lesson went on with a different teacher. It was a struggle to concentrate, and it must have been hell for the teachers.

What sticks out most in my mind were the war games we played, even in the infant school. Most children opted to play *British* soldiers, they being the goodies who would win the war. I, however, liked to play the villainous *German*, even though he got shot in the end, because a German could snarl, do the goose-step, and salute smartly while bawling out 'Heil Hitler!'

I played this game all by myself once at my aunt's house, using a seaside bucket for a helmet and a wooden spade for a gun as I marched in a goose-step round and round the sitting-room. But when, finally, I tried to get the bucket off again, horror upon horrors, it wouldn't budge. My aunt couldn't get it off either, nor could my cousins. "It's stuck," I howled. "What'll I do?"

"Don't cry. I'll get Dai from number 55. He'll sort it out," Aunt Blod said.

Dai arrived and, using a cutting-tool, sliced off the bucket-handle. Free at last. He laughed. "I'll bet you won't do that again in a hurry."

There was hardly any bombing in our area, though we were all given gas-masks: rubbery contraptions, fun to try on but hardly comfy. Some people, for extra safety, built air-raid shelters in their gardens. These were often cobbled-together affairs and didn't look that safe to me.

The Blackout was another precaution. I vividly recall Gran's rolling down the black blinds each evening to shut out the light and avoid giving Hitler's pilots any clues of their whereabouts. But with us danger was slight. We were lucky to live in an insignificant small community of little use to the Germans. The one and only air-raid I remember was when a mansion half way up the mountain got bombed. As the sirens wailed and a bomb crashed through its roof, Gran sat in the cupboard-under-the-stairs, with me on her lap, murmuring over and over, "Dear God, help us! Dear God, help us!"

During these tough times food was scarce and had to be rationed. Bananas were so rare my mother once acquired one as first prize in a raffle. Every family had a ration book. The government allowed you only so much cheese, eggs and meat per week, and if you'd used up all your coupons, bad luck.

Astute folk, like the Lloyds next door, supplemented their meagre rations by growing their own vegetables and keeping chickens. Rationing went on till well after the War. It was such a relief when it ended and ration books were dumped.

I was ten when the news came over the wireless that the war was over. Most children were in bed at the time but parents pulled them out and carried them into the street to dance with the jubilant grown-ups. Even pianos were dragged out, as people sang, danced and feasted. I shall never forget the exhilaration of that night.

During the early years of the war, my great grandmother, Mary Ann Hall, was still alive, and Gran took me to visit her from time to time. She was ninety years old and lived in a street high on the mountain slope with her unmarried daughters, Katie, Martha and Unna. She had given birth, Gran told me, to eleven daughters and one son. Tragically, the son died shortly after birth. Most of the girls survived. We called the old woman 'Gaia', this being a shortened version of the Welsh word *Mamgu* meaning grandmother.

Gaia, at the time I knew her, was small and frail, her voice hardly more than a squeak, her teeth scarcely visible below her gums. She always wore a black dress with a woollen shawl over her shoulders, looking the typical 'little old woman' of the Victorian fairy tale. While Gran chatted with her, Katie and Unna, Martha sometimes entertained us with a hymn on the organ in the front room. I'd get restless by that stage and start to wriggle, yawn or tap my feet on the carpet. "Is it time to go yet?" I'd whisper to Gran. "Ssh! Eat your cake," she'd whisper back.

When I'd finished my fruitcake and got bored with wiggling my toes or counting the ornaments on the what-not, I sometimes left the oldies to their chats and walked a little way down the mountain to visit Aunt Agnes, Gran's youngest sister. There I would meet her daughter, Maureen, and we'd play roly poly down the grassy slopes.

At other times, we'd visit Gran's friends from Moriah chapel. There was Mrs Jones the Post, a plump, slow-moving woman with a pronounced swelling on the neck. Gran called it a *wen*. Then there was Mrs Jones, the Dairy. She was a thin, earnest little woman with a thin sort of voice to match, and a fox fur draped over her shoulder. She often wore this to Sunday School where she taught ignoramuses like me to read the bible in Welsh, a language few youngsters spoke or understood. She also told us stories of Jesus, describing in lurid detail his crucifixion. "Just imagine those nails being driven into his flesh," she'd say with a dramatic intake of breath. "They might even have been rusty." Her words made such an impact on me, that for years afterwards I couldn't look at a cross without shivers running up my spine.

Most of Gran's friends lived in Tonypandy, the other side of the river. The main street of this mining community ran along the floor of the valley and was crowded with shops. There were also several pubs, competing for space with a fair number of chapels – mostly Methodist or Baptist. There were, moreover, two dance halls and three cinemas. There was a lot of cinema-going. We called it 'going to the pictures'. I spent many a Saturday morning at the Plaza with scores of other kids watching *Tarzan* or *Donald Duck*. The noise was sometimes deafening but the whoops and cheers didn't seem to bother us any more than did the endless rustle of toffee paper.

Cousin Joan often walked with me to Tonypandy. A favourite haunt of ours was Hathaway's, the fish-and-chip shop. Ordering two pennyworth of chips each, we'd sit in the restaurant upstairs and wait for our chips to arrive on the dumb-waiter. The dumb-waiter was like magic to me. I loved the whirring sound as ropes pulled it to the upper floor till, with a jolt, it reached the top, holding two plates of chips all ready for us to pick up and consume with lashings of vinegar and salt.

So many things seemed to be invested with magic in those days. I remember the first time I saw a moving escalator. I was staying with my Aunt Ivy and Uncle Tom in their new house in Cardiff. One day my aunt took me into Queen Street. It was a splendid place, I thought, full of exciting new sights and smells, and enormous shops, much grander than those in the valley. It was in Howells, the department store, that I spied the escalator. I could scarcely believe my eyes.

"A magic staircase!" I gasped. "Please let's climb it."

"No, I don't need to go upstairs," my aunt replied, "so stop pulling at me, and be a good girl."

She was a smart, sensible lady, especially strict about matters such as hygiene and getting value for money. She was also one of those who made you eat up your greens, wash your neck properly, and wipe your feet, so I knew that pestering her any further would be a waste of time.

But I felt droopy with disappointment at missing a climb up the magic stairs. If I'd been with Cousin Margaret, I thought, *she'd* have let me climb them. I might as well have stayed at home with her and Uncle Tom.

Uncle Tom preferred to pass his spare time banging away at the piano in the front room while bawling out musical hits from *The Desert Song* or *The Chocolate Soldier*. Sometimes, I and Cousin Margaret joined in, standing each side of him while we sang. This sort of musical soiree often went on amongst families well-off enough to buy a piano.

The event of the year I most looked forward to was the Sunday School trip in August to the seaside – usually to Barry Island or Porthcawl. Both places had sandy beaches and a fairground with thrilling rides like the Scenic Railway and the Big Wheel.

A week before the trip, I'd be pent up with excitement, my mind full of sea-spray, sunhats and donkey rides. "I can't wait for Saturday," I'd say to Mam.

"It's sure to rain," she'd reply.

My mother could be a right old Eeyore. She was one of those whose cup was never half full, or even half empty. More often than not, it was *totally* empty.

Even so, she was almost always right – about Sunday School outings anyway. It usually did rain.

During the train journey on that special day we peered out of carriage windows, waiting for fields of cows to come into view. When they did, we greeted the sight either by cheers or groans.

"They're standing up," some kid would yell. "Yippee, it's going to be fine."

Another time our cries were more subdued. "Aw. They're lying down. That means rain." Which way round it was I can't remember, but rain or no, we still managed to enjoy ourselves.

Looking back, I don't think we children appreciated the amount of freedom we had. In my view, this wonderful freedom more than compensated for the absence of TV, mobile phones, chat lines or computer games. For many of us were free to roam, without anxious parents always tagging along with us. From the age of six or seven we walked to school and home again, either alone or with our friends. We visited parks, caught buses, scrambled up mountains, sometimes did dangerous things, not always without mishap.

Freedom was easier then, of course. There was less traffic on the roads. And no TV news presenters to scare parents witless with the spectre of paedophiles lurking round every corner.

Not that paedophiles didn't exist. Once, one sat next to me at the Saturday cinema and, after offering me toffees, put his hand up my skirt. I couldn't understand why he should do such a rude thing, but I didn't complain. I just moved to another seat.

I didn't tell Gran or Mam. Sex talk was usually avoided or met with embarrassment. We children were conscious of this, so unless seriously assaulted, we kept quiet. Parents did give the occasional warning but often such warnings were put so obliquely, they left us baffled.

"If a strange man should offer you a penny," Gran said mysteriously one day, "say 'no thank you', and walk away." No explanation of what might happen if I *accepted* the penny.

Few of us, as infants, knew where babies came from. We weren't short of theories. "You order them from Woolworth's," one little girl said. "Don't be daft," said another, "they're made by the government."

There was no sex education to speak of. We obtained the facts of life from other, better informed children who delighted in shocking us. At school, sexual facts were limited to the behaviour of frogs or rabbits.

Reaching sexual maturity, we had no contraceptive-pill, while abortion, with few exceptions, was against the law. At the same time, social attitudes were strict. A wise girl seldom risked being 'up the duff' unless sure marriage would follow.

Thinking back to my childhood, I remember the joy, not only of outdoor pursuits with other children but also the joy of being alone, engrossed in activities indoors.

Modelling houses out of shoe-boxes kept me occupied for hours. So did drawing and painting. While painting pictures I escaped into a fantasy world where children slid down rainbows or flew on magic carpets. Gran liked to show off my creations, especially to the insurance man who often asked to see them.

"Well, how about that!" he used to exclaim, a suitable expression of wonder in his tone. And Gran would purr with pleasure.

When I learned to read, another magical world opened itself to me: the world of story-books.

Soon, I was writing stories myself. Whenever I got an idea, delicious prickles of excitement ran up my spine. I couldn't wait to put pen to paper.

I started making up stories when I was seven and in 1A of the junior school. My teacher, Miss Martin, soon saw I could be useful. "Read one of your stories to the class, Shirley," she'd say. She'd then busy herself with marking, or swan off to visit another teacher.

Often, instead of *reading* my stories, I'd make them up as I went along. Though I never knew what would happen next, an idea always seemed to pop into my head at the right time.

Much later, in the secondary school, I managed to win first prize each year in the school essay competition. Not that I should pat myself on the back and think 'clever little me.' There's no great merit in winning a few prizes if you're attending a second-rate school filled with under-achievers like yourself.

I became embarrassed, almost guilty, about winning these prizes, especially since George Powell, my number one enemy was thirsting for revenge at being only a runner-up each year. The last time I stepped forward to collect my five shillings, therefore, I stepped *cringingly*, trying to make myself as small as possible – a bit difficult, since I was pretty small anyway!

George Powell wasn't slow in getting his own back. He grabbed my exercise book one day and scribbled 'the witch' in brackets after my name on the cover.

"What's this? Shirley Stephens (the witch)?" a teacher asked, frowning, as he passed me my exercise-book.

Sniggers broke out. I could have sunk through the floor in embarrassment.

It's odd to think that this old woman I see in the mirror today is the same person as that child with all her hopes and dreams of the future. But even as that child, I was aware that the future would end in old age and finally death. I can remember pondering on these thoughts when no more than nine years old and walking slowly along my aunt's garden path. "One day I shall be old like Auntie Blod," I said to myself. "And then I shall grow older still like Gran. And when I'm that old I shall remember walking down this garden path and thinking about it."

I always have remembered.

CHAPTER SEVEN

A SKELETON IN THE CUPBOARD

(December 2011)

"How was your week?"

I shrug. "Okay, I suppose."

Yes, a week has gone by and it's time for another session with Frieda.

She's wearing a grey polar neck sweater. It's a bit baggy and the colour doesn't suit her, but it looks nice and warm – ideal for winter. Anyway, I don't think Frieda is that concerned about her appearance. She's probably confident enough to expect people to accept her as she is. I wish I were like that. Now the weather's got colder I've started wearing my white woollen hat and matching scarf. The funny thing is that, since I've been wearing them, nobody's been offering me a seat on the tube. Does that mean that white makes me look younger? If so, I shall wear white all the time.

There I go again, obsessing about my looks. Concentrate. Frieda is waiting for a response. 'Okay, I suppose' is hardly informative. I'll try to elaborate.

"I've been going to the U3A as usual. We're busy practising for the Christmas concert. One of my classes is putting on a mini-pantomime – Jack and the Beanstalk. I'm Jack."

I see her smile into her notebook. She probably thinks it hilarious – a load of old biddies putting on a pantomime.

Then she looks up at me, still smiling. I see now that there's nothing mocking about her smile. It's almost as if she's impressed. Or is she surprised at my nerve?

"I'm sure you'll make an ideal small boy," she says at last. I believe she actually means it.

"I'm a bit long in the tooth, I know. But I *am* small and I can do the voice. Anyway I don't mind making a fool of myself, if it's to entertain." I give an awkward laugh then go on. "Jack's 'mother' is one of the *men* in the group, and he's a really good actor. He'll be wearing a wig, of course, and petticoats. At one point he has to whack me with a stick. That should give the audience a few laughs."

She chuckles, but soon her expression is serious again. "Talking of mothers, you've said very little about yours. I've heard a good deal about your grandmother, but nothing about your relationship with your mother. Why is that, I wonder?"

Ah. Now we're coming to the nitty-gritty.

I'm silent a moment. "It wasn't a bad relationship," I say, after some thought. "It's just that – well – my mother would hardly have got any prizes for Personality of the Year."

I cough, feeling self-conscious. That wasn't a nice thing to say about my mother.

"What do you mean exactly? Was she unpleasant?" She taps at her chin with her pencil.

"No." I rush to my mother's defence. "She was gentle. Kind. It's just that she seemed to have – well – no real substance – to be more a *shadow* of a woman. She was a timid, passive creature and so reserved, you never knew what she was thinking or whether she had any thoughts at all."

"You make her sound like a non-person."

Is that reproof I detect in her tone? A feeling of shame sweeps over me. I'm making my mother seem vacuous, an empty vessel. She wasn't that, not under the surface.

I try to explain, to justify my criticism. "It's just that when a person seldom passes an opinion or voices a thought, you get the impression that…"

"That there aren't any thoughts to voice?" She gives an enigmatic smile. "Go on."

37

I clasp my hands together, searching for words. "You'd call her a depressive, I suppose. Life appeared a burden to her. But she never tried to *change* things, to make things better for herself."

"Perhaps she couldn't. Maybe she felt trapped." Frieda's voice has dropped to a whisper, as if she's thinking aloud.

"Gran did all the cooking and organising. My mother helped out with the housework, but she'd spend most of her time escaping into romantic novels."

I am conscious of my voice rising. "I wanted a mother who would *guide* me, take charge. But my mother couldn't take charge even of her own life. She left it all to fate, or to other people. It was partly her upbringing, I suppose. From childhood onwards, she was babied by everyone. My Uncle Tom and Aunt Blod shielded their little sister from all the knocks of life. She never needed to fend for herself."

I pause. "That's why, I suppose, I've always tried to take charge of my life, to make changes if I could, and to be independent. All the time, you see, I'm struggling against my upbringing and the genes I've inherited. I don't want to be like my mother, pulled this way and that by other people and by circumstances. I want to have some control over what happens to me."

I give a hesitant smile. "I didn't hate her, I assure you. With the cruelty of youth, I suppose I let myself get irritated by her very qualities – her gentleness, humility... I came to appreciate such qualities later in life."

She scribbles something in her notebook. "Did she show you love and affection?"

"When I was younger, yes, though she was never very demonstrative. I still had warm feelings for her and she for me, I think... until..." I pause and bite my lip.

"Until?" She looks up from her notebook.

I run my tongue along my mouth. "Until I was twelve or so. Then something happened that made me turn against her."

"Ah, so? It wasn't merely the case of a child growing into a critical teenager then? There was something else."

I open my mouth to respond, then quickly close it again. There are some things about my childhood I've always kept private. This is one of them.

Frieda leans forward, encouragingly. "Well?"

I take a deep breath. "She died around forty years ago. She was only sixty – not old, by today's standards. The funeral was a pathetic little affair– just a few close relatives, a couple of neighbours… Then, back at the house, I visited my mother's old bedroom again. That's when I caught sight of the hatbox. It brought it all back: the family secret that changed my feeling towards my mother."

"Hatbox?" Frieda lets out a murmur of surprise.

"Yes. It's funny how an object like that can trigger off so many memories."

The room becomes little more than a blur as I sit there, letting the past become the present, reliving the day of my mother's funeral.

I am thirty-six when she dies. It's 1971, and I've journeyed down from London to attend the burial service. Going up to her bedroom afterwards, and seeing the hatbox, takes me way back to my childhood. I gaze at it, hypnotised by its mottled colour and curved shape as it stands there under the dressing-table. It belonged to my grandmother once, as did the bedroom. And it's standing in the same place it had stood more than twenty years before when, as a girl of twelve, I first opened it.

Would I ever have found out the truth, I wonder, had I not looked inside that box?

A voice calling from downstairs breaks into my thoughts. "Take something home with you, Shirley, to remember your mother by." It's John, my stepfather.

"Thanks," I call back. He can't hear me. He's almost totally deaf. I wondered how he'd cope without my mother's support, and with Diane, my mentally disabled half-sister to care for?

I move over to the dressing-table to choose a memento. Amongst the clutter of porcelain bowls and bottles of scent stands a figurine of a dancer. I pick it up. A cheap souvenir, but pretty. My mother had liked pretty things. I put it down. Not for me.

I look at the hat-box again and feel my eyes glaze over as I relive that time in 1947 when I had opened it.

It was boredom and curiosity that drove me to it. I knew there were hats inside, old-fashioned straw ones with straggly feathers or ribbons for tying under the chin. No one ever wore them. I'd seen Gran try on one or two before going out, but she'd always end up wearing one of her old faithfuls – the felt, no-nonsense sort she kept on the wardrobe shelf.

"I'll have a bit of fun with them," I muttered, "It'll be something to do."

I took them out of the hat-box, one by one. That's when I noticed the pool of letters and documents lying at the bottom.

I looked at them in surprise. What were they doing in a hat-box? Had they always been there?

I settled myself on the rug, unfolded a grey, official-looking document and started to read it.

My hand began to shake as harsh words leapt out at me: 'On 24th of May 1935 Miss Sydna Stephens of 205 Ynyscynon Road, Trealaw gave birth to a bastard girl…'

I sat staring at the document, heart thumping against my rib-cage. "24th of May. That's my birthday," I murmured. "It's about my mother. And about me."

I couldn't read any more. The writing had grown blurred and my eyes wouldn't focus. *Bastard*. The word had an ugly ring. My best friend, Joan Jones, once told me that if anyone called her brother, Maldwyn, a bastard, he would punch him for insulting his mother.

And *I* was one of those, and had *that* sort of mother. I got angry then. They'd told me lies all along. They'd said my father had died before I was born. Admittedly, I found it odd that my surname was the same as Gran's, my mother's mother. "Mam married a cousin," Gran explained. More lies. I'd never trust them again.

I flung the document back in the hatbox, ran downstairs, curled up on the sofa and wept.

My grandmother found me there, her forehead lined with concern.

I said nothing for a minute or two, then blurted out, "I looked in the hat-box. I know everything."

She stared at me, frowning. "Hatbox?" At last, the penny dropped. She whitened. "You had no business poking about in there."

That was all she said. No explanation. No move to comfort me. I watched her turn and scurry out.

Five minutes later, she was back, followed by her friend from next door.

She spoke without meeting my eyes. "Here's Mrs Davies, Shirley, to have a talk with you. She knows all about it." She hurried out again, leaving her neighbour to deal with the problem.

Mrs Davies plonked herself on a nearby chair and leaned towards me, her double-chin wobbling as she talked. "There, there, Shirley, love," she began in her gravelly voice. "It's not the end of the world. Your father came from a respectable family."

"Why didn't they tell me the truth?" I blubbed.

"They thought it was for the best." Mrs Davies drew from her pinafore-pocket a handkerchief smothered in the scent of eucalyptus. She passed it to me. "Dry your eyes now. No need to feel ashamed. It's not *your* fault, as I tell our Nellie or anyone else who points the finger."

So people pointed the finger. Worse and worse. "Then everybody knows?" I faltered.

41

"No, no. Not everyone. Only a few of us living here in this street."

I hate myself for it now but I began to despise my mother. My one excuse is being a child of my time, when a woman who 'got herself in trouble' was rated as only a step or two up from the criminal classes. She's brought shame on herself and on me, I whinged.

I knew she couldn't be what people called a *hussy*. She was too much of a mouse. That made it worse somehow. It made her seem too stupid and weak to look after herself. I didn't want a mother like that.

I wanted to be like other children. In those days that meant having two parents, married to each other, and a brother or sister, all living in a nice, tidy family.

On the other hand, being different made me feel kind of *special*. Perhaps my father was handsome, capable, talented, just like the fathers in story-books. Maybe he was cleverer than my quiet, slow mother who seemed to be frightened of everything and accomplished at nothing.

I longed to meet him.

"You can't," Gran said, pushing back a wisp of hair straying from her bun. "He's far away. In London, I think." She tightened her lips.

"Forget about him," Aunt Blodwen snapped, her eyes flashing. "He let your mother down. And he's a no-good drunk."

My mother said nothing. She went about the house, cleaning, dusting, a bleak expression on her face. I could almost feel her heart sinking.

But there was no let-up in my coldness towards her. For weeks I gave her hardly a smile or a friendly word. I cringe now when I recall the shabby, indifferent way I behaved towards her, probably driving her self-esteem even lower than it already was.

I continued to fantasize about my father. Perhaps he wasn't in London, as my grandmother supposed. Maybe he was here in my home-town. Often, as I walked along the streets, I'd find myself scanning middle-aged men, wondering if one of them could be my father. If he were bald, fat or loud-mouthed, I'd mentally shake my head. It couldn't be him. If, on the other hand, he looked elegant, clever, and a cut above the others, I'd smile and think, perhaps he's the one.

Two years before the hatbox episode, my mother had married, her husband, John, moving in with us. I didn't care for my new stepfather. He was quiet and ordinary, like my mother, and worked in the pit. There weren't any parents like that in the books I read. Years later, I came to realise I read the wrong sorts of books. I should have read more Dickens or Hardy and less Enid Blyton.

Determined to track down my real father, I pleaded with Aunt Blodwen to tell me where he was. I felt sure she knew. I pestered her till at last she flung up her hands and gave way. "Okay, if you're that keen, I'll arrange something. But on your own head be it."

She frowned and went on, "He's left London and his wife. Typical. And he's back down here, like a bad penny."

My heart began to thump. Being back down here wasn't exactly a good omen. The smart ones usually left and they didn't come back. Still, you never know. I crossed my fingers.

My aunt was true to her word and made the arrangement.

We met in a café, further up the valley, with red check cloths on the tables and a strong smell of hot pies. I was too excited to eat, and made do with a lemonade.

I sat there sipping it, enjoying its frothy tang, and staring curiously at the man who was my father. He's not bad-looking, I decided. Not bald or fat. And he doesn't put Brylcream in his hair.

He seemed to shrink under my gaze. He uttered an awkward 'Well, well...' and made a business of adjusting his tie. At last, he said, haltingly, "I've often wondered about you,

43

and – er – how you were getting on." He fumbled in his pocket. "And, I've – I've – brought you a present."

He held out a wrist watch. I gave a squeal of delight. I'd never had a wrist-watch before.

I asked him what he did. Being the little snob I was, I prayed he wasn't a labourer or working in the pit.

He didn't answer straight away but rummaged inside his jacket for a cigarette. I noticed his hand tremble as he lit it. After a few drags, he appeared to relax.

"What do you do?" I asked again.

He made a vague gesture with his fingers. "Oh, this and that. I'm a bit of a butterfly. Not like the rest of the family. There were seven of us, you know." He gave a wry smile. "I was the black sheep"

He went into a long spiel about his brothers and sisters. "Most of them went to University," he told me. "Your Uncle Arthur went to Oxford. Dan became a doctor, and your Aunt Glenys, a dress designer. My brother, Llewellyn, went into business. He owns some of the houses round here."

I felt a thrill of satisfaction. So I had successful relatives. Great.

"But what about you?"

He paused again. "I played in a band once."

"So you're a musician. That's nice."

"And I've been a carpenter. And an insurance clerk…." He ticked them off on his fingers.

We talked some more. Finally, he paid the bill and gave me an awkward kiss before parting.

I met him several times after that. We never bonded though. I was never able to call him *Dad*.

My aunt was right about his drinking. Almost every time I called I'd find him with a beer in front of him, his speech slurred and his movements unsteady. And with his drunkenness came a mean-spiritedness and a tendency to growl and snap about some trifling let-down he'd suffered in the past.

44

As my disappointment grew, so our meetings got fewer, until soon they ceased altogether.

I didn't tell Aunt Blod. I know what she'd have said.

My stepfather calling from below brings an end to my reverie. "Shirley, are you okay? They're all asking about you down here."

"Coming."

I think again about my mother and her crushed, pushed-aside life, the presents she sent for my birthday, that she couldn't afford, her mild manner towards me, in spite of my cold looks and my slights. I did try to make amends later on, but things were never the same.

And now she's gone. My reminiscences bring a lump to my throat, and I cry at last. She could have given me up. I wouldn't have blamed her. They were hard on unmarried mothers in those days.

I wipe my eyes. I must join the others. But first there's something I'd like to do.

I cross to the dressing-table and pick up the porcelain dancer from the top. As I gaze at the figurine it seems to let out a strange, unearthly glow. I catch my breath and gaze a while longer.

Then, gently, and with a lighter heart, I slip it in my handbag and go downstairs.

The screeching of brakes outside Frieda's window hustles me away from my mother's funeral, out of my childhood, and into the present. I shake back my tears and try to assume an expression of ease. "Hope I didn't bore you with all that stuff. It's a relief to get it out of my system. I've felt too ashamed to talk about it up to now. Absurd, isn't it? As if anyone gives a damn about that sort of thing anymore. So many children are born out of wedlock nowadays, it's become the norm."

Frieda looks up from her notebook and smiles. "I'm glad you're feeling happier about it."

"I still feel bad though about the mean way I treated my mother. I could have helped her, made an effort to build up her confidence and self-esteem. I did pay off her mortgage. That's something, I suppose. But giving her some love and respect might have been more helpful."

"We all have regrets about what we should or shouldn't have done. You couldn't help the way you felt." She looks briefly at her notes. "You had no father at home. And when you met him those few times, you were disappointed. Do you think that is why you have always been more interested in *older* men than in those your own age? You've been searching for a father-figure?"

She gets up. "I won't be seeing you again until after Christmas. My receptionist will arrange times. Think about the father-figure question."

She's looking at the clock now, anxious for me to go. No wonder. We're five minutes over the hour. And there'll be another client waiting.

I make a hurried exit, remembering that I'm only *one* of her clients. I wonder if she ever gets sick of listening to their problems. Perhaps she has enough of her own…

CHAPTER EIGHT

MORE THINGS IN HEAVEN AND EARTH

That my mother seldom expressed her views on life didn't mean she lacked independent thought. For instance, some years after leaving school, I asked her why she'd never joined Gran and Auntie Blod on their visits to Chapel. She didn't answer at first but, after my persistent badgering, blurted out, "I don't believe in God, that's why."

I gave a gasp. In the mid-fifties, most valley people were believers, and chapels were full. Yet here was my passive little mother going her own way. She was evidently more independent-minded than I'd given her credit for.

Not that I should have been surprised by her lack of belief. She was a pessimist. How could she believe in a loving God watching over her? Or in a heaven ready to welcome her when she departed this life? It all sounded too much like wishful thinking.

Today, a good number of us might agree with her. Even so, religious belief is still pretty universal. It also goes so far back in time, I sometimes think that many of us might be hard-wired by nature to believe in those ideas of God or gods passed down to us, and to go on believing them, or revised versions of them. Perhaps it's nature's way of providing us with a security blanket. After all, a supernatural being, especially in the form of a personal God, gives us purpose, the protection of an eternal parent, as well as the hope of life after death.

(1940–1945)

Belief in God was very important in my life as a child. My grandmother saw to that. "God is watching," she warned whenever she caught me doing something I shouldn't. "His eyes are everywhere."

"Even while I'm in the bath?" I asked in dismay.

"Just be a good girl, and you'll be all right."

Her religious belief was simple enough. If you followed the moral rules, and said your prayers regularly, God would love you and welcome you into Heaven when you died. You'd get an even better chance if you kept away from drink, swearing, and singing 'comic songs' on Sundays.

If you were badly behaved, on the other hand, God would punish you, and send you down to Hell – a terrible place where people were tortured and burned in fires.

Gran was a Baptist. Baptists focused on *preaching* and studying the bible and its ethics. Unlike Catholics or Church of England Protestants, they were vague about such ideas as the Holy Trinity. They regarded Jesus as the son of God but I can't remember ever being taught that they were other than separate beings. There was no baptism of babies. Baptism to become a full member of the chapel took place only when the individual was sure of his faith.

For Gran, Moriah Chapel was more than a place of worship. It was a community of which she was an active member. On Sundays she often attended morning as well as evening worship. On Wednesdays, there was 'sewing class' and at other times activities such as Singing, Band of Hope or Magic Lantern. In addition, there were 'socials' organised for adults and children.

Not only did Gran send me to Sunday School. She sometimes dragged me to morning or evening worship as well. I found it a terrible grind, and was never short of excuses for staying home.

"I got a terrible tummy ache," I would say, or "I'm feeling sick and my head's aching."

Gran would give a snort of impatience. "All the more reason to go to chapel," she'd reply. "You can ask God to make you better. Now hurry up and get those shoes on."

Gran was a hard task-master. As soon as I could read she would make me memorise verse after verse of biblical psalms, and spend hours testing me afterwards till I was word perfect.

This wouldn't have been so bad if the text had been in English. But being in Welsh, a language I couldn't understand, it was like learning a load of gobbledygook. The problem was that Welsh seemed to be dying out in the valley. Old people still spoke it. So did those adults attending Welsh chapels like Moriah. But it was seldom spoken at home. And though taught at secondary school few youngsters chose to study it.

Whatever the problems, I was soon reciting at special chapel services, standing on a chair in front of the congregation. After my rendering, adults would smile indulgently and murmur 'Ahh'. And Gran would sit there beaming, in her best hat, and looking as if she would burst with pride.

When I reached eight or nine, I began to feel that these performances were beneath my dignity, especially when, with half a dozen other children, I had to do 'actions' at appropriate places in the text, such as pointing to my heart or to the birds in the sky. "Doing actions is babyish," I protested.

I didn't go so far as refusing to do them. But when people in the congregation smiled at these gestures and said 'Ahh', I'd turn down my mouth and glare at them.

The only services I enjoyed were baptisms. At such times, in the area below the pulpit and facing the congregation, the floorboards were taken up, exposing a pool of water. One by one, barefoot and dressed in simple white gowns, those waiting to be baptised would be helped into the pool by the minister who would say a prayer then dip them in the water. I used to hope the water wasn't too cold and didn't go up their noses.

People usually wore their best clothes for chapel-going. There was Mrs White, the Butcher, wearing her prettiest hat with the feathers, Mrs Jones the Post, looking formidable in her black suit and strings of pearls and, of course, Mrs Jones, the Dairy, with the usual dead animal draped over her shoulders. My Aunt Blod used to whisper, "They only come to show off their finery. It's all swank."

I was not the only child dragged to morning or evening service. Plenty of youngsters were there, including Joan and Mair, and my two boy-cousins, Tudor and Kerry. None of us could speak Welsh so we were all bored out of our minds.

The boys brought pencils and paper and secretly drew aeroplanes during the service. Sometimes I dozed off but then woke with a start as our minister, in an effort to drive home some ethical point, raised his voice to a crescendo of passion while bringing his fist down on the pulpit.

Our preacher was called Washington Owen. He was handsome and charismatic, and even though I couldn't understand Welsh, I could still enjoy listening to him. The richness of his voice was awe-inspiring, while his dramatic gestures, and the fire in his eyes held you spellbound.

He was blessed with a handsome son called Peredith and a beautiful black-haired daughter, Rhiannon, who looked like an Arabian princess and who tragically died of cancer in her twenties.

When I was grown-up and had ceased chapel going, I heard from Gran that Washington Owen had been dismissed from his duties by the deacons. It appeared that he'd been carrying on an affair with a woman who wasn't his wife. "It's a wicked rumour," my Aunt Blodwen said, loyal to the last, while Gran said, fiercely, "God will punish them for their lies."

(1945–1950)

I don't think there was any real substance to my belief in God. Until I reached my teens, it simply didn't occur to me that I had the option *not* to believe. But when I got to fourteen, we had a new teacher at school called Mr Swayne. He was a young man with a broad face and hair that flopped over his forehead. He also had dark, serious eyes that looked straight at you, and a bearing that commanded respect.

"Never take at face value everything you read or are told," he said to us. "Always examine things critically, even the bible and talk about God."

Suddenly my eyes were opened. There was another option. I didn't *have* to believe. I could work things out for myself, make up my own mind about religion or anything else.

Most of my fellow-students went on believing, and are still believers so far as I know. I, together with a few others, lost our belief, and did so on the day Mr Swayne gave us permission to think for ourselves.

For all that, I would agree with Hamlet that there are more things in Heaven and Earth than are dreamed of in our philosophy. Below is a case in point.

Just before the arrival of Mr Swayne, a new church from America, Elim Temple, came into our area. It became very popular, especially with teenagers.

At the secondary school, I was one of a group of girls who always hung out together. There was my best friend, Joan Jones, two other girls, Lilian Visor and Jean Samuel and a plump, freckly girl, a year older than the rest of us named Gladys Ford. It was Gladys who introduced us to Elim Temple.

"I've seen the light," she announced one day, face glowing with passion. "I've been to Elim and been saved by Jesus. You must all come."

In a couple of weeks Joan, Lillian and Jean had become fervent members of the Temple. They no longer went to the cinema or talked about dancing or boys. They talked about Jesus and how to avoid the temptations of the devil. Gladys would say things like, "Get thee behind me, Satan" and "Thy sins will find thee out." She was a strong personality, and soon had the others following her like sheep.

They visited Elim Temple almost every evening and eventually persuaded me to go along. With a sigh of reluctance

I went. At least it will be in English, I thought, I doubt though if I'll see any 'light'.

Nevertheless, I shall not forget that evening. One member after another stood up and related with ecstasy his religious experiences. Each told how turning to Jesus had changed his life, how sorrow had changed to joy, how evil had been replaced by good.

When I looked round at the rest of the congregation I noted, awestruck, that there was not a dry eye to be seen. Every man, woman, girl and boy was weeping and shaking with passion. "Why," I asked myself, "am I, and I alone, *unmoved* by all this? What's wrong with me?"

But tears of passion were nothing compared with what happened next. Following the public confessions, one person after another was struck by the 'baptism of the Holy Ghost' or the ability to speak in tongues. This vocal eruption was in no way like Welsh or any other earthly tongue. And there was nothing bogus about it. The outpouring of a language that sounded alien to this planet was, I would argue, totally spontaneous. It streamed out of people's mouths, as automatically as if some strange power had seized each person and spoken through him. Fifteen-year-old Gladys was affected similarly. After speaking with passion about 'being saved by Jesus' she too started talking in tongues.

I looked and listened in a daze. What was happening to her? What was happening to everyone? Why the glazed eyes, the weeping, the loss of control over speech? Thinking back on this incident, I wondered if emotional or spiritual excitement had stimulated some little known part of the brain and set off this kind of reaction.

I don't remember attending another service. As for the rest of the group, enthusiastic attendance at Elim Temple soon turned out to be little more than a flash in the pan. Gladys, the most zealous of the group announced quite suddenly, "I'm going to the pictures again. Dancing too." These pastimes were denounced by the evangelical church as pastimes of the devil. However, Gladys's announcement was a cue for the others to follow suit and drop their frequent church going. Two of the group, Lillian and Jean, remained faithful to the evangelical Church, though less fervent in their approach. My best friend, Joan Jones, soon lost her enthusiasm and stopped attending altogether.

Coming back to Hamlet's remark to Horatio, there is surely something strange about the 'speaking in tongues' that I encountered. But I remember other happenings of a supernatural kind that I have found puzzling. Here is an example:

A group of girls from my class met one evening to have a go at a ghostly game we'd heard about, using a wine glass and letters of the alphabet. We placed the carefully cut letters in a circle round the table and an upside down wine glass in the centre. Then all we had to do was each place a forefinger on the bottom of the wineglass, ask the spirit, or whatever it was, a question, and the glass would move to particular letters till it spelt out the answer. Forefingers had to be kept quite still on the glass. The idea was to let it move of its own accord.

Common questions were: "Is Derek Williams interested in me?" or "What is the name of the man I'm going to marry?"

The game gave rise to several disputes. "You're pushing the glass" and "You *made* it go to the letter 'y'. I could feel you pushing it. That's cheating."

When it came to my turn, there was no dispute, only strange looks. When I asked the name of the man I was going to marry, it spelt out the name *Godfrey Ronald Fry*. Nobody could be accused of pushing the glass, for no one, including myself had ever heard of him.

We had another go, to make sure it wasn't a fluke but again it spelt out the same name – *Godfrey Ronald Fry*.

I forgot this incident until, some years after leaving school, I played a similar game with my friend Olwen, this time with a large door key tied, except for its handle, between the pages of the bible at the Book of Ruth. You recited the verse which began: *And Ruth said "Entreat me not to leave thee or to return from following after thee..."* At the same time you both kept a finger on the handle of the key. Then you asked Ruth the question: 'Who is my husband going to be?' You would then call out the letters of the alphabet. The key would twist round on a certain letter and the bible fall. You would continue until it spelt a name. For me, these years later, it spelt out the name – *Godfrey Ronald Fry.*

In both cases, the spirit or whatever was giving the answer, was obviously in error. I never married a Godfrey, nor had a boy-friend of that name. There's still a chance I'll meet him, I suppose, if such a person exists. I must have another go at surfing the Internet.

Reflecting on belief in God, it's curious to me that some religions demand worship of him sometimes several times a day. But why? Out of gratitude because he is benevolent and created us? Out of fear, because this all-powerful being commands it and will punish us if we don't?

That he is benevolent seems a bit of a joke. He can at times make Hitler sound like the Good Samaritan. And even if he did create us, did we ask to be created? For many living beings, life is a burden rather than a joy and, as I see it, more suited to curses than prayers of gratitude.

As for worshipping a God who commands it, and who punishes you if you don't, would you willingly fall to your knees before such an egoistic tyrant?

I wouldn't. But maybe I haven't that optimism or hard-wiring to throw away reason and depend purely on faith. I can, though, believe in an impersonal, creative force, working through nature. If we see God this way, then questions as to why there are famines, floods or disasters like that in Aberfan those years ago, become irrelevant. God is neither good, nor bad. He just is.

We might agree with Hamlet that there are more things in heaven and earth than are dreamed of in our philosophy but whether they are anything to do with God in the traditional sense of the word is open to question.

CHAPTER NINE

ANOTHER SKELETON

We're now into January 2012. Christmas is over, thank goodness. It's not much fun on your own. This year wasn't bad though. I stayed with the Glovers, newly discovered relatives of mine living in Bournemouth. They wouldn't allow me to help with the Christmas lunch or with anything else so I had a nice, lazy time chatting with the children, Rachel and Amy, and watching them open their gifts.

"We've had a wee," Rachel shrieked in great excitement. Naively, I wondered what was so exciting about having a wee until her father explained that a Wii was a technological device for playing games on your television screen.

Ten-year-old Amy got angry with her mother at one point. "You've put down a Catholic school as my first choice for next year," she complained, close to tears. "Don't I get a say in the matter? I'm not Catholic. I don't even believe in God."

Rachel had no such problem with choice. She took the exam for the grammar school last year and passed. Amy took it last month but is sure she has failed. I feel for her. She is less confident than her sister but equally bright.

There are few grammar schools left in the UK. I can't say I'm sorry. I'm dead against a system of selection that determines a child's future at the age of ten or eleven.

This brings me to the second thing in my childhood that, up to now, has remained a shameful secret: failing the 11+.

(1945–1946)

Until I reached ten years old and joined Mr Cording's class most teachers seemed to consider me an able pupil. I was always in the top stream. And in the end-of-term exams I was, so far as I remember, never below fifth in order of merit, even with more than thirty in a class.

But then things changed. About six of us 'jumped' a class and had Mr Cording for our teacher. We were a little younger than the others. They had been with Mr Cording the year before and had already learned to do algebra and geometry, subjects we six had never done.

Apart from Brian Williams, the rest of us never caught up in maths. I began to hate the subject, and finally to hate going to school altogether. Mr Cording became my bogey-man. He asked me questions I couldn't answer, making me blush with embarrassment. Soon, I began to feel sick with worry whenever my turn to answer came up.

Instead of asking for help, I gave up trying and did my best to disappear from view, sitting at the back of the class, hoping Mr Cording wouldn't notice me. Anything written on the blackboard for us to copy and work out, I would copy from Iris, the girl next to me. I was too short-sighted to read the board from that distance. While sitting there I would sink into day-dreams and wake up only when a piece of chalk or board-rubber was flung at my head with the shout, "Attend, girl!"

Mr Cording began to treat me like a moron. I began to act like one, sometimes even unaware that he had asked me a question.

In order to miss school I tried to make myself ill. When my cousin, Joan, had chicken pox, I went secretly to visit her, saying: "Touch me. Breathe on me, please!" But it was no use. The only infection I ever caught was mumps, and that was long before I'd got to Mr Cording's class.

I trudged to school each day, overwhelmed by a feeling of dread, crossing my fingers that Mr Cording would forget my existence. In the end of year exam, I came not fourth or fifth as usual, but fifteenth, and even that was better than I expected.

I knew I was doomed to fail the 11+. I would do my best in English but a good mark in English couldn't possibly make up for a zero in maths. I had already decided there was no point in filling a maths paper with guess work. I might as well leave it blank.

That is exactly what happened: a completed English paper and an empty maths one.

On the day successful children received their letters of acceptance to the grammar school their whoops and yells in the classroom were deafening. They even sang the chants of their new school. The confident ones had already learned them by heart.

Mr Cording, all smiles, allowed them to let off steam, before settling the class down.

Those with no letters sat quietly in their seats, trying to look as if they didn't care.

I wanted to shut out the cries of triumph, go straight home and flop down on my bed, letting the tears flow. No chance of that. I had to tough it out with the other failures.

"Did *you* get a letter, Shirley?" Eleanor, one of the successful girls asked.

I put on a phoney smile. "I don't know yet. I left before the post came."

A few of the others glanced across at me. A likely story, their eyes seemed to say. I kept the phoney smile sticking like plaster to my face. But my stomach churned and I wished I were dead.

I turned away from their probing, feigning rapt attention to the book on my desk. They knew I was lying. I might as well have had the word FAILED stamped in big, bold letters on my forehead.

Anyway, what was the point in hiding things? Soon, the local paper would be out and all our names would be published there, winners and losers. The names of those who had passed would be at the top of the list in descending order of merit, followed by the failures who continued to the bottom. Before long, everyone would know I had failed.

On the day the paper came out, Gran scanned the list carefully. "That Vernon, opposite, is right at the top," she said. "You'll never hear the end of it from Mrs Peedon. She's a real old bragger."

I gave a snort of irritation. "If you're looking for my name," I said, "don't bother. It'll be on the last page, at the bottom."

"No, you're quite high up," Gran said, adjusting her glasses. "There's hundreds after you."

"That's no help," I snapped. At the same time, I knew that, having handed in a blank maths paper, I must have done pretty well in English to have been 'quite high up'.

It wasn't long before the successful children were chatting about their sports gear and smart new uniforms. They all looked forward to flaunting them on their first day to grammar school. We Secondary Modern children had no uniform. Just as well perhaps. No point in advertising the fact that we were going to a school for failures.

On the first day of the next term, I and other sec-mods joined them on the bus that took us to our different schools. Their smart uniforms and distinctive school badges served to reinforce the divisions between us, visually distinguishing winners from losers. I felt my shoulders sag under the heavy shame of my ordinary clothes as if they bore the blunt sign 'not good enough' scrawled over them. I kept my eyes averted from the grammar school children, seeking the comfort of obscurity at the back of the bus. From the corner of my eye, though, I noticed a couple of them glancing at us rejects, before whispering to each other behind their hands. I imagined them saying, "Poor things. They're off to the dumping-ground for no-hopers."

(1946–1950)

At Trealaw secondary school I came first, second or third in all the end-of-term exams with hardly an effort. Few of us made much effort. What was the point? Our future, after leaving school, was destined for some rubbish-job.

Nevertheless, I enjoyed my years there. I got on well with most teachers and, with their help, acquired new interests such as singing and music appreciation. I developed a facility for games and more skill in gymnastics. My spirit soared when Miss Evans, the gym teacher, asked me to demonstrate my rope-climbing to every class.

My favourite time of the year at school was March 1, the day of the eisteddfod when every school abandoned lessons to celebrate St David, the patron saint of Wales. On this day school houses competed against each other in poetry, singing and folk dancing for the glory of winning the St David Shield. I was in my element, taking part in everything, determined my house, Dyfud would win. I always got first prize in recitation. But it was the prize for singing I most coveted. Sadly, I never got higher than second or third, whereas Cousin Mair, my rival in singing, always came first at her school. I have to admit that, bitchy or not, she *did* have a lovely voice. People claimed she sang like Deanna Durbin, a glamorous singer and film star of the time.

Although at school, I skimped on science lessons, cookery and maths, I worked hard at the subjects I enjoyed. I might have worked harder at everything, but always there was that fly in the ointment – the memory of Mr Cording and the way he'd humiliated me. On top of that came my failure of the 11+. Such memories held me back, leaving me with feelings of low self-worth that lasted years afterwards.

I tried not to think of the end of it all – of the pointless, daily grind that would face me for the rest of my life. It didn't bear thinking about. At the same time, there remained a tiny grain of hope that wouldn't disappear – the vague and distant fantasy that one day I might do something interesting and creative, like acting or writing children's stories.

Some hope. When, at the end of our four years, the Careers Adviser came, he had few suggestions for poor sods like us. Not a word about further education or second chances. My friend, Joan Jones, badly wanted to become a nurse. The careers adviser suggested factory work. When Joan, shattered, expressed her disappointment to Miss Davies, our sewing teacher, Miss Davies commented, "You surely don't expect a hospital to accept a secondary modern girl? A nurse has to be trusted with people's lives."

I winced. She made being a nurse sound as out of reach to us as being Prime Minister. Were we so worthless?

When it was my turn to see the careers adviser, I said, boldly, "I'd like to be an actress one day." He raised an eyebrow but made no response other than to say, "You look like a smart girl. I think you might do well as a shop assistant."

Well, what did I expect? We were classified as morons, weren't we? What right had we to harbour expectations above our status?

Our schools and careers advisors gave us no information of possible opportunities or encouragement to set our sites higher than menial, low-skilled work. We were left to find out for ourselves. For some, finding out came after long dreary years of monotonous work. For others it came too late.

Either way, whatever we achieved later in life, the more sensitive among us could never wipe out the feeling of shame bred by this early failure. It clung to one like a leech, even after its cause had been forgotten.

CHAPTER TEN

ADVENTURES IN MUSIC AND DRAMA

*I still feel pangs of shame as I recall that early failure. It will be a
pity if Amy fails too. I believe she already feels she walks in the
shadow of her sister. But failure shouldn't hurt her unduly.
Today's comprehensive offers more chances of success than the
old secondary modern. Anyway, how do you define success? One
definition perhaps is the ability to cope with disappointment.*

*I push thoughts of education out of my mind as I potter about
my flat, trying to find homes for the Christmas gifts I've received.
There are toiletries galore as well as all these chocolates...*

*It would help if I got a bigger place. This though would mean
leaving central London. Prices here have rocketed, and you're
lucky to get a two-bedroom flat for less than a million. It's partly
to do with rich foreigners paying vast sums for property and
pricing the rest of us out of the market.*

*But it's so convenient here in W1. Besides, it's a comfortable
little flat. It's set in a block with an elegant Nash frontage, and
when you step into the entrance hall, you feel you're stepping into
a palace. The illusion vanishes directly you take the lift and visit
the flats. They are much humbler affairs – the dustcarts following
the Lord Mayor's show.*

*Directly I've finished tidying I shall glance through Sheridan's
'The Rivals' the play we're reading at the U3A when the term
starts next week. After that, I'll make myself a coffee, settle on the
sofa and listen to an old LP of Beethoven's seventh symphony. I
don't listen to music half as much now as I did when I was young.*

(1945-1950)

It was in my early years at the secondary school that my
interests in drama and music came to the surface. I put this
down to the passion conveyed to us by some of the teachers

there. The school itself might have lacked challenge but it was saved by some worthy, enthusiastic teachers.

Miss Jones was one of those. An English teacher, fond of Shakespeare, she gave us parts in his plays and urged us to read with feeling. Some of us learned by heart quite long speeches, for *fun*. I still remember Macbeth's 'Is this a dagger which I see before me?'

She encouraged me and my friend, Joan, to join a drama group at one of the local youth clubs.

The trouble was that the one we joined consisted mainly of grammar school children, most of whom were older than we were. From the outset we felt ill at ease mixing with this group of lively young people with their superior knowledge and social skills. It wasn't that they were unfriendly, or that they deliberately drew attention to our inferior schooling. It was just that we were so acutely aware of the differences between us. *They* had passed for the top schools. *We* had failed. These differences *showed*.

The grammar school children displayed their success in their self-assured manner and speech. We, on the other hand, exposed our failure by the way we hovered uncertainly on the fringes of the group, speaking in low, hesitant voices, while trying unsuccessfully to cover our diffidence with inane smiles or nods of agreement.

How could we possibly fit in with these mature, sophisticated teenagers? They even had opinions about politics and the courage to express them.

When the General Election came round, a girl called Ann said of the group's star actress, "Natalie Price claims she's a Conservative. What do you think of that, Maureen? After all Mr Atlee's done for the country."

Maureen tossed her blonde curls and stuck out a contemptuous chin. "Huh! What has *she* got to conserve? Her father's *only* a teacher, same as mine."

I had little idea what a conservative was. I couldn't remember ever having met one. I gathered from Maureen's words though that it was someone who *owned* things and wanted to hang on to what he owned. And that if you owned nothing, there was no point in being a conservative.

What puzzled me more was Maureen's remark – *'only* a teacher'. I'd assumed teachers were pretty well top people. If, instead, they were considered lower rank types with nothing to conserve, what did that make a pit worker, like my stepfather? An unskilled nobody? For the first time, I became aware of social class and my own lowly place in it.

I soon learned that some members had professional or business parents. There was Biddy Fisher whose dad was a doctor, others whose fathers were lawyers or funeral directors. But to me, the girl whose father had the most spectacular occupation was Ruth Jones.

"He's a detective inspector," Joan told me in a dramatic whisper. I gave a gasp of awe. I wasn't envious of Ruth herself who had stick-out teeth and couldn't act for toffee. But how I'd have loved to boast that my father was a detective inspector, working on a murder case, like Paul Temple in the current radio serial!

I didn't venture to argue or express an opinion. I grew increasingly aware that I knew next to nothing to have opinions about. I'm an outsider, I reflected, my chest heavy as lead, but if I join in more, I'll only expose my ignorance.

When I read aloud my first part – lady-in-waiting to Elizabeth 1 – surprised murmurs broke out "She's not bad," some whispered. They evidently expected little from a girl so gauche and ill informed. But although I played competently, I could never really *lose* myself in a role. My feeling of not measuring up made me hopelessly self-conscious. This interfered with my ability to *be* the character. For all that, I still hankered after acting. Perhaps one day...

I had other out-of-school activities apart from drama. One of our teachers, Hayden Davies, inspired in me a passion for music. He played us records of work by Bach, Mozart and

Beethoven. "Lay your heads on your desks," he'd say, his voice falling to a whisper. "And listen. Just listen."

Soon, I became an enthusiastic listener of the Third Programme on the BBC and, after leaving school, I never missed a concert that performed in our town.

At the same time I became obsessed with singing. I practised every day in my room, warbling 'Cherry Ripe' or 'Who is Sylvia?' at the top of my voice. I hoped the neighbours wouldn't hear and grit their teeth the way *I* did when Vernon, across the road, scraped away at the strings of his violin.

"You should join the Co-op choir at Ynyshir," someone said.

I did. It meant a long bus ride, and a fair walk – not that pleasant on winter nights – but so what? It was a small price to pay for a whole evening of singing.

The choir consisted of some forty girls. Our first choirmaster, Mr James, was a thin, no-nonsense man with a black moustache and a fierce way of brandishing his baton.

Soon after I joined, he arranged for us to sing on the BBC. My heart pounded at the news. The BBC! The wireless! Everyone would hear us. We'd be famous. I couldn't wait to tell the family. Aunt Blod said, "Now, before you sing, give a little cough like this – hrmm – then I'll know it's you."

I can recall few details of this event. I know that we travelled to the BBC studio in Cardiff, and that the presenter, a charming woman with a voice like warm syrup, told us we must watch for the light to come on. "That means we're on air," she said. I was on air in more ways than one. My plan to become an acrobat quickly faded. I was going to be a singer as well as an actress.

Mr James retired some months after I joined and a Mr Edwards replaced him. We all adored our new choir master. Though grey-haired, fifty, and with a bulging waist-line – a feature he often joked about – he was full of charm, with a smile that instantly won your heart. I was twelve at the time and had an intense crush on him.

Sometimes, we caught the same bus to Ynyshir and it thrilled me to share his seat even though I was too shy to engage in what you could call 'conversation'.

After attending the choir for six months or so, Mr Edwards chose me and two other girls, each to sing a verse of a song, while the rest joined in the chorus. I felt on top of the world. I would be singing solo in a concert. It was only one verse, but that was quite enough to excite me and to make me feel special in the eyes of my adorable Mr Edwards.

Later, we started rehearsing for the International Eisteddfod in Llangollen. Apart from the thrill of competing, there was also the excitement of the journey and of staying there for two whole nights. I'd never been so far from home before.

The weather was beautiful. So was Llangollen, with its tranquil, green landscape, and mountains in the background, mountains so much higher and more majestic than those of our valley. And in the middle of it all, the kaleidoscope of colour and culture produced by the competitors, especially the dancers, who laughed and chatted as they swirled around in their national costumes.

The Spanish dancers performed for us out in the open, tapping their feet, clicking their castanets, inspiring me with the hope of becoming a dancer one day as well as a singer and an actress.

When it came to our turn to perform, we found we were competing against numerous other girl choirs from all over Europe. We'd have to sing our very best if we wanted to win.

To me it seemed we did just that, sang really well.

Not well enough as it turned out. Hours after our performance there was much gnawing of nails and crossing of fingers as we awaited the results.

We were doomed to disappointment. A choir from Austria won first place. Tension mounting, we prayed we might come second or third. Sadly, we were not even runners up but placed near the bottom. When I saw the look of anguish on Mr Edwards' face, my heart bled for him. I wished I could think of something to say that would cheer him up.

The Co-op couldn't forgive him for this failure. At our next rehearsal we found to our surprise that both Mr Edwards *and* Mr James, our previous conductor, turned up. Mr James threw Mr Edwards a look of such scorn that none of us girls could possibly have missed it.

Then, turning to us, stiffly he said in a voice like steel. "After your woeful performance in Llangollen, I've been asked to return to remedy the matter. You've clearly slipped into bad habits."

That last remark was meant for Mr Edwards, of course. A deliberate put-down.

I seethed at his humiliation. So, I think, did most of the girls. Mr James turned to the other man with pursed lips. An argument broke out. It should have been private but we could hear every word as their voices grew ever louder and more strident. At last Mr Edwards picked up his briefcase, faced us and said, "I'm sorry, girls, if I've let you down. But not anymore. I'm leaving."

Instantly, a girl in the middle row, jumped to her feet and cried, "So am I." With that, she strode from the room.

Gasps broke out at this dramatic turn of events. I wondered if others would follow. But no one did. Perhaps no one else had the guts. Instead, we remained stiff and uneasy on our chairs, awaiting the next move.

Mr James, a look of grim determination on his face, rolled up his sleeves and gave the order for song sheets to be handed out. Soon we were singing, 'All in an April Evening'. After the first few bars, he stopped us. "Put your song sheets down," he commanded. "Who taught you to sing like that?" He was clearly having another dig at poor Mr Edwards.

I soon left the choir. Mr James was a first-rate choirmaster, I suppose, but he was quite without warmth, and I couldn't forgive him for the way he'd humiliated Mr Edwards in front of us all.

Anyway, I had other chances to sing. I had started singing solo at chapel and at concerts organised by the youth club as well as at the school eisteddfods so, although I *missed* choir rehearsals, I wasn't deprived of singing activities altogether.

Fast forwarding to the present, I try singing 'All in an April Evening' as I make myself a coffee. My God, is that me? I ask myself. What a pathetic apology of a voice! I haven't sung for years, that's the problem, and with singing, it's a case, not only of ageing lungs, but of taking note of that sage advice, 'use it or lose it'.

Still, no use regretting the past and what has or hasn't been done. The now is more important. And the now means that, having tidied up, I shall drink my coffee and read through `The Rivals', as planned, before immersing myself in the glorious music of Beethoven.

GROWING UP AND LEAVING

1950–1961

CHAPTER ELEVEN

TO BE OR NOT TO BE

Trealaw Secondary Modern might have been considered a rubbish school, but when, in 1950, it was time for me to leave, I wept for three days. I wept at the loss of my friends, at the loss of my place in that safe little community. Most of all, I wept at the loss of my childhood.

The adult world felt hostile, bleak, an unpredictable world of never-ending drudgery which offered no escape. But I was fifteen, grown up, more or less, and I had to serve my time as a grown-up and do what was necessary to survive. That meant taking a job, whatever was available. My grandmother couldn't go on supporting me.

I dragged myself from one job to another, unable to settle at anything. The first was a clothing factory. Day after day, from eight to six, I stood at the factory line, chalking out the shapes of men's collars, cutting them, and passing them down the conveyer belt. My legs ached from standing so long in one spot, and I grew corns on my fingers from holding the scissors. My wage was one pound six shillings a week, but after setting aside money for fares and factory lunches, as well as for my keep, there was little left for anything else.

Each night after dinner, I was too tired to do anything but sleep. Each morning, when I woke up, I wished I were dead.

One evening, after work, I planned to kill myself. There seemed no future, no hope. I couldn't tolerate the thought of slaving away day after day at one mind-numbing job after another. If this was what life was about, it wasn't worth the bother. I wanted out.

I made my way to the river which was only a ten minute walk from the house. The water looked dark, uninviting. The thought of drowning myself filled me with dread, but so did other options: cutting my throat, hanging myself, jumping off a quarry in the mountain.

I stood on the bridge over the river for half an hour, staring down at the black water, trying to summon up the will to jump in. I couldn't make up my mind which was worse: the hell of living or the hell of dying.

Soon, my mind was made up for me. Miraculously, Gran appeared on the bank with my friend, Joan Jones. Spotting me, they began to gesticulate, shout and run towards the bridge. "Thank God! At last!" Gran was saying, as she puffed her way towards me. "We've been looking for you everywhere." Her voice was high-pitched with anxiety. "Silly, silly girl! What are you doing here, by the river?" I didn't tell them. But they must have guessed. Why else would they have come this way? They took me firmly by the arm and marched me home. I went without a murmur.

Soon after this incident, Gran had a chat with Mr Isaacs who ran the Co-op. He offered me a job in the office there. I postponed committing suicide though I didn't drop the idea altogether.

The Co-op offered more variety than the factory, and the wage was two pounds a week with no bus fares to pay. That meant a pound for me and a pound for Gran.

I stuck this a year, sorting, filing, pasting dividend slips into customers' books. It was boring but not unpleasant. That couldn't be said of some of the girls who were a bunch of prize bitches.

Word had got round that I was a shameless flirt. "She has a different boy every night," I heard one whisper to another. It's true that, since working there, I had started going to dances and flirting with boys and, admittedly, I liked a bit of variety. I was flattered by the attention, and the more attention I got, the happier I was. But a different boy every night? That implied all sorts of goings-on that were well outside my experience. All it amounted to was that a boy escorted me home from dances each Saturday. If, most times, it was a different boy, so what? I liked to ring the changes.

Gossip got ever wilder. "I'm told you go out with married men," a girl called Irene said, with a smirk.

I gaped. "News to me."

It seems that one dance with a married man was quite enough to indicate a scandalous affair.

A less sensitive person might have laughed it off or shut them up with a witty retort. But I felt bruised by the sly looks and whispers of these straight-laced, gossipy girls. I decided to move on.

My next job was in Cardiff working for a football pool company – Shermans. It was almost as bad as the factory but I stuck it for several months. The reason was that I had discovered close by an Evening College where I could take a language course. There was nothing of that kind in the Valley so I decided to enrol. I still felt an uneducated dimwit and hadn't forgotten my excruciating shyness when mixing with grammar school children.

I attended the college straight after work three evenings a week, studying German, French and Spanish. The classes were full of ex-grammar school students but, surprise, surprise, I came top of each class every week, even though I hadn't studied languages before. My confidence soared.

The pity was that in order to carry on with classes, I had to travel to Cardiff and also put up with my job there. This became a no-no. I decided that stuffing football coupons into envelopes was not my goal in life. Nor was the tedious journey to and from work. Or the nightmares I kept having about making a terrible blunder and sending thousands of pounds in winnings to the wrong people.

I chose to quit. Dropping my classes at the same time wouldn't be the end of the world, I thought. I could study on my own. I'd borrow language books from the library, history books too. I'd start educating myself with a vengeance, simultaneously, I hoped, winning some self-respect.

After two more crappy jobs too unmemorable to write about, I started work as a psychiatric nurse. I stuck this for nearly two years – a record in my case.

I must confess that, unlike Joan Jones, now happily training to be a midwife, I had no aspiration to become a nurse. I was interested in people but wouldn't have described myself as the hands-on type. I also had serious doubts about my practical skills. Could I cope with dressing wounds or giving injections?

But, having served notice at my last job, I was out of work again. The job of psychiatric student nurse was available. And, hell, I thought, nursing was a step up from factory or routine office work.

Besides, the word 'student' was encouraging: I might learn something.

My job application went to an institute in Llantrisant. It housed people called in those days *mental defectives*. However, I was to spend the first few months at Bridgend Mental Hospital. There I would study, observe and take my preliminary exam before moving to Llantrisant. Taking exams no longer bothered me. "You did okay at Cardiff Tech," I told myself.

The patients in Bridgend Hospital were not mentally defective. They were broadly classified as either *neurotic* or *psychotic*. The neurotics were voluntary patients. They suffered from the milder disorders such as anxiety, and had not lost touch with the real world. They were housed in pleasant open wards and seemed to have a great time, painting, exercising or discussing their problems. If that's therapy, I thought, I wouldn't mind some myself.

The locked wards of the sectioned, psychotic patients were another matter altogether. They seemed more like part of a prison than of a hospital. I watched aghast as long-term

Schizophrenics and manic depressives paced up and down those dreary day-rooms. The more elderly and chronically ill often sat in a large circle, chairs set against the walls, still and silent as zombies.

Even when taken out for exercise, they were confined to a locked yard. And all they did there was walk, backwards, forwards, round and round, sometimes muttering to themselves, occasionally screeching at other patients. The ward sister, often a hefty woman, marched up and down like a prison warder, a bunch of keys dangling at her belt.

Many psychotics, I heard, had been there for years with little hope of getting out.

They could be treated roughly. Once, I saw nurses trying to force medication down a patient's mouth till it bled. Even then she spat it out. Later, I tried gentle persuasion. It worked.

Most of the treatments given, eg. ECT, lobotomy, insulin coma therapy, were largely hit and miss affairs. Sometimes they worked. Sometimes, they did more harm than good.

Preliminary student nurses had little practical work to do on the wards other than bed-making or blanket-bathing. Much of our time was taken up with lectures on anatomy as well as on basic nursing, in preparation for the exam.

I enjoyed the studying and passed the exam with ease. And now it was time to transfer from the psychiatric hospital to the Institute for the Mentally Defective.

Hensol Castle, near Llantrisant looked an impressive place. An eighteenth century Gothic mansion, it stood in attractive grounds, surrounded by trees, flowers and a lake crossed by a bridge. I learned from Nurse Jennings who showed me round, that it became a 'colony for mental defectives' in 1930.

As we walked through the castle grounds she pointed out several wards, a school, a laundry, workshops. The 300 to 400 residents, she explained, were usually admitted because they couldn't be cared for at home.

They were housed in about eight different wards, and divided by sex and grade. The medical terms for classifying these grades sounded shocking to me, a bit like the insults we toss at each other in temper or irritation. At the top were the *feeble minded* – patients with IQs between 50–70; below, the *imbeciles* – moderate to severely retarded: and at the bottom, the *idiots*. They had mental ages of two or less. There was a further grade called *moral defectives*. These were mainly unmarried mothers and those given to anti-social behaviour or petty crimes. They were housed with the feeble minded. The lowest (idiot) grade resided in a special unit called the Villas. This was situated over the bridge, on the other side of the lake.

My first sight on visiting that unit was of a twelve-year-old boy squatting on the ground. He looked normal enough except that he was rocking backwards and forwards and bleating like a sheep. Behind him, other patients, sat or tottered about, making meaningless gestures accompanied by squeals and grunts. And over all hung the distinctive and competing smells of urine and disinfectant. You'll get used to it, I assured myself, but my stomach turned over at the thought of ever working on that ward.

The high grade residence, J, was, by contrast, clean and orderly. The patients there worked, some in the laundry or kitchen or as cleaners in nearby houses. Others helped look after patients on the low-grade wards, a task they were stuck with from early morning to late evening. I couldn't understand how some of them landed there, especially those whose only crime was to have a child out of wedlock. They had no autonomy to speak of or motivation to govern their own lives.

I saw little in the way of treatment, though I know that LSD was used on certain patients. Epileptics received medication to control it. Others had daily doses of amphetamine – presumably to make them more sociable, or tranquilisers to calm them.

The lowest grade patients often couldn't walk or even sit up. They needed constant care to avoid bedsores.

It was care that was paramount. This was easy when dealing with Down's syndrome children. They were often lovable and able to learn. But you had to be really dedicated to care for lower grade patients. Many were incontinent, unable to communicate or use a knife and fork, and often had unattractive habits such as grunting, dribbling, throwing food around or tearing off their clothes.

My thoughts and feelings of revulsion when working with these patients appalled me. What are they for? I kept asking myself. They can't communicate, feed themselves, can't even escape from danger when there's an obvious escape route. All they can do is guzzle, soil themselves and make meaningless noises. They're nature's mistakes, and there's no point in their existence.

I tried never to allow my negative feelings to get in the way of my caring. And most nurses, I'm glad to say, treated them kindly and with gentleness.

But there was some abuse. Cyril Jones, a young man who had been a student with me, said casually one day, "If a patient plays up, we give him a thrashing then plonk him in a cold bath to stop the bruises." I should have reported this but didn't have the guts. Anyway, I thought, Cyril would be sure to deny it. Years later, I heard he'd given up nursing mental defectives to become a prison warder.

The work was tedious, and I was so tired when I got home, I sometimes fell asleep in the middle of a meal.

I was just as tired getting up in the morning. Gran rose before me. She'd yell up the stairs, "It's five o'clock." "Coming," I'd yawn, and go straight back to sleep, dreaming I was getting washed and dressed, until she called again: "Shirley, get up. You'll be late."

My heart would sink to realise my preparation for work was only a dream and I'd have to go through the whole process again. Some mornings I'd have this same dream over and over before forcing my eyes open and willing myself to face the world. Often I rose so late there wasn't time for breakfast. That's when I'd run like hell to the bus-stop, munching a piece of toast on the way.

In my second year, I passed my Part 2 exam, This qualified me to take charge of a ward, if Sister was off sick. It meant more responsibility: writing reports, seeing to medicines, and so on. It was more interesting than working on the ward the whole time. On the other hand, I hated telling nurses what to do, especially when they were older and more experienced than I.

I wondered if I could stick another year. I could then take my finals and become a qualified nurse. It would be nice to be qualified at something. But could I stomach another year? And what would be the point? It wasn't my intention to carry on nursing for the rest of my life. I wasn't cut out for it. In fact, I'd begun to dread going to work each day, my heart sinking every time I faced those poor, vacant-eyed, deformed creatures who had no hope of a cure for their disabilities.

I began to wonder what the devil was wrong with me. Why couldn't I stick any job I took? Other people did.

For me, however, the whole process of living had come to be a matter of stepping from one hell-hole into another.

Dark thoughts thrust themselves into my mind. Maybe I wasn't meant to live. Maybe I too was a mistake of nature – unable to settle, whatever I did. The old longing for oblivion returned. Once more, I wanted to curl up and sink into a dreamless sleep from which there was no waking.

And this time there was a chance I could do it, in a comfortable, non-violent way.

A plan began to form in my mind: I would steal some sodium-amatol from the dispensary. I often visited the place to collect drugs for the ward. I could do it easily. No one would find out.

I can't remember exactly how I pulled off this stunt. But I did.

I took my stolen pills home. There were twenty. I'd take the lot, swallowing them down with orangeade, after Gran had gone to bed.

Things didn't go quite according to plan. After swallowing nine, I came to a halt. My gullet refused to take more. Each time I tried, I heaved and sicked the pill back up.

Nine wasn't enough to achieve permanent oblivion, but I did get a long sleep. The following afternoon I woke, feeling sick and half dead. My grandmother was shouting and shaking me, but I could scarcely move or utter a sound in response. I saw her in a kind of fog, clasping and unclasping her hands, as she muttered, "Oh, my God, what are we going to do?"

She guessed what I'd been up to and didn't phone a doctor, too afraid police might become involved. Suicide was a criminal offence.

At least I missed two days of work. Not that I enjoyed them. I felt too sick.

On the third day, I struggled back and put up with a couple more months.

During that time, while sitting in the canteen one day with other nurses, I heard something to make my pulse quicken, something that would change my life.

"Our Rose is taking her GCEs at Cardiff Tech," Nurse Jennings told us. "She failed most of them at school. Too busy playing around."

"I wish my Derek would do that," one of the others commented.

To say I was all ears is an understatement.

"Can anyone take their GCEs?" I asked, "even if they didn't go to grammar school?"

"Of course. Why not?"

I felt myself blush under their sudden scrutiny. Affecting a casual air, I said, "It's just that I know a girl who'd be interested, that's all." I wasn't about to confess who the girl was.

Nurse Jennings frowned. "I'm sure there's no rule about what school you went to," she said. "So tell her to apply. If she does well, she can even take her 'A' levels and go to university."

"Really?" I smiled. The darkness in my mind lifted. Suddenly, life seemed full of hope again.

The following day, I gave in my notice.

CHAPTER TWELVE

EDUCATION, EDUCATION, EDUCATION

I left Hensol Castle in the summer of 1955 when I was twenty years old. While serving my notice, I spent one of my free days in Cardiff and enrolled for GCE evening classes at the Technical College. I also found myself a day job, a short distance away, at Dolcis, the shoe shop.

A wild, insane joy swept through me. I almost skipped to Cardiff station for the train home. I wanted to sing and shout: I have another chance, a chance to go to college and change my life."

I arrived home, bursting to tell Gran my news.

"Good luck to you, love," she said. "You'll be dead beat though, working every day and studying every night. And there'll be all that travelling again, back and fore to Cardiff."

"I'll be okay, don't worry," I said.

A week later I started at Dolcis. The work was by no means a doddle. In those days shoes were not displayed on racks and left for customers to try on for themselves. Instead, they were hidden away in boxes. The assistant had to scrabble through box after box for the colour and size the customer required. On busy days, you might be serving three customers at once, each wanting to try on about ten pairs of shoes.

On quieter days, though, you had time to chat with the customers and help them decide between one pair of shoes and another. "I think I prefer the suede on you," I'd say. "Suede is so fashionable too." I became a pretty good saleswoman and soon started earning commission.

For once, I had little to grouse about. The other assistants were pleasant and full of banter and jokes. And there were all those lovely shoes to buy at a discount. On top of that there were the evenings of study to look forward to.

Evening classes started in September preparing you for the GCE exams in May and June. I studied a different subject every evening, taking five altogether – English, History, Biology, Art, and Human Anatomy and Physiology. No maths of course. Mr Cording had put me off that subject for good.

The students were mostly ex-grammar school types who had either left school early or failed one or more GCEs. I found them a friendly bunch, and the teachers helpful.

Most of my studying I did on the train; homework, on days off. I seldom studied on week nights since I often didn't get home till ten o'clock. It was hard work but never left me feeling drained. I put this down to motivation. I was determined to succeed and beginning to enjoy life for a change.

In Art, besides Object Drawing and Still Life, I also chose Life Drawing. No one else opted for this, so there were no classes, and I had to take the exam alone and provide my own model! Luckily, I had a friend delighted to help out. Her father was an artist and she often posed for him.

When the exams came round, Dolcis gave me time off to take them. I left for the Technical College on these days, full of trepidation. Suppose I couldn't answer the questions? Suppose I failed? I broke out in goose-bumps at the very possibility. However, once I started writing, I lost some of my nervousness and actually began to enjoy myself.

"I finished all my papers," I told Gran. "I *might* pass. You never know."

During the next couple of months I took things easy, meeting friends and going dancing in my spare time. I'd acquired a new boy-friend called Ieuan who was a medical student. We used to walk home from dances on Saturday nights, absorbed in arguing about religion. He had recently converted to Catholicism and would have liked to convert me.

He had about as much hope of that as I, of converting him to atheism.

Then came August, month of the exam results. When the post arrived, I sat for some time with the dreaded brown envelope lying closed in front of me. Dare I open it? I ran my tongue along my lips. I'd worked so hard. I must pass. I *had* to, if only to make up for failing the 11+ those years ago.

At last, gritting my teeth, I tore it open and unfolded the slip of paper inside. It showed my marks for each subject. Hardly daring to breathe, I read through them, and let out a huge sigh of relief. I'd obtained between 70% and 80% in everything except Art, which got me only 58%. No matter. The important thing was I had passed in all five subjects. I began to breathe again.

Gran was cock-a-hoop at my news, especially when I told her I intended to go to college. She set about making some ginger beer and Welsh cakes to celebrate. "You wait till I tell that Mrs Peedon," she chortled. "She'll soon see that her grandson isn't the only one round here with brains."

It was too late now to apply for teacher-training. I would try next year. In the meantime, I'd stay on at Dolcis and in the evenings study for one or two A-levels. I'd need them if I decided to go to university later on.

I wasn't sure I had any real vocation for teaching. It was the long holidays that attracted me – several weeks a year to do what you liked in! Bliss compared with the paltry fortnight you got with most jobs. And there was the time at college beforehand to study. Now that really appealed.

I was a bit sick of travelling backwards and forwards to Cardiff, though, and decided to find a way out of this. I wrote to my Uncle Tom and Aunt Ivy and asked if I might stay with them for a year, assuring them I would pay for my keep. Uncle Tom wrote back to say yes, so the following month I packed a case and off I went to Cardiff.

My aunt and uncle lived in a small street called Violet Place. It had the personality of a violet, I thought. It was made up of neat, unimposing little houses with tiny gardens front and back. The whole stood shyly at the bottom of a lane, well away from the main road.

The house was my aunt's pride and joy, her palace. She and my uncle treated it with loving care, keeping it spick and span, painting and decorating it regularly, and sparing no expense when renovation or refurbishment was due.

I suspect that most of their money went on the house. Yet they were by no means well off. Aunt Ivy was a housewife; Uncle Tom, a factory supervisor whose earnings were hardly top drawer.

My aunt, however, was a good housekeeper and particularly good at managing money. To do this, she often scrimped on basics such as hot water and electricity. When you had a bath, two inches of water were quite sufficient, in her view. To save electric light you sat together in one room on dark evenings and went to bed at 9.30.

For all her stinginess, I couldn't help admiring my aunt. She was a straight-backed, elegant woman, shrewd, smartly dressed, always efficient at everything she did. I could see her running a successful business, running several businesses in fact. But Aunt Ivy had a secret, a secret she managed to hide from everyone.

She couldn't read or write.

It was years before I found this out. She was so clever at hiding it. "What does that say?" she'd ask, squinting over a set of instructions. "My eyesight has got so bad. I'll really have to get glasses soon."

According to my Aunt Blodwen the reason for her illiteracy was that she'd had so little schooling as a child. She'd been kept at home to help bring up her younger brothers and sisters.

But her parsimony about matters such as electricity made things almost impossible for someone who had only evenings to swot for exams. I was soon wondering how, in this situation, I could pass an 'A' level in less than a year, in a subject I'd not done before, when there was so little chance to study.

I had decided to take English Literature. It was lucky in the circumstances I'd opted to take one subject rather than two. Even so, there were loads of books to read, including Chaucer, two plays by Shakespeare and five novels.

This meant a lot of studying. But there was nowhere to study in peace. The television blared away each evening. I could hear it even when I sat in the kitchen.

"Can't I stay up another hour?" I asked when bedtime arrived, "I shan't forget to switch off the light."

My aunt frowned. "No. Too much studying is bad for you. You'll ruin your eyesight."

"But it's the only time I have. I'm at work during the day."

She tightened her lips and wouldn't budge. I wanted to scream with frustration.

I tried reading in my bedroom, but my aunt spotted the light under the door. "You must switch off the light as soon as you get into bed," she said.

But I had a neat little plan. I bought myself a bicycle lamp and, after going to bed each night, studied under the bedclothes. At last, I was able to concentrate and learn something.

My bicycle lamp meant I could study for a whole hour before going to sleep, longer still when I went to bed early.

Even so, I didn't manage to write a single essay.

"Essays are so important," our tutor warned, "Neglect them at your peril."

My heart sank at his words. It sank even further when one of the students said, "If I don't pass English Literature *this* year, I might as well give up. I've failed it twice."

But she's a bright student, I thought. She's always got something clever to say during lectures, whereas I say nothing at all. If she's failed twice, what hope is there for me?

I arranged to have my holidays two weeks before the exams and spend them back in the valley studying at Gran's. There, I set to work writing essays on the set books.

When it was time to take the exam, I felt confident enough about tackling the paper on Shakespeare and Chaucer and the one on novels. But there was a *third* paper, and that one terrified me. It was a paper on pure literary criticism, mainly poetry, and you didn't know in advance what the poems were going to be.

I felt myself break into a sweat as I stared down at the sheet. We had not studied poetry in class and I had no idea how to go about writing a criticism. I managed to scribble off a page or two but it was pretty poor stuff, I thought, and I'd have to do amazingly well in the other papers, if I wanted to pass.

Some months before the exam, I had applied to the Clearing House for an entry form for teacher-training college. My first choice was Goldsmith's, London. Going to London was my dream. I had visited the city with my friend, Joan Jones, when we were fourteen, staying with relatives of hers. We had fallen head over heels with the place, and it was my great ambition to live there one day.

I travelled to London, full of hope. But the woman who interviewed me soon squashed it. She had my application form in front of her. "We can't take you, I'm afraid," she said.

"Why not?" I asked, "I had good marks for my 'O' levels, and I'm taking an 'A' level in May."

"Oh, I can see you're a clever little girl," she said, patronizingly, "but we can't accept you. You've had no sixth form experience."

I got the train home, close to tears. Why, I thought, hadn't they made it clear beforehand what they wanted, instead of letting me waste my time and money traipsing all the way to London?

When, shamefaced, I told my aunt I'd been turned down, she said, "Oh, dear, after going all that way!" She sounded sympathetic enough. But her look told me it was the outcome she'd expected.

My second and third choices didn't invite me for an interview. I'm still not good enough, I sighed. Perhaps, though, if I pass this 'A' level, I'll be accepted for *next* year. I can wait.

As things turned out, I didn't have to. A few months later, Shenstone College in Worcestershire offered me a place in September of that same year.

Shortly after that, I received a letter to say that I had passed my 'A' level in English Literature.

CHAPTER THIRTEEN

BOYFRIENDS PAST AND PRESENT

Before moving on with the story of my education, I'd like to return briefly to the present.

I'm with Frieda again. I missed last Tuesday's session. Forgot all about it.

She gives the clock on the wall a quick glance, adjusts her glasses and turns over a few pages of her notebook. Then she smiles across at me, all ready to scribble down more of my secrets. I wonder what secrets *she* has. I know nothing about *her* at all. I don't even know if she's married and has children. Or if, like me, she ever gets into a panic about growing old. I shouldn't think she's much younger than I. Those are pretty deep lines around her mouth, and her hair is more grey than brown.

I take a breath. "I'm sorry about last week. It's not like me to forget appointments."

She gives me a piercing look, eyes narrowed, head on one side. "Could it be that you wanted to forget?"

Oh no. She's dishing out that Freudian stuff again. I answer with a sharpness unintended. "It was no defence mechanism, I assure you. I'd got out of the weekly routine, that's all, due to the long Christmas holiday."

She gazes at me intently.

I drop my eyes, feeling flustered. "Anyway, I had things on my mind. And I'm not sleeping."

Her expression changes to concern. "I see. Can you think of any reason why it's got worse?"

I sigh. "No, it's the same old thing. Disappointment at not having made my mark in life. Being alone..." I pause. "That does have advantages, I know. Gives one freedom, space. But when I'm feeling low, I have this need to have a man around, someone I care for and who cares for me."

"You do have men friends, I believe."

"Companions, yes. People I see from time to time. There's no intimacy between us."

"Is that what you're looking for, intimacy?"

"I suppose so, but emotional, more than physical. A mutually caring sort of intimacy."

"And you don't have that with the men you go out with?"

"No. There's no real warmth. We're just friends. Friends are important, I know, but I'd like someone who's more than just a friend."

I think in turn about them, beginning with Julian. "He's a professor of natural history," I say, "specializing in amphibians. He discovered a new genus of frog once which was named after him."

"Hm. He sounds interesting."

"I suppose so, if you like frogs. The trouble is he has the emotions of a frog. I search his face, listen to his voice, for signs of joy, anger, surprise. There's nothing. He's kind and reliable enough, but the only affection he shows is a peck on the cheek. I think he expects the advances to come from me."

"Perhaps he's shy. How about the others?"

"Well, there's Colin. He's a linguist. Teaches Chinese, Japanese, French and Dutch. He's also interested in Science. He was friendly with Stephen Hawkin when he was at Oxford, also with Richard Dorking. He can be good company, so long as you don't discuss language. If you do, he'll talk non-stop till your eyes glaze over."

"Is he as cold as Julian?"

"He's livelier, and he's certainly not backward in coming forward. He's even dropped hints about my going to live with him. He has two quite decent properties: one in London, one in the country. But step inside either of them and you're stumbling over books, boxes, and all manner of rubbish. I couldn't put up with that. Anyway, there's no romance there, no passion."

"He must have some feeling for you if he's asked you to live with him, don't you think?"

I roll my eyes. "With Colin, one woman's as good as another."

Her smile suggests she's taking that with a grain of salt. "What about the third? No use either?"

"Oh, Hugh's nice – a happy, cheerful sort, mad about music, and a lot more generous than the other two, won't let me pay for anything. He's not badly off, I think, has a beautifully kept house and garden, drives a Mercedes…"

"So, what's wrong with that one."

"Well, he's ten years younger than I. Colin's *five* years younger – though he doesn't know it – and that's bad enough. It's funny but I've never been able to really fancy a man who's much younger than myself, though it's quite convenient in a way. I'd probably die first and he'd be able to arrange a good send off."

She laughs. "It's always good to look on the bright side." She studies her notes and says quietly, "So Julian's too dull, Colin's too messy, Hugh's too young. A bit picky, aren't we?"

"Perhaps. But I'd put up with a lot if I felt romantic about any of them." I stop, embarrassed. "I'm being pathetic, aren't I? Like a teenager. I should be past that sort of thing at my age. But I keep getting this empty feeling. I try to fill my life with interesting activities but always I'm aware of something missing. I have family, friends, but they're not enough."

"What about your time at the U3A? You must meet plenty of potential men friends there?"

"No. Let's face it, most men my age are either married or dead. I know few live single ones who'd attract me. And even those who appear suitable turn out to be gay."

I pause to reflect.

"There is one man I'm attracted to. I sometimes travel with him on the train and we chat. I wouldn't mind a romantic liaison with him. He's married, of course. Quite unobtainable. Anyway, he's probably not the slightest bit interested in me."

"Maybe you're interested only in those who are unobtainable?"

"So I don't have to commit, you mean?" I frown as I roll that over in my mind. "Perhaps you're right."

"Has it always been like that?"

"Early on perhaps." I think back to my youth and to my first experiences with the opposite sex.

The first young man I remember going out with was a Ukrainian watchmaker. His name was Dimitri and he rode a motor bike. I went out with him because he was good-looking. And being foreign as well as older than I, added to his charms.

The trouble is that, having been brought up by women, I looked upon men as a different species. I put them on a pedestal, judging them to be more god than human. So when Dimitri took me to the seaside one day and suddenly said, "Excuse me but I'm going for a pee," he immediately fell off his pedestal. My god-like man didn't 'go for a pee'. If he did, he wouldn't say so, especially in that coarse way.

My next young man was a naval officer called Gareth whom I met at a dance. He was only two years older than I but looked so smart in his uniform I forgave him that, and we had a romantic liaison that lasted at least six months. We couldn't meet often but he wrote me long and passionate letters from abroad, letters which thrilled me to the core and made me long for his return. Unfortunately, his feeling for me was deeper than mine for him, and when, on returning from one of his voyages, he said he was madly in love with me, my romantic feelings suddenly and inexplicably evaporated. From that moment I didn't want to see him again but was too cowardly to say so.

I had started going out with other young men while he was away. They were little more than casual flirtations, but Gareth found out. His final letter was full of bitterness in which he wrote, 'I should have known that a leopard never changes its spots'.

My grandmother was disappointed. She liked Gareth, and whenever he had called, she deliberately left us alone together. She obviously trusted him and hoped we would marry.

She was less enthusiastic about my next boy-friend, Ted. He was well into his twenties and, if I remember rightly, worked for an insurance company. His great ambition, however, was to become a writer. Having tried his hand at a novel or two without success, he remained hopeful, deciding to have a go at non-fiction. When I met him, he was in the middle of constructing a course of lessons in his spare time called 'How to be Happy'. "I think home tuition is my forte," he said. "When the course is completed, I'll get it published. And it will help thousands of miserable people to find happiness, as well as make me some money."

I was less sure. As for Gran, she scoffed at his ambitions. "He's full of dreams, that one," she said. "You should have stuck with Gareth. He was a nice boy, with a good job and prospects. That Ted now…" She clicked her tongue. "He's going nowhere."

Poor Ted! No one took his ambitions seriously, not even his own family. He lived with his sister and brother-in-law and their children in a poky, terraced house. When he talked about his writing, his sister would sigh and roll her eyes as if to say, "There he goes again. When is he going to start living in the real world?"

Perhaps, later in life, he surprised them all by realising his dreams. I didn't remain his girl-friend for long enough to find out. He too showed signs of becoming serious, and, again, I lost interest. I was by no means ready to settle down. I wanted to educate myself first, and then perhaps meet and marry a clever and charming professional man.

It was while I was studying for my GCEs that I met Ieuan, the medical student. He was a thin, serious young man with strong, religious views. I liked his company, despite our different viewpoints. We both enjoyed a good argument and discussed endlessly such matters as the existence of God, the ethics of blood sports, homosexuality and other controversial issues.

"How can you possibly visit a bull fight in Spain, and enjoy watching a poor beast being tormented?" I asked him once.

"But the bull's bred for it," he replied, as if this were reason enough. "And think of the bravery of the Matador. That's surely good to see?"

I gave a snort. "It's as disgusting as the 'sport' of seeing a fox being torn to pieces by hounds."

Another point on which we differed was homosexuality, illegal in those days. "It's an abomination," Ieuan said, "and I hope it never becomes legalised."

In spite of our differences, we kept up a friendship of sorts even after I left for College. I always hoped that one day I'd manage, through argument, to water down some of his dogmatic opinions and bring him nearer my own point of view. But our relationship had cooled by that time and never regained its initial energy.

While I was studying A-level Literature, he was preparing for his fourth year medical exam at University. When his results came out, I could tell from the grim look on his face and the flatness of his voice that he had failed. "I'll have to give up all hope of a medical career now," he said with a sigh.

I learned later that he had taken a temporary job as a milkman, before finding work as a public health inspector.

A cough from Frieda makes me start. Heavens, I've been jabbering away, my mind so far back in the past, I'd almost forgotten her presence. I glance at the clock. Five minutes left.

She frowns down at her notes, a hand resting on her chin. "Would you have considered marrying Ieuan, if he had *passed* his examinations?"

I hesitate, fiddling with the brooch pinned to my collar. "I don't think so. I was too interested in educating myself to think about marriage. Anyway, I couldn't marry someone who has no compassion for animals."

I break off. That wasn't the whole story.

Feeling my face redden, I say, "At the same time, becoming a health inspector, rather than a qualified doctor did make him less attractive in my eyes as a potential marriage partner. It just shows, doesn't it, how shallow and snobbish I was in those days? Even though I had nothing to be snobbish about."

Frieda shrugs. "You wanted to get on in life. Climb out of poverty and failure. And you wanted a man who would help you do this – someone successful whom you could look up to – a father-figure, perhaps, who would compensate for the one you didn't have. Ieuan, I'm afraid, fell off his pedestal by failing his examination."

I smile doubtfully. "He was only a year older than I. Hardly a father-figure."

"Nevertheless…" She closes her notebook and looks thoughtful. "You did have a stepfather once. Did you not look upon him as a father-figure?"

She gets up. "Perhaps we can talk about that next time."

CHAPTER FOURTEEN

MY STEPFATHER AND OTHER RELATIONS

Since my last session with Frieda, I've been thinking a lot about my stepfather. His name was John Lewis, and, despite the passing of years, I remember clearly his thick-set build and florid complexion; the shock of auburn hair brushed back from his face; his wide mouth. Unimpressive to look at, he was, furthermore, quiet and shy, like my mother. This was partly the result of a childhood illness that had left him deaf. Deafness limited his options not only in finding well-paid work but in making friends.

We had no relationship to speak of. If there was one, it was one of indifference. I didn't *dislike* him exactly, but nor did I admire him. Being poor and deaf and not even good looking, he didn't at all measure up to those clever, successful fathers I'd read about in story books. Thus, with the harsh uncompromising judgement of a child I labelled him *not good enough* and turned my back on him.

It was towards the end of the war that he became friendly with my mother. I was nine or ten at the time and growing uneasy about the progress of this friendship, especially when Mam began to make herself cosy on John's lap. "How would you like a new Daddy?" he asked me one day.

I turned away, appalled, and ran from the room. "Not one like you," I muttered when out of earshot. "You're stupid. And you look like George Formby. All you want is a ukulele."

They married in Moriah Chapel, the only time I ever saw my mother in a place of worship. Afterwards, they settled in my grandmother's house, in rooms separate from hers. No father-daughter bonding developed between John and me. *My fault, I suspect.* I gave it so little encouragement, spending most of the time in my grandmother's part of the house. When John was at work though, I hopped in and out of both apartments, as did my mother and grandmother.

In just under a year my brother David came along. I'd had little interest in babies up to now, often wondering why women became so dotty about such dull little creatures. Their only abilities seemed to be to cry, scream or be sick. And you could scarcely tell one from another, in spite of all the talk about 'having his father's nose' or 'his mother's eyes'.

My feeling for David, however, was anything but indifferent, especially when he approached his first year and had started to walk and talk. To me he was the prettiest, most charming little boy in the whole world. He had pale, blond hair, blue eyes, and such a sunny nature he would laugh and sing all day long while running up and down the sitting-room in the little grey rompers Gran had made him.

He was so advanced too, I thought, learning to walk, and talk before his first birthday, progressing much faster than most of the other babies in the neighbourhood.

Sometimes, when John wasn't at work, he would make a special concession, and carry him to meet me from school. I would rush forward, bursting with eagerness to give the child a hug, at which David would laugh, jump about in his father's arms and shriek, "Shirley a' come."

My mother's next child, born a year later, was a girl. She was to be called Janet. Sadly, I never got the chance even to see my new sister. She died shortly after birth.

I was fifteen when my mother's last child was born. My mother was ill following this birth and she and baby Diane remained in hospital for some weeks afterwards.

When I saw Diane for the first time, my heart sank. I knew something was wrong. She looked dull, vacant. There was not a spark of liveliness in her eyes.

Unlike David, she didn't start talking before her first birthday. Even when reaching three all she could do was babble or let out the occasional 'Da' or 'Ma'.

"You'd better take her to the doctor," I said to Mam. "She's either deaf or mentally backward."

Mam said nothing but Gran sprang to her feet. "Nothing of the sort," she said, mouth set in a stiff line. "Our Katie, didn't start talking till she was four. You can't stop her now."

I gave a sniff of contempt. "That's no argument. Everyone knows Auntie Kate's not quite sixteen ounces."

But when, at four, Diane still wasn't talking, my mother, together with my Aunt Blod, finally took her to the clinic. It turned out she was indeed deaf, deafness being part of the brain damage she'd sustained at birth.

Years later, I learned that her condition was the result of RH Factor Incompatibility between my mother and stepfather. This often had serious consequences for a second or third child, and required a complete blood transfusion. In those days it could also leave it mentally subnormal or with other deficits.

Diane has never been able to work or to look after herself without assistance. She can talk a little now, though not in sentences, and her pronunciation is hard to decipher. She can also write a few words, including her name. To add to this, she is clean, orderly, and remembers birthdays.

When, at the age of sixty, my mother died, Diane was twenty or so, and John gave up work to look after her. My attitude to John had softened over time. I also began to take more interest in Diane, inviting her to stay with me now and again. I also tried to help her gain some independence by teaching her how to handle money and how to read and write.

Following my mother's death, I felt sorry for John. Having given up work, he had little money coming in. And money was badly needed. His house was becoming more and more ramshackle, the furniture more dilapidated.

From time to time I travelled to the Valley to visit them, staying overnight with my cousin, Joan. Once, I remember visiting during a snowy winter and seeing John and Diane huddled up in coats before a non-existent fire.

"No coal," John explained, shaking his head.

"Couldn't you have got central heating put in?" I shouted, trying to penetrate his deafness.

He shrugged in a helpless sort of way. I sighed. Of course. No funds. That was the crux of the matter.

I felt a pang of guilt. "I should help," I told Joan. "John is so hard up, I should fork out some money to make things easier for them. They can't live without heating in weather like this."

"Why should *you* feel responsible?" Joan asked. "If anyone should help, it's David."

"David's hard up himself."

"Just the same, you did your bit when you paid off the mortgage. You've nothing to feel guilty about. I don't suppose John feels guilty about the way he used to treat you."

My mind flew back to that time. I was difficult, I know, but *he* hadn't been great either. He treated me as if I were *Gran's* child and nothing to do with him or my mother. If Mam bought me the odd skirt or pair of socks, she had to do it in secret. Funnily enough, I didn't feel hurt by this. We were, after all, little more than strangers. And with no love between us, what did his neglect matter?

Now, as an adult, I could feel only pity for him. He's had a hard life, I thought, being deaf, and unable to earn much. And now, stuck here, poverty-stricken, with only a subnormal girl for company...

I decided that as soon as I returned home, I would sort out my finances and do something. Perhaps I could send him some money or arrange with Joan for central heating to be installed.

Too late. Before I had got round to helping, my cousin phoned to say that John had been rushed into hospital. Three days later she reported him dead following an operation to remove an ulcer.

My stomach churned as I asked, "What's going to happen to Diane?"

"Don't worry. It's all settled," Joan replied. "*I'm* going to take care of her."

Weeks later, at the funeral, I muttered, "I should have helped. John was so hard up."

My cousin gave me an odd smile and shook her head. "Don't you believe it."

I gaped at her. "But…"

It was then that I heard the news of my stepfather's secret.

This apparently penniless man had left behind hoards of money, discovered by the family after his death. I listened in amazement as Joan recounted the story.

"David found thirty-five thousand pounds stashed away in a suitcase in his bedroom," she began. "Then there was at least twenty thousand in the building society. That's fifty-five thousand."

"Fifty-five thousand," I echoed. "You can buy a house with that. Even in London."

Surprise turned to indignation. Again, I thought of him and Diane sitting in a ramshackle room, shivering in coats, the snow falling outside. And, all the while there were thirty-five thousand pounds lying upstairs in a suitcase. What use was it up there? His children would benefit, of course, now he was dead. But was the future so much more important than a bleak, uncomfortable present?

"He pleaded poverty," I murmured. "Made us feel guilty. And all the time…"

But soon my anger subsided. I thought, what else did he have, this solitary man, other than money? He had few friends. Money perhaps represented friendship as well as security, something tangible to cling to. It must have been hard making friends when he was so deaf. I remember seeing the ill-disguised irritation on people's faces when trying to talk with him, his blank expression when asked a question he couldn't hear, the intense strain shown on his face when attempting to decipher what people were saying.

He was abandoned. Alone. David visited, but not often. There was only Diane for companionship. However, he had *money*, his secret friend, hidden away, untouched.

John died around 1980.

He made no Will, so it was left to the solicitor to divide the capital between David and Diane.

Cousin Joan, being Diane's carer, used her share partly to extend and renovate her house so it would be large enough for another member of the family.

Much of David's money went on financing the divorce and settlement between him and his ex-wife.

Some years later, David remarried and now has a sensible, competent wife called Angela who adores him. He never fulfilled his early promise of doing well at school, then getting a worthwhile career. Instead, he left early and went into the building trade.

His daughter, Caroline, married and became a successful chef, winning several prizes for her cooking. As for David's two grandsons, their step-grandmother Angela tells me proudly that the older one, now twelve, is nicknamed 'Prof', and is a wizard at maths. She insists he's a child protégé, with his younger brother not far behind. But then Angela has never been given to understatement.

She is a governor of the local primary school and has a strong community spirit. She and my brother have spent much time organising out-of-school activities and in setting up a youth club so that young people have somewhere to go.

They visit Diane regularly, taking her shopping and out to lunch. Diane has moved away from Joan who is too ill these days to act as carer, and she is now settled in her own flat in a sheltered housing block. Healthwise, she's much too obese for her own good. Standing together we look like the female equivalent of the two forties' comedians, Laurel and Hardy. But she so loves food. And being deaf, she has little else in life to keep her happy.

By contrast, my cousin Joan, once a plump extravert, now has only a thin layer of skin to cover her bones. To add to that, this people-person of the old days has become an almost total recluse. She started going downhill when she lost her beloved daughter-in-law to cancer some years ago. After that, she also lost her appetite, turning more and more to alcohol and cigarettes for sustenance. And she won't see a doctor. She appears to have given up.

I hope I never get like that. My cousin's condition has taught me one thing, though. It is easier to get over a loss if you keep up your interests as well as your friendships, and can turn to them for comfort; easier too, if you never depend so much on the love or friendship of one special person that you fall to pieces once that person is gone.

When I think of Cousin Joan, I like to remember her, not the way she is now, but the way she used to be: plump, sociable, and one of my best friends.

I like to remember the Valley too, the way it used to be. Impoverished and down-at-heel though it was in the forties and fifties, it had a vibrancy, a kind of energy that no longer exists.

I am of course looking at things through the eyes of my childhood, through the sparkle of nostalgia and the magical mists of time. But time cannot stand still, in the Valley or anywhere else. Nor can we.

The Valley people are surely better-off, more comfortable now than they were then? And although a good number are out of work, and continue to be poor, with some young people turning to drugs and crime, life is easier for the majority than in the past. Splendid new roads have been built and streets smartened up with better lighting. Most inhabitants own their own houses and drive their own cars.

But time has stripped it of its character. The High Street is empty, dead. People no longer meet there to mingle, laugh and chat. They seldom even shop there anymore. They prefer to whiz along the new roads in their cars to shop in more fashionable districts with bigger stores. The cinemas, dance halls, chapels and working-men's clubs that once existed have crumbled and died, along with the mines.

But I still think with affection of the old place and of the friends and relatives I once had. My life has changed so much over the years, and I could never leave London to live in the Valley again. At the same time, my roots are there and I never want to abandon them.

CHAPTER FIFTEEN

THE JOYS OF COLLEGE LIFE

Surprise, surprise! Amy Glover phones me right in the middle of breakfast. "I passed for the grammar school after all," she announces, voice quivering with excitement.

"Wow, how about that! And after all those tears and all that talk about how badly you did."

Little spurts of laughter come rippling over the line.

Though no promoter of grammar schools, I am pleased she got in and will now be joining her sister. She needed a boost to her confidence.

Both girls are already ambitious. Rachel wants to become a doctor, Amy, a writer. For all their dreams, life will not be easy for them. If later, they go to university, there'll be fees to pay as well as living expenses, and if their parents can't foot the bill, they'll have to fund themselves.

How much easier it was for me and my generation! Not only were there fewer students, so less competition for places, we also had our student grants to keep us going!

Memories like these take me back to 1957 when, as a mature student of 22, I began my studies at Shenstone College in Worcestershire.

The mishmash of buildings that made up this establishment was tucked away in a rural area some five miles from Kidderminster. Constructed out of World War II barracks, it looked it. But the leafy walks round and about were a delight. My favourite was a footpath edged with shrubs and wildflowers that twisted its way to a small lake called 'Captain's Pool'. Here, in this quiet glade, you could study in solitude while dipping your toes in the water.

Teacher-training colleges offered only two years training after which you obtained a diploma, not a degree. This qualified you to teach in primary and secondary schools but not at grammar school level.

The discovery that Shenstone was a ladies' only college came as a bit of a blow. Nevertheless, going to college at all was a step up the ladder and I was proud to be there. I was especially proud to sport my new college scarf with its gaudy stripes. Most students wore college scarves in those days to distinguish them from the mass of young people (about 90% at that time) who didn't go to college or university. With my lowly background I was particularly keen to show off mine. I had after all, become one of the privileged!

Whatever its drawbacks, I recall the place, on looking back, as an idyllic blur. Like childhood, my college years represented for me one of the happy periods of my life, a time when I lived in a tight little community into which I belonged and played a role. It felt like being part of a large extended family, tutors being parents, aunts or uncles, students, sisters or cousins. What troubled me was the realisation that one day I would have to leave this little community and actually teach.

During my first year, about a dozen of us had to lodge out rather than live on the campus. I and two other Welsh girls shared accommodation in a house in Kidderminster. Our landlady, Mrs Vingo, was a widow with a strong Birmingham accent. Fat and in her fifties, she was very funny in a coarse sort of way. She kept a budgerigar called Tommy who, she insisted, was oversexed and frustrated because he didn't have a mate.

When he fluffed up his feathers, she'd say, "Look at the naughty little devil. He's masturbating again. Just you stop it, Tommy. I'm watching." We students gaped at each other. Whatever would she say next?

She herself had a boy friend she was forever raving about. She called him 'Uncle Cyril'. No surprise there, we thought.

He looked at least ninety. Was he her real uncle or a pretend one, we wondered. Whatever the case, we girls thought it hilarious that a woman her age should still be interested in romance and actually have a boy-friend, however ancient.

Jasmine, one of my fellow-lodgers, was a solid, good humoured girl with bobbed hair and dark-rimmed glasses. She wasn't a bit like her name, there being nothing flowery about her at all. Homely in looks and mild in manner, she wore sensible shoes and tweed skirts. But beneath her staid appearance lay a warm heart and a talent for seeing the funny side of things when anyone got too earnest.

Ann, the other girl, was moody and I liked her less. We were the same height with similar hairstyles, called *bubble cuts*. Because of this, people often got us mixed up. Ann complained bitterly about it. "Why do people keep mistaking me for you? I'm not a bit like you," she whinged.

I became annoyed that *she* was annoyed. Did she consider it such an insult to be mistaken for me?

The childhood memory of being 'that plain little girl from across the road' came back to haunt me.

Ann didn't stay for more than a term. She came to me one day in tears saying she was homesick, missed her boy-friend, and couldn't cope with all the essay-writing. "I want to quit." she sobbed.

"Oh, come on, Anne. It's early days yet." I tried to jolly her up, even offering help with her essays. It was no use. The only help she wanted was in writing a letter of resignation to the Principal.

She left at the end of term.

I was fond of Jasmine, but my best friend at college was a slim, dark-haired girl called Wendy Newton who, at the age of twenty-six was an even more mature student than I was. We both lived out and studied English Literature as our main subject.

I didn't care for Wendy at first. She struck be as snooty and self-opinionated. But first impressions are not always true ones. I soon found her to be good-humoured and full of life. What particularly warmed me to her was that she, too, had obtained her 'O' levels at a college of further education. She talked nostalgically about this place, always beginning with "When I was at college in Norwich…" For some reason this used to send the rest of us into gales of laughter.

Those who lodged out were given the opportunity to live in during the second year. Wendy stayed put at her lodgings but Jasmine and I seized the chance to move into college. It meant a better social life and the chance to join more societies such as the drama club, the choir, or the debating society.

But house rules were strict, and I doubt if young people today would tolerate them. However, our submission was more apparent than real.

For example: We had to be in our houses by 10 o'clock on week nights and were each obliged to sign the house register brought out between nine and ten pm. It was then returned to the house tutor. Some of us got round this by forging each other's signatures and staying out later. It seems I had a talent for this, so that girls wanting to break the rule would come to me begging to sign them in. I was flattered that they sought my expertise and wondered if I might do better as a criminal than a teacher.

At first, some of us thought it a great lark disobeying the rules. But then something happened to make us think again. One night, the fire alarm went off. Startled out of sleep, we scurried to the Great Hall in slippers and dressing-gowns, trying to guess where the fire might be. We'd surely not be dragged out of bed at midnight merely for fire drill?

We stood, tense, curious, in the Great Hall as our names were read out.

The P.E tutor, Miss Cavendish, ticked them off as we each answered.

Then she came to one that got no answer. "Susan Lock?"
Silence.

"Susan Lock?" Miss Cavendish peered around the hall. So did everyone else. A chorus of whispering and murmuring erupted, accompanied by much bobbing of heads and shuffling of feet.

Jasmine gave me a nudge. "She's off with her boy-friend. Oh dear, they're sure to find out."

They did. A quick investigation soon proved that Susan's room was empty.

Two days later in Assembly, the principal announced that Susan Lock, had been sent down.

Gasps broke out, sympathetic mutterings. Poor Susan Lock!

There was no mention of any fire. Had we been dragged out of bed then simply to catch a wayward student?

Whatever the case, we'd think twice about breaking rules in the future.

I planned early in my first term to take History and English Literature as my main subjects. But my heart sank at the long lists of books we had to read. To ease the burden I decided to drop history at the end of the term and take a nice practical subject: Art.

My art was pretty mediocre. It did improve as time went on, though my oils continued to look like water colours however bold I tried to be with the paint brush.

Luckily, our tutor, Mrs Long, was good-humoured and very patient. When looking at our work, she often said in slow, languorous tones, "Fascinating, my dear. Absolutely fascinating."

I was rather shy of her, mainly because I felt I was there on false pretences. For me, art was an easy option. I had no ambition to teach it.

One thing that sticks out in my mind was the extra-curricular Life class we attended one evening a week. I looked forward to this, especially as the model was a young man with rippling muscles dressed only in a pair of leopard-skin briefs.

We all thought him a real hunk, that is, until in the interval, he began to chat with us. As soon as he opened his mouth, his sexy image shattered. He had the high, squeaky voice of a prepubescent boy, a voice that didn't at all match his muscly body.

I preferred English Literature to Art and worked hard to achieve 'As' for my essays.

Some students grumbled that Mrs Mitcheson or 'Mitch', as we called her amongst ourselves, favoured me above the others, and let me get away with murder. A sure sign was that she called me by my first name but addressed the others formally and often frostily by their surnames. "Come along, Miss Newton, pay attention, do," she'd say to Wendy in her ultra well-bred, well modulated voice – the kind that went out with the lorgnette and gaiters. And to Myra: "This is the second time you have been late, Miss Baines." To me, when I'd lost my place in whatever book the class was reading, she'd say with an indulgent smile, "Shirley's having her little nap again."

What I particularly remember about this course was the thrill of performing the morality play, *Everyman*. Initially, when the parts were dished out, I wanted to weep with disappointment. Mrs Mitcheson gave me the part of Five Wits, a most dull role, I thought. I longed for a character part such as that of Kindred, an old man. Then I could put on a wheezy voice, pretend to be deaf and hobble about with a stick. Pat, the student given that part, didn't care for acting, and simply *recited* it, giving it no character at all. I felt like screaming at her to put some life into it.

One day, however, during rehearsals, and shortly before the performance, Pat didn't turn up. Mitch frowned. "No Kindred? Oh dear." She turned to me. "Would you…?"

In less than a heartbeat I was on that stage, casting off my youth and slipping into the character of an old man. After my reading, Mitch paused, stroking her chin.

At last she said, "Hm. Perhaps you'd better play Kindred as well as Five Wits." I wanted to dance for joy. Good old Mitch.

But things did not run as smoothly as I'd hoped.

Wendy had difficulty memorising her lines, so I spent time helping her. The trouble was, there was a line in her speech similar to one in mine. The result was that during the performance when that line came up in my speech, I carried on with the rest of Wendy's lines instead of my own.

I began to sweat as the truth hit me. Wrong role. I tried to forget the darkened auditorium with all the students and tutors watching as I searched frantically through my memory. After a muddled effort to ad lib I managed to recall my last few lines. Was I mad though to miss out the best bits of my part? That damn prompter! She might have done her job of prompting instead of leaving me flailing about talking nonsense.

The incident didn't put me off acting. I still dreamed of a career behind the footlights, holding an audience rapt. I was still in love with the stage.

We had three teaching practices which were each, as far as I remember, three weeks long. Most students looked forward to them. I looked forward to them about as much as I looked forward to going to the dentist and having a tooth out.

In spite of my dread, I was, so Mrs Mitcheson told me, heading for a distinction. The reason, I believe, was that my lesson plans were well constructed and my teaching, when observed, a bit like an actor's performance. I had an audience and was putting on a show.

Unfortunately, my third and last performance put paid to any hopes of a distinction. My special tutor for the final teaching practice was a gruff, straight-from-the-shoulder north countryman called Percy Crossland. Tutors could come any time to watch you teach. And you never knew when.

Percy arrived at the wrong time.

I had asked my supervisory teacher at the school, Mrs Hill, if, instead of teaching the English lesson I'd prepared for that day, I could observe her taking a class in drama.

Neither of us expected a college tutor to come and check on me last lesson on a Friday. So when he walked into the classroom, I almost fainted. Mrs Hill greeted him, then quietly left. Percy sat at the back of the class, waiting.

My mouth went dry as I gazed nervously around me, hoping an idea would pop down from the ceiling or through one of the walls. What the hell was I going to do? The children were expecting drama and I had nothing prepared. I couldn't suddenly transfer from drama to English. Not when the whole classroom had been rearranged for acting. I'd have to ad lib my way through as best I could.

I can't remember the details but I know it was a rubbish lesson. I'm no good at doing things off the cuff. I have to prepare.

Mr Crossland strode over to me afterwards holding out his copy of my lesson plan.

"You had some excellent work here," he said, jabbing at it with his finger. "What's the point in writing it out and then not using it? It wastes your time *and* mine, as well as the children's."

He sounded so cross, I burst into tears.

He softened a bit and lent me his hanky. But I knew that after this there'd be no distinction.

I'd be lucky to get a credit.

When the two years came to an end I shed even more tears. The thought of leaving was unbearable. The thought of teaching, odious.

I passed with credit as expected. And although I didn't look forward to teaching, I felt it my duty to do so, having received a government grant.

My first job was at a primary school in Redditch teaching 1C. I worked like a Trojan there for a year. It was worth the slog.

After leaving, I learned that six of my children had moved from 1C, the bottom stream, to 2A, the top stream, and that the whole class had made good progress.

Nevertheless, I had no intention of teaching permanently. After moving from Worcestershire in the early sixties, I worked as a supply teacher so I'd have time for other things such as drama classes.

Meanwhile, I kept up my general education, gaining more 'O' and 'A' levels over the next years.

By the time I reached my thirties, I decided to read for a degree. Without one I began to feel only half educated, though I must confess it was the continual put-downs of an obnoxious boyfriend I had at the time that pushed me along this path. "Damn him!" I fumed, "He thinks I'm not good enough."

That's when I started studying 'A' level Economic History, aiming for at least a B grade. This would qualify me for entry into UCL. It was there that Claude Wedeles, the obnoxious man I obsessed about, lectured in anatomy. Maybe I would meet him. And wouldn't he be surprised? I'd pointedly ignore him, of course, cut him dead. Or perhaps I'd freeze him with withering politeness. But stop. Husbands and lovers belong to another chapter. For now, let's stick to education.

Having passed my entrance exam for UCL I was provisionally accepted for the Anthropology degree course. Fortunately, I achieved a good grade in my 'A' level and was admitted in the autumn. Less fortunately, I decided in my first year that Anthropology wasn't for me. Also there was no sign of Claude Wedeles. No one in the Medical Department had heard of him. And I was still obsessed. It was years later that I finally took my degree, achieving a two-one in psychology and philosophy. Better late than never, I suppose.

Now, in my old age, I'm still studying, but at the U3A there is no homework and no exams. I don't think my poor brain could cope with exams these days. However, I do give the occasional talk, and this often demands a fair bit of research. All helpful to those little grey cells. I hope.

CHAPTER SIXTEEN

HEADLESS CROSS AND MRS RIMMER

(1960–61)

It was while I was teaching at my first school, Headless Cross, in Worcestershire, that my grandmother died. She was eighty and had been suffering from cancer for some months.

"It's a blessing she's gone," my Uncle Tom said.

You're right, I thought, but that doesn't make it less sad for those who loved her.

What haunts me still is that I missed her funeral. She died in winter, a particularly hard one. On the day she was to be buried, Redditch was covered in snow. There was talk of trains not running.

"You'll freeze to death, trying to get to Wales this weather," my landlady, Mrs Rimmer said, "especially with trains so unreliable. And it's going to get worse."

I glanced at the snowflakes spattering the window, torn between the shame of not attending Gran's funeral and my reluctance to brave the weather to get there. "Even if I manage to reach Cardiff," I told myself, "I'll probably get no further. Ten to one, I won't arrive in time for the funeral anyway."

Convinced by my own argument, I took the easy way out and stayed where I was.

A couple of days later I received from Cousin Joan a letter that sizzled with disapproval. 'After all Gran's done for you over the years,' she wrote, 'and you couldn't even spare the time to go to her funeral.'

I stared down at the letter, angry tears misting my eyes. I instantly wrote back. Did she think I wouldn't have done everything in my power to get there, if I could? What about the transport problems? Was I expected to walk? I rammed my reply into the post-box.

Later, when I'd calmed down, little tendrils of doubt began to creep in. *Had* I done everything? If I'd been a loving granddaughter, I'd surely have braved ice, snow and everything else to attend Gran's funeral, instead of ranting on about transport problems? I deserved my cousin's disapproval.

Joan, however, nice, good-natured Joan accepted my explanation and we stayed friends. I was relieved. I couldn't bear the thought of a rift between us.

I plodded on with my teaching job determined my class should make as much progress as possible. Teaching, I soon discovered, was no easy option. Even the long holidays were not truly free. They were times for preparing lesson plans and visual aids for the following term.

Two things that stick out in my mind about Headless Cross were school assemblies and the school concert. Being a Church of England establishment, the day began with morning Assembly, the headmaster or deputy head conducting it. But one morning a week ordinary teachers, in turn, had to take on this task. This included me. And, like it or not, I couldn't get out of it. The proposition struck me with horror. Me, the religious sceptic, rattling on about the glories of God? Sermonising? One might just as well ask a Marxist to enthuse on the glories of Capitalism.

Well, I wasn't going to be a hypocrite. I worked at my 'sermon', focusing on moral behaviour, the unacceptability of violence and bullying, and the value of kindness and helpfulness. I managed to not mention God once, not even in the 'prayer' that followed.

I wondered if I'd gone too far, but neither the headmaster nor any of the teachers complained. However, one teacher, a middle aged woman, whose name I can't recall, peered at me over her glasses and remarked, "Clever little what's it, aren't you?"

The second thing that embedded itself in my mind was the school concert, prepared each year for Parents' evening. Each class was expected to put on a show lasting about 10 minutes. It could be singing, verse-speaking, a sketch or short play. I chose verse-speaking for my class, and determined that, although it was only 1C, its performance would be a credit to the school.

Rehearsals were hard, frustrating work. But I'd given the children a difficult task, especially those who were in no way natural actors. The main poem *Night Mail* demanded variety in pace, pitch and volume to imitate the sounds and rhythms of the train. This took much repetition and a lot of sweat to get right. The short poems performed by small groups and individual children involved plenty of acting and movement.

By the time of the performance, everything had come together. The children all knew their parts and acted them well. In fact, they performed brilliantly. Together with the top class, 4A, my little 1C children put on the best show in the school, making the audience cheer and clap for minutes at a time. The congratulations afterwards and the smiles of triumph on the children's faces made the whole uphill effort worthwhile. I was proud of them and would remember their achievement long after I left the school in July.

I would remember my landlady, Mrs Rimmer, too. She was a large, elderly widow, practical, sensible, with a crisp, ex-boarding-school accent. But she had no illusions about herself. "I was a duffer at school," she said one day with a laugh. "Always near the bottom of the class."

Like most of her neighbours she had bought herself a television set and enjoyed watching it in the evenings, especially the new series 'Coronation Street'. I found it rather dull myself, though I sometimes watched it with her, while eating my dinner.

Watching television one evening, news came over that the unexpurgated version of Lawrence's *Lady Chatterley's Lover* had been published. It soon became the talk of the country.

Mrs Rimmer immediately bought herself a copy.

"Well, really, Mrs Rimmer!" I said, putting on a shocked voice.

"Oh, don't worry, I'm skipping the rude bits," she assured me with a casual flap of her hand.

I wondered how she could tell which the rude bits were without reading them first.

Mrs Rimmer's late husband had been a pharmacist. She carried on the business after his death though I doubt if it made much profit. Not being a qualified pharmacist herself, she wasn't permitted to deal with prescriptions. This must have been a huge drawback.

Once, while her assistant was off sick, she asked me if I'd mind looking after her shop for an hour while she kept an appointment across the road. She showed me where everything was and how to operate the till. "There won't be many customers this time of the day," she assured me.

Shortly after she left, a flashy looking fellow with a red spotted tie and black moustache appeared at the counter. He rested a pair of bold eyes on me. "Hullo. Where's the old girl then?"

My bright, business-like smile vanished. "Can I help you?" I asked, primly.

"Packet of Durex please."

I felt myself colouring. Blast. My first customer and he has to ask for *that*. And now I'm showing myself up by blushing. Worse still, I can't bloody well remember where they're kept.

"S-so sorry," I stammered, flinging open drawer after drawer, feeling my face turn a deep puce. "I can't seem to find them." God, what an idiot he must think me!

"You're looking in the wrong place," he chuckled, "They're in that cupboard." He bent over the counter and pointed. "Like me to get them out for you?"

"I think I can manage, thank you," I answered, trying to sound dignified but failing.

After he went, I sat behind the counter, hoping he was the first and last customer I'd have to deal with. He wasn't. Several more arrived, mainly men, all wanting the same thing: a packet of Durex. At least, I knew now where to find them, and I'd stopped blushing.

"Everything go all right?" Mrs Rimmer asked when she returned.

"Right as rain," I answered.

"Good. I expect they all wanted the same thing?"

"Well, there was one who wanted some aspirin as well. He said his wife kept having headaches."

Mrs Rimmer tittered. "Huh! That old chestnut."

LONDON AND THEATRE LIFE

1961–

CHAPTER SEVENTEEN

LONDON, HERE I COME

July 1961. End of term – almost. And then my move to London, the bustling metropolis where everything happens. I could hardly wait.

Where to live, where to work – it was all sorted. And soon I'd be there, realising one of my early dreams: to live in the capital of England – capital of the *world* in my book.

Precious memories of my first visit at fourteen came rushing back: Joan Jones and I strolling down the Mall, escorted by her Uncle Paul, on our way to view Buckingham Palace – how thrilling if we caught sight of King George, we thought, or one of the princesses; then the excitement of visiting Piccadilly Circus with its theatres, cafes, eager tourists squinting up at the statue of Eros. And afterwards, moving on to Trafalgar Square, gazing at the fountains, watching pigeons mingle with people, perching on shoulders, fluttering for crumbs. And how could we forget the grandeur of Westminster Palace and Big Ben? Or the delicious quivering in our stomachs at the wonder of it all?

London wasn't all glitz and glamour, I was well aware of that. I'd seen down-and-outs sleeping rough in the street, as well as middle-of-the-road types going about their daily tasks.

And my visits hadn't always been pleasant. Apart from my joyless trip to Goldsmith's College in 1957, I had made another visit, not altogether pleasurable, some time before, when I was nineteen and still nursing at Hensol Castle.

Let me digress a moment from the story of my move to linger a while in 1955, the year of that visit. It was prompted by my love of music. Attending an opera at Covent Garden

121

became a must. So as soon as I'd saved enough money, I went to a theatre agency and booked seats for *Rigoletto* one night, *Carmen* the next. I also arranged overnight stays at a B&B in Paddington recommended by one of the nurses.

But the trip wasn't an entire success. To begin with, I hadn't timed things well on my first night, and missed Act One of *Rigoletto*. Despite this, the evening wasn't a total wash out. At least I arrived in time to enjoy the rest of the opera.

That couldn't be said for the next evening. No, I didn't arrive late. I simply found to my annoyance that that stupid theatre agency, instead of booking me a seat for *Carmen*, had booked me a seat for Wagner's *Tristan and Isolde*. Worse, my seat, which I'd thought was so highly priced, was situated at the side of the upper circle. From there, I could see only half the stage.

The performance lasted three and a half hours and for most of it I sat in bum-numbing boredom. On top of that I badly wanted to blow my nose. However, I didn't dare for fear the noise might be heard by the whole audience, causing every head to turn with fury in my direction. I'd also forgotten my handkerchief. The result was that I was reduced to wiping my nose surreptitiously on something in my bag that served as a hankie – I think it was a glove – while doing my best to avoid sniffing.

Covent Garden seemed a very grand theatre with its spacious foyer, chandeliers and plush carpets. Before the performance and during the interval equally grand people from the stalls and the dress circle stood in groups chatting in well modulated, superior voices. The women, clad in evening dress of silk or velvet, some with fur wraps draping their shoulders, emitted little trills of laughter from time to time as they chatted with their friends.

I looked down at my dowdy self, heart sinking. With this crowd of well-heeled sophisticated people I felt pretty much like Cinderella turning up at the ball but still in her old clothes and without a grand coach to take her there. They must think me a piece of underdressed low life, I thought, a gauche, uninitiated outsider who's barged into their exclusive circle by mistake. At any moment I expected a tap on the shoulder and a voice enquiring in polite but firm tones, "Excuse me, but are you sure you're in the right place? If you want Lyon's Corner House, it's further down the road."

But I needn't have worried. Nobody even noticed me.

I gave myself a mental pep talk. "Stop this. You've paid for your ticket. You've as much right here as they have." I pushed back my shoulders and began to walk up the carpeted stairway, sticking a determined smile on my face as if going to the opera at Covent Garden was a regular occurrence.

My smile didn't last long. Half way up, at the mezzanine level, was an archway. I prepared to step through, swerving slightly to avoid colliding with a person walking towards me, a person as small and shabby looking as myself.

Then, "Oops!" came a voice from behind.

I had bumped my nose on sheer glass. What I had thought was an archway turned out to be a mirror, the shabby girl walking towards me, myself.

"Your name must be Alice," chuckled the smartly-dressed gentleman behind me. "Are you okay?"

"Yes thank you." I turned hastily to my left and hurried up the rest of the stairs. My second night at Covent Garden and I'd forgotten my way to the upper circle. What an idiot I must have looked! Like it or not, I would have to start wearing my glasses.

I put the whole thing down to experience. I was younger then, uneducated, and easily overawed. Now, at twenty-six, I have more savoir faire. I've been abroad twice, have some knowledge of French, German and Spanish. I've even read Plato's *Republic*. I won't be intimidated by the opera-going set or any other group when I go to London. I'm more confident now and better able to measure up.

Things started off reasonably well. During the school holiday I became a chambermaid at the Garrick Hotel in the Charing Cross Road. Hardly stimulating work, I admit, and I wasn't that eager to start the day at 6 o'clock in the morning. But, hell, it was only temporary. And there were pluses as well as minuses. Meals and accommodation came with the job, so the whole of my wage, including tips, was mine to do as I liked with. On top of that, the hotel manager and his wife paid me additional cash to help their daughter with her English exam.

My employers were pleasant, helpful people; the other chambermaids, both Irish, unpredictable in temper but not impossible to work with. One of them, I remember, was a middle-aged spinster and zealously religious. This was not only in regard to regular attendance of Mass but to the exact way sheets should be folded and pillows placed. The other, Nora, also unmarried, was younger, taller, with a shock of red hair and a habit of flying into tempers over next to nothing. She was losing some of her teeth, I noticed, and had developed a distinctive pot belly. I suspected she was pregnant.

I was right. According to the manager, she claimed she'd had nothing to do with men and couldn't understand how it had happened. An immaculate conception? Ignorance about the birds and the bees? Whatever the case, a woman in her thirties, I thought, could surely take better care of herself?

While at the Garrick Hotel, I had time to plan my next move. I already had a teaching job for the following term and had now also found – I could hardly believe my luck – a bed-sitting room, rent free in return for a little housework. I'd be settling there in two weeks. Talk about everything going my way.

During the time I had left at the Garrick, Nora suggested a night out at the Hammersmith Palais.

There I danced with a short, stocky man, young-to-middle-aged and slightly bald. I didn't find him attractive, but I quite enjoyed his company. He was a scientist who had emigrated from Russia while still a child. I've forgotten his name but, since he was Russian, I shall call him Boris. Boris had plenty of stories to tell and I was happy to listen.

But I didn't want to meet him again, so when he suggested dinner, I made an excuse.

Unfortunately, I had told him where I worked. As a result, he kept phoning for me at the Garrick hotel until I finally ran out of excuses. Instead of being brutally frank and saying, "Sorry but I don't fancy you" I met him for lunch. Just this once, I told myself. And that'll be the end of it.

But it wasn't. As we left the restaurant, it began to rain. "My flat's just across the road," he said, "You'd better shelter there till it stops. Then I'll take you to the tube."

"I'd rather not, thank you," I said, doubtfully.

"Why? Think I'm going to rape you or something?" He laughed.

I won't go into detail about what happened in his flat. Suffice to say that he plied me with drinks and when I reached the required woozy state, made his advances. I struggled to escape but he was a lot stronger than I. He had in any case locked the door.

Back at the hotel I could have punched myself for being such an idiot. "You're in London now, not the Rhondda Valley," I fumed. "You've got to be careful."

I tried to push the incident out of my mind.

At the end of August, I moved into my new room. It was situated in what looked like a council block in the area of Southwark, hardly the most fashionable part of London. "It's not forever," I told myself. "Think of all the money you can save living rent free."

I bundled my things into the small, feminine-looking room, with its pink flowered wallpaper and matching bedspread. The flat was owned by a middle-aged, well built man called Mr Barclay. He sounded pleasant enough, but after my experience with Boris, I was on the alert. Suppose he had

125

an ulterior motive? What finally decided me to go ahead was the cunning little bolt on my bedroom door. There was also the fact that he worked for *The Times* and would be out, he told me, for most of the day. Good. I'd have plenty of privacy. That he worked for *The Times* did rather surprise me. He didn't sound particularly well educated or well informed, and surely, his salary would enable him to do better than live in a council block in Southwark?

Perhaps I was being snobbish. I gave a mental shrug. Where Mr Barclay chose to live and what he chose to do for a living was his own business.

But there were other things that puzzled me. Letters arrived for Mr *Bloom* rather than Mr Barclay. "Bloom's my pen-name," he said. I wondered about that since he seemed hardly the type to hide his light under a bushel. He was forever showing off about himself and his achievements – the important things he'd done, people he'd met, how *The Times* couldn't do without him… Some of these tales didn't add up and I began to wonder if they were more fantasy than reality. Then something happened to bring my suspicions to the surface.

One morning, after he'd gone off to work, I did something very stupid. I slipped out of the front door to pick up a bottle of milk. As I did so, the door slammed shut, locking me out. I'd forgotten to leave it off the latch. I groaned. I was still in my nightgown and slippers and stuck outside the flat. I'd probably be stuck there all day. How could I get to work?

I made my way downstairs to the flat below. Mr Barclay, I knew, was friendly with the people there. I knocked on the door.

"I'm from number 23, the flat above," I began. I tried to smooth back untidy strands of hair falling over my face. I must have looked a fright.

The little grey-haired woman standing at the door immediately guessed my predicament.

"Locked yourself out, Ducks? Don't worry. I'll phone Selfridges. Harry Bloom drives a van there. If I catch him, he might be able to slip back with the key." She ushered me in.

"Selfridges? But I thought he worked for *The Times*."

"What? Harry Bloom? He's having you on. Old Harry's been driving a van for Selfridges as long as I can remember, and that's a very long time."

I managed to get to work that day with the help of my landlord's kindly neighbour who lent me money and clothes, which almost fitted, as well as the use of her bathroom to tidy myself up in.

But my suspicions about Mr Barclay-cum-Bloom were confirmed. What a liar! Was he trying to impress me? If so, why?

I soon found out. Cleaning his flat a couple of times a week was not all he had in mind when offering a rent-free room. "The place doesn't need much cleaning," he told me. "A bit of hoovering, a flick of the duster, and you're done." He leered. "How about something extra?"

"I could bring you a breakfast-tray in the morning? Or do some shopping?" I said.

He waved aside my suggestions and glowered down at a magazine on the coffee table. But he said nothing more on the subject for a while.

I knew perfectly well what he was getting at but I wasn't letting on just yet. However, putting him off became more and more difficult. Subtle suggestions with sexual overtones increased. I tried to ignore them, pretending to be too thick to catch on. At the same time I began a frantic search for alternative accommodation.

While this was going on, there was something else bothering me, something that sent me scuttling to the doctor.

He confirmed my fears. I was pregnant.

So there I was, alone in London, having a baby I didn't want and stuck with a predatory man I'd begun to loathe. What a mess!

Meanwhile, Bloom's suggestions became more overtly sexual. One evening, he presented me with an ultimatum. Either I gave him sex or out I'd go.

I left there and then with my two suitcases, my landlord not knowing and apparently not caring if I had somewhere to stay or if I was reduced to sleeping on a park bench for the night.

After securing a place at the YWCA, I was ultimately rescued by a fellow-teacher who gave me a room to rent for a couple of months.

My only feeling for the child growing inside me was revulsion and a desire to get rid of it.

"If that's what you want," my GP said, "just knock on a few doors in Harley Street. Someone's sure to help. But you'll have to plead mental illness. And it'll cost."

I didn't tell him or anyone else I'd been forced. Who'd have believed me? I blamed myself. Where was my sense, entering the flat of a relative stranger, and then allowing him to ply me with drinks? And there I'd been, harshly judging my mother as well as the Irish girl as fools for being unable to look after themselves. Now I was in the same boat.

I couldn't summon up the nerve to knock on doors in Harley Street. Anyway, I was too ashamed to let anyone know of my condition. I went through the ordeal with the help of an elderly welfare advisor called Mrs Forster. At the same time I carried on teaching until I was seven months pregnant, giving myself a false name by pretending to have got married.

With the help of Mrs Forster, I spent the last two months at a Mother-and-Baby Home. By this time I was resigned to bearing a child whom I intended to have adopted as soon as possible. The only member of my family who knew my secret was Cousin Joan and I made her swear to tell no one else.

I had no morning sickness or any discomfort other than anger with myself for getting into such a mess. The actual birth was a different story. I wanted to scream my lungs out, but the nurse on duty ordered me to shut up and stop disturbing other patients. She also kept addressing me as 'Miss'. It was spiteful of her, I thought, letting on to everyone that I was unmarried.

I gave birth to a baby girl on 3rd May, 1962. I felt too unhappy and worn out even to look at her for two days. All I wanted was to sleep.

A nurse finally persuaded me to hold the child. It was then that the maternal instinct kicked in. She was a beautiful baby with masses of dark hair and large blue eyes. And she would be mine for six weeks, after which time her adopters would take her away.

Looking after her at the Mother-and-Baby Home, I grew more and more attached. It was thrilling to see her first smile, and later, to hear her start to babble. I named her Juliet Amanda.

I wanted to go on looking after her. But would that have been fair? I wondered. What sort of life would a child have with a single parent, pinching and scraping to bring her up and with no proper roof over her head? It would be sheer selfishness, wouldn't it, especially when she had a chance of two parents to provide for her?

The first would-be adopters changed their minds, I was later told, on seeing her at the Adoption Agency and learning her father was Russian. "We don't agree with mixed parentage," the woman said, "and she does look foreign."

The Adoption Agent handed Juliet back to me, offering comforting words. But I didn't need comforting. It was such a relief to have her back.

At the end of another two or three weeks, she was finally adopted, this time by people who were thrilled to have a child, whatever her parentage.

After the parting, I behaved like every other unmarried mother at the Home. I wept till I felt I had no tears left.

CHAPTER EIGHTEEN

WANTED: WELL EDUCATED PROFESSIONAL GENTLEMAN

At my next session with Frieda, I let out the secret of Juliet Amanda. It had been on my mind.

She doesn't bat an eyelid. Until, that is, I mention adoption. Her mouth drops open. "You gave her away?"

I shrug. "What else could I have done? I was on my own."

She pauses, frowns, lips narrowing into a tight line. Is it surprise or condemnation I read on her face?

"It would have been difficult for you, I see that," she says at last, "but there have been plenty of women in the same boat. Would many have considered adoption, do you think?"

She speaks softly, but I sense disapproval in her tone.

Damn her, sitting there relaxed on that comfortable chair, judging me. She's supposed to be neutral, not judgemental.

My voice sharpens. "Yes. Many. Things were harder for single mothers in those days, you should know that. They were often *pushed* into it for the good of the child."

She says nothing, just leans back, looking at me, or, rather, studying me as if I'm a specimen she's dissecting.

I feel my blood pressure rise. "Do you think I didn't *want* to keep her? For God's sake…"

Her eyebrows arch. "Why are you being so defensive? That's not what I was thinking at all. I'm sure you had good reason for making your decision." She pauses to flick open the pages of her notebook. "I can't help remembering though the story of your mother. She had *you* when she was unmarried, didn't she?"

I feel like slapping her. "I suppose you think I'm following in my mother's footsteps."

"Not quite. She didn't have you adopted."

"It might have been better if she did. A different parent might have given me some guidance, more chances of success." I bite my lip. That was uncalled for. But I hate being compared with my weak little mother.

"Is that why you didn't keep your baby? You were afraid you'd be an ineffective parent like your mother?"

"No, it wasn't. And I *did* want to keep her. I even tried to get her back."

"Really?" A flash of interest lights up her face. "How did you go about that?" She picks up her pen and begins to write.

I make an effort to calm my ruffled feelings and to recollect my memories of that time. Soon, I am ready to tell her my story…

Although I'd given up my baby, I still dreamed of getting her back. First though, I needed a husband, someone who would be a father for her. This to me was imperative. But I'd have to find one fast – within three months to be precise. If I ran over that time limit, I'd lose the option of getting her back.

There was another problem: the adoptive parents' growing attachment to the child. I expressed my unease about this to Mrs Forster, my welfare advisor but she was quick to point out that I too, had grown attached to my baby before feeling obliged to give her up. My doubts melted at her words and spurred me into action.

The fastest way to find a husband, I thought, was to place an advertisement in the *London Weekly Advertiser*. This popular paper had hundreds of advertisers seeking friendship or marriage.

I can't recall exactly how I worded the advertisement, though I do remember describing my preferred man as 'educated' and 'professional'. And I didn't leave out the fact that there'd be a child to support. My box number received about seventy replies.

I set about reading them. Letters written on lined paper I quickly binned, suspecting the writers to be uneducated or lacking in taste. Where a stamped addressed envelope was enclosed, I replied briefly but politely that I was now 'suited'. From the pile I had left, I chose about twelve possibilities. The one that attracted me most was the letter from Peter Bessell. I rang his number and arranged to meet him.

He turned out to be handsome, charming, in his early forties, with a house in Cornwall, an office in Clarges Street and a flat in Dolphin Square. I could scarcely believe my luck. Good looking, well-educated and clearly *rich*, I thought. What more could a girl ask for?

There was one snag.

"I must be honest with you," he said, as we seated ourselves in a stylish-looking restaurant near the river. "I am in fact married, but not for much longer, I hope."

He went on to tell me that he was a Liberal candidate for Bodmin in Cornwall, adding, "I'm hoping to get into parliament at the next general election. When I do, I'm determined to bring about a change in the divorce law."

He seemed sincere enough as well as being devastatingly attractive. I was already beginning to have romantic feelings for him. We appeared to have lots in common, including a love of Beethoven.

"I hope we can meet again," he said as the evening ended and he drove me home. "I've enjoyed tonight so much." He kissed me, and I thought I felt passion behind the kiss.

My head was in a whirl as I went to bed that night. What a wonderful evening! What a wonderful man! He might be married, but not for much longer. And married or not, he was irresistible. I longed to meet him again.

I never did. I waited and waited for his precious call. It never came. At last, I rang him. It hurt my pride to do so but I had to find out why he hadn't made contact.

He had seemed so keen.

"I did want to see you again," he assured me in reply to my call, "but I didn't dare." He paused. "Things have happened, and I have to be extra careful just now not to put a foot wrong. The faintest whiff of scandal and I'm out on my neck. And that'll end all hopes of getting into Parliament."

"You might have phoned or written to explain," I said.

"Yes, I'm sorry, but there it is." His voice took on a brusque tone and I could imagine his dismissive shrug at the other end of the line as he turned to more important matters.

I didn't waste time. I started meeting other candidates on my list of possible husbands.

From time to time though, Peter Bessell's name cropped up in the news. He had got into Parliament as a Liberal MP in 1964. Later on, the divorce law was changed and passed, though I don't think Peter Bessell was an important contributor to the change.

Some time afterwards, I heard of his involvement in several scandals. There were fraud allegations relating to his business ventures; also his participation in the trial of Jeremy Thorpe, the liberal leader accused of attempted murder. The judge described Bessell's evidence for the prosecution as 'a tissue of lies'. Bessell himself only just escaped prosecution.

He spent most of his last years, trying to pay off his debts. Perhaps I'd had a lucky escape.

Back in 1962 his future had seemed assured. Even so, I had no intention of breaking my heart over a man I'd dated only once.

I began fixing dates with other possibilities on my list. In some cases, after a few meetings, we realised we weren't suited. In others, so little interest was sparked off during that initial coffee and chat there seemed no point in arranging further meetings. I found no one as attractive as Peter Bessell, no one I could feel romantic about. And could I possibly consider marriage when there was no grain of romantic feeling behind it? Such a marriage would surely end in divorce, I thought. And for me, divorce meant failure and wasn't an option.

But there were two or three men I went on seeing for some time in the hope we might eventually click. The first of these was a retired army captain called John Speight. He was a tall, thin, man with intense dark eyes and a neat fringe of moustache lining his upper jaw. Aged forty-five and not bad-looking, he was divorced, and keen to remarry. What is more, he fell in love with me. Great. So why didn't I grab him?

The truth is, I couldn't. I never fell for him. He was so generous too – always buying me presents, taking me on outings, wining and dining me. And what did I give in return? Sweet nothing. He gave. I took. But I got my comeuppance. Here's how:

I had started seeing Robert, another 'suitor'. At the same time I told John I couldn't consider marriage with him, though I was happy for us to meet now and then.

"That's not really what I had in mind," John said looking crestfallen. "I wanted a proper relationship. I thought that's what you wanted too. Didn't you say you needed a father for your little girl."

"I did," I said with a sigh, "but it's no use. Sorry, John. I do like you. And you've been good to me."

He gave a wry smile. "Being good doesn't get you anywhere, though, does it?"

The next time I visited his flat I found that he'd bought himself a little dog – a poodle. He named it after me. I felt choked. He'd lost *me*, so got himself a puppy. Poor man. I'd so hurt him.

It surprised me when, shortly after this, he called at my digs in Kenyon Street, without even phoning first. His face was a picture of worry. "I'm in dead trouble," he faltered, "and I wondered if you could help out." He passed an anxious hand over his forehead. "Could you lend me twenty-five pounds?"

Well, what could I do? He'd been a good friend and all I'd done in return was dump him. I'd just received my month's teaching salary. I counted out twenty-five pounds and gave it to him.

That was the last time I saw John. He disappeared. Disappeared from his flat in Bayswater. Disappeared from his place of work. No one seemed to know what had happened to him. I never got my money back.

I think during those three months of searching for a man, I met everyone on my list, at least once. There wasn't one I could consider marrying. Most of their names I've forgotten now but there was a Michael whom I stayed friends with. And there was Robert.

I actually fell in love with Robert in a mild sort of way. Unfortunately, a deepening of feeling on my part came too late. It didn't happen during that crucial period when there was pressure to find a husband. Not that Robert would have been suitable. He lived in a tiny flat in Chelsea Cloisters and showed no inclination ever to consider swapping it for a family home.

Goodness knows why I fell for him at all. He was, in truth, rather ugly. On top of that, he lacked warmth while, money-wise, he was even more careful than I was. This was in spite of the fact that he was an investment banker. But perhaps investment bankers weren't that rich in those days.

On the other hand, he was clever, witty and well educated. A point in his favour was the fact that he went to a posh public school, followed by Oxford. And at that time, such superficial status symbols attracted me like a magnet. Furthermore, he wasn't at all stingy when it came to musical events. He wouldn't stint on booking the best seats at Covent Garden when one of his favourite operas was being performed or taking me to any number of concerts at the Royal Albert Hall.

But during the early days I had little affection for Robert, being more aware of his unimpressive looks and lack of generosity than of his intellect. I decided I didn't want to marry him.

Before the three months were up, I realised that my prospects of finding a marriage partner in such a short time were close to zero. There was no way I could face tying myself to a man I had no real feeling for. Anyway, it wouldn't have been fair to him. He would want a loving wife, not someone who was merely using him as a convenience.

So at the end of that time I had to reconcile myself to the fact that Juliet Amanda would be staying permanently with her adoptive parents. The crucial three months had elapsed.

I heave a sigh as I bring my story to a close.

Frieda looks up from her notebook. "And there wasn't one man amongst those you met whom you felt you could share your life with, if only for the satisfaction of bringing up your daughter yourself?"

I shake my head. "Not one."

I read sympathy on her face now. "It must have felt wretched, knowing she was out of your life for good."

"It did, believe me." I'm silent a moment, recalling how my heart sank at the thought of all the things I'd have to miss in giving her up: I'd never be able to hear her first words or see her first tottering steps... never have the pleasure of telling her stories after tucking her into bed each night, never have the chance of watching her grow up...

I feel a tightness in my throat. "But I had to think of *her*," I say at last, "not of myself and my own pleasure."

"Yes, I see that. You were trying to do the right thing." Her voice has softened, and a smile touches her lips.

"I hoped so. Hoped with all my heart that her new parents would help her grow into a happy, well adjusted person. Maybe, one day, I thought, I'd get a chance to meet her again. I might even be able to trace her."

"And did you?"

I glance at the clock. My therapy should have finished five minutes ago but, for once, Frieda hasn't noticed. I button up my jacket. "I'll have to tell you about that another time."

The session ends. I feel strangely relieved. Few people knew the secret of Juliet Amanda. Now at last I'd got it off my chest.

CHAPTER NINETEEN

NO NAME, NO FACE

(1962–63)

During the first few months of my daughter's adoption, I received several letters from the Adoption Agency to report how well she was thriving with her new parents. They had apparently decided to keep the name *Amanda* but drop the *Juliet*. At the end of six months they sent me a photograph of her, plump and smiling. I framed it and kept it on my dressing table.

I didn't want to forget her. I couldn't anyway, though cramming my life with activities did help.

By this time I had found myself a bed-sitter in a terraced house in Kenyon Street, off the Fulham Palace Road. The rent was only two pounds ten shillings a week, giving me a chance to save part of my income. The house was owned by a pleasant, easy-going woman called Mavis and her Polish husband, a man with a roving eye who needed careful watching. I made sure I was never alone in his company and my bedroom door was always locked.

Mavis introduced me to her two other tenants, both young women around my own age. One of them, Margaret Maney, was a nice, quiet Catholic girl from New Zealand. I soon found though that her tranquil manner was a surface trait only. She liked the occasional drink, and after one too many, she'd surprise you by giving vent to an outflow of passionate feelings, often lashing out at her mother, calling her a bitch and ranting on about how she'd ruined her life. She'd also tear to pieces the Catholic Church, the Pope, the priests, even God.

On asking her why, if she felt so strongly she didn't give up religion, she'd reply in her half-tipsy state, "Well, you never know, do you? There might be a God, there might be a heaven. I don't want to take any chances and risk landing in the wrong place."

While living in Kenyon Street, I carried on teaching, supplementing my income by modelling in my free time. Does that mean that the ugly duckling (me) grew into a swan? Not quite. However, my figure was decent, I had lost my freckles, and, with the help of combs and cosmetics, I managed to satisfy the camera-man.

Being too short for fashion, I sometimes modelled for book-jackets, often posing for the covers of detective, gangster or murder-mystery novels. I might be pointing a gun at the reader or lying dead in a ditch. Such poses, I confess, appealed to my sense of drama. There was also commercial modelling where I'd be asked to advertise photocopying machines or wonder hair-curlers. The work was often boring, but the money wasn't bad. And, since at the back of my mind was the idea that one day, I might achieve my goal of buying a flat in London, this would require a good deal of money and a lot of hard work.

To acquire more interesting assignments as well as, hopefully, more cash, I also attended an evening course in television modelling. This was said to be highly paid with opportunities to act as well as pose.

The course turned out to be a waste of money. It was supposed to act as an agency as well as a school, but it did little to find you work.

This, however, is not the point of my story. The important thing is what happened to one of the students there after the course had ended and how I became involved.

It all began with a phone call. I was still half asleep when Mavis called, "It's for you."

I groaned, threw off the bedclothes, and trailed, barefoot down the stairs, my dressing-gown wrapped around me. Who on earth, I wondered, could be calling at nine o'clock on a Sunday morning?

Mavis thrust the phone into my hand.

"Miss Stephens?" a male voice enquired.

"That's me," I croaked, stifling a yawn.

"Sorry to disturb you. This is Inspector Lucas – Saville Row Police Station."

I was wide awake in an instant. Had I done something illegal, immoral or what?

"I'm ringing about an acquaintance of yours, a Miss Barbara Haldane. You've probably read about her in the papers. She was a clerk at the Admiralty."

I let out a sigh of relief. It wasn't about me then. As for my knowing anyone called Barbara Haldane... The police had obviously made a mistake. Got me mixed up with someone else.

"I've never heard of her," I murmured. "Why? What's she done?"

He paused. "She was murdered. Two weeks ago. Stabbed to death near Soho Square."

I clutched at my dressing-gown. "Murdered? That's terrible. But..." I tried to control the wobble in my voice. "But what am I to do with it?"

"We believe you might be able to help us." Another pause, then a faint rustle of paper over the telephone.

"Does the Stuart Academy, off Piccadilly, mean anything to you? You were a student there some months ago, we understand, at the same time as Barbara Haldane. You were in the same group."

A flash of recollection. "The Academy? Ah, yes."

So. She was from there. Some poor, would-be fashion or TV model. Faces flashed before me. Jo, the star of the group; Sally, the blonde with the funny laugh, Jill... I remember everyone, don't I?

"It was only a short course," I said, "one evening a week. I got to know most people, but the name Barbara Haldane doesn't ring a bell at all."

"Never mind. You're sure to remember once you've seen her photograph. Can you come to the station this afternoon or some time tomorrow?"

"I'll be over tomorrow after work, if that's okay. About five."

"Good. You know where it is?"

"I'll find it." My hand shaking, I put down the phone.

At work the following day, it was hard to concentrate. I kept wondering who Barbara Haldane was; searching my mind for names and faces.

Of the twelve students at the Academy, I managed to recall nine names. There were two others whose names I couldn't recall but whose faces I saw clearly in my mind. One was a tall, slim girl with a mole on her chin, the other a bubbly little person with frizzy hair and a Cockney accent. Could Barbara Haldane be one of them? Or was it the twelfth student, the one with no name and no face?

I arrived at five on the dot and soon I was sitting in Inspector Lucas's office. He was middle aged, well-built with sandy hair and feathery moustache. Not a bit as I had imagined from his voice on the phone. He greeted me pleasantly, took a file from his cabinet and pushed across a photograph.

It was black and white, postcard size. I scanned the face and straight away I recognised her. It was the twelfth student, the one for whom I could find no face and no name. But I remembered her now. I remembered the fuzzy, non-descript hair, anxious eyes, vague smile. So this was Barbara Haldane?

I felt suddenly choked. We were fellow-students. Yet I hadn't even taken the trouble to remember her name. I don't think anyone had. We all wondered why she attended these classes. She was such a little mouse, shabby, not particularly attractive or talented. Some girls tittered at the way her petticoat always seemed to hang below her skirt. One student, I remember, called her a non-person.

I felt sorry for her but never did get round to having a chat, other than to say 'hullo' or 'how are you enjoying the course?' And I'd even forgotten her name. It was too bad of me. She was a person, damn it! She had a life, a job, a home. What right had anyone to call her a non-person?

"Well?" Inspector Lucas looked at me expectantly from behind his desk. "You remember her?"

I nodded. "Yes, I remember. But I don't think I can help much. She was a quiet sort of person, you see. We didn't really chat." I handed back the photograph.

He frowned, obviously disappointed. "Don't you remember anything about her? Are you quite sure you didn't get into conversation at some time and discuss family matters, say, or boyfriends?"

I shook my head. "No. I'm sorry but as I explained, she was a quiet, timid sort of person."

He gave a grunt. "Not as timid as you think. Did you know she was unmarried with two illegitimate children? She was no innocent, I assure you." He smiled, grimly. "And she wasn't too timid to spend some of her evenings wandering round Soho, for what purpose one can only guess."

I gaped at him, at the lines of disapproval on his face. "It doesn't sound at all like the person I knew. Poor girl. What a terrible way to die! Do you think you'll find the killer?"

He threw up his hands. "It's hopeless. Street murders late at night are almost impossible to solve, especially with no witnesses. All we know is that the murderer is male and might have been having an affair with her. However, no one can tell us anything about her affairs."

He closed the file with a thud. "As if we haven't enough on our hands, we have to waste time on some cheap little... Women like that are just asking for it."

"Asking for it?" I felt a surge of anger rise to my throat. "Asking to be stabbed to death?"

He fiddled with his pen a moment. "No one deserves to die that way, I admit. She was stabbed nineteen times, apparently. Shocking. Still…"

He shrugged, picked up the file and put it back in the cabinet. "What did she expect, leading a life like that? It's giving us one hell of a job I can tell you."

I felt my face burning, the anger growing. He doesn't give a damn about her, I thought. To him she's just a cheap little nobody, undeserving of police time.

I wanted to lash out at him, to yell, "So, she's given you a tough job. Not the killer, but she, the victim? Why this way round, I wonder? Because she was some poor wretch, struggling to bring up two children without a man's support? Because she'd got her life in a mess?"

But I said nothing. Too polite. Afraid perhaps I'd go over the top.

I couldn't help wondering, though, if he'd be so dismissive, were it someone rich or well-connected who'd been murdered in the street. But perhaps I was being unfair. Maybe it wasn't Barbara Haldane he was mad with, but a case that gave him so little to work on.

"Have you interviewed anyone else from our group?" I asked.

"A few. But no one as yet has supplied any useful information."

"Pity. Well, good luck with the investigation."

I rose. He saw me to the door.

As I sat on the tube to Hammersmith, a hundred questions chased each other round my brain. Why, I wondered, was she roaming the streets late at night. Was she a part-time prostitute, desperate for money? Or was she lonely, urgently seeking love in whatever way she could?

And why was she murdered?

I don't suppose I shall ever know. Her case is clearly hopeless, one that will probably be filed away and eventually forgotten.

But I shan't forget. And it will always sadden me that I never talked with her, and that, for me too, she was once the girl with no face and no name, someone to dismiss and dump into oblivion.

View of Rhondda Cynon Taff

Dunraven Street, Tonypandy

Me, at age 7

My brother, David,
going to the seaside

Cousin Margaret

My stepfather with David and me

Shopping in Cardiff with Gran and Auntie Ivy

147

At a theatre party with Mitzi and Jean

Sir Frederic and I outside his house in Welwyn Garden City

In the Garden with Patrick

A Christmas party with the family: Patrick, his two daughters, Pauline and Debbie, his ex-wife Patsy, and her new husband David

The wives of Patrick: Patsy, Joan and I in Cumbria

I and my late partner, Bill, outside a restaurant in Soho

I and my friend Wendy, on a day out in Bournemouth (2014)

The Life Story group at the U3A

CHAPTER TWENTY

A LUCKY BREAK

The pressure to find a man having subsided, I dumped the London Weekly Advertiser, deciding to leave romance to the will of the gods. At the same time, I determined to be more circumspect. "Watch for predators!" I warned myself. "You don't need another Boris or Bloom messing up your life."

Don't get me wrong. I wasn't averse to the odd flirtatious glance or look of appreciation. But anything beyond that sent warning bells ringing.

Today, with the passing of youth and middle age, I no longer need to be wary of predators, at least not of that kind. As for flirtatious glances, now I've reached the riper end of maturity, people seldom look at me at all. That's something I miss about being young: Getting noticed. It sounds horribly vain and self-absorbed but I can't help it.

Sometimes my play-reading group gives me a chance to be young again. If there's a twenty-year-old or even a child in the play, I'm sure to get the part. I can do the voice.

I'm probably a better actor now than when I was young. I'm more able to lose myself in the role. Achieving this is a real joy. It's like having a holiday from yourself.

During my time in London, the urge to act was like an itch in my system. Modelling was okay as a sideline but couldn't be anything more. What I really wanted was to TREAD THE BOARDS. It was one of my life goals.

I abandoned the sessions I'd begun at the Guildhall School. As a part-time student all I would get there were qualifications to *teach* Drama. And I wanted to *act*.

I started lessons at the Roselli Academy, an agency as well as a school. It wasn't that easy though juggling lessons with teaching and modelling jobs.

At the Academy, I learned to dance, sing songs from the musicals and light opera and practise audition pieces from a book called 'For the Actress'.

Now I'm not a great optimist, always expecting lucky breaks, so when, one day, Miss Roselli said, "Do you fancy being in pantomime?" my heart stopped for a couple of seconds. "Sorry it's such short notice," she went on, "but one of our singers has dropped out. Would you mind taking her place?"

Would I mind? Immediately, I contacted schools and model agencies to tell them I'd be away for a month or so. I also gave notice to quit my room in Kenyon Street. The panto was in Wolverhampton, and I saw no point in paying rent in two places.

The show, *Mother Goose* was to be performed at the Grand Theatre, the leading lady being Beryl Reid. There was another comedian called Ted Rogers who, later on, ran his own television show.

The singers: Jean, Pat, Mitzi and me, formed a quartet. We also had to do some movement and acting. Jean was the oldest and Mitzi the youngest. I took to Mitzi straight away and we became good friends, sharing digs together in Wolverhampton.

Mitzi and I spent our first evening settling into our new lodgings with an elderly woman called Mrs Bailey. She seemed thrilled to have us there. I think she was lonely and hoped we'd bring a bit of colour and excitement into her life. The following day we started our week of rehearsing.

All I remember about this was that the whole theatre was a hive of activity. Every corner, besides the stage, was utilised by cast members practising. I enjoyed it, enjoyed the whole run, in fact. The scenery, actors, the crowds watching... all was magic to me, more like a dream than reality.

At the Grand Theatre, we singers shared a dressing-room with some of the dancers. They were a lively lot of girls and we got on well together.

One of the most popular acts in the show was a group called the Dallas Boys. They made the audience roar with laughter when they did a send-up of the Beatles. Their leader was a tall, fun-loving extravert called Stan.

Stan was Welsh. And not only did he come from the same valley as I, he also came from the same street!

The show, like so many pantomimes, had a Squire and a Dame. Here, at the Grand, these were two gay men who shared a dressing-room. Some of the dancers had a crush on the squire who, though middle aged, had lost neither his looks nor his charm. They flirted with him shamelessly, hoping, I think, that their allure might be strong enough to convert him from gay to straight. They were doomed to disappointment. Though ever charming, ever polite in his responses, he maintained his usual orientation, staying faithful to the Dame.

Another character of interest was the wicked magician, a tall, thin, solemn man who kept himself to himself. I never once saw him smile though he certainly knew how to roar at the audience and startle the kids.

One evening, on passing his dressing-room before going on stage, I noticed that the door was part open. I couldn't resist a peep inside. And there he was, the wicked magician, in his tall, pointed hat and star-spangled cloak, sitting in solitude, knitting.

Knitting? I crept away. The wicked magician knitting! How weird is that? I couldn't wait to tell Mitzi.

These are mere fragments of my period in pantomime.

But in trying to sort out the details, to build up a picture of it all, I can recall little more. So much has become an enchanted haze in my mind, a vague impression.

I would have nothing more to write about were it not for the page-a-day Diary I discovered on moving house some years ago. I remembered then how Mitzi and I made a New Year resolution for 1964 that we would each keep a diary for that year.

DIARY EXTRACTS – 1964

Wednesday, 1 January

Very tired after New Year's Eve party. Don't get to bed till after 5 a.m. Two of the Dallas Boys come, also Ted Rogers and the Orlander acrobats.

One of the acrobats appears to have a crush on me. Has offered to do an extra somersault in the show tomorrow, if only I will go out with him. He keeps trying to kiss me. I wish he wouldn't. I couldn't possibly be interested in one so young, especially an acrobat.

Mitzi is in ecstasies because Bob, one of the Dallas Boys is here. I can see there's going to be trouble, if she's not careful.

Saturday, 4 January

Have lunch with Edward, a spotty-faced youth, badly in need of a haircut. He's reading philosophy at UCL, but helps in the flies at the Grand Theatre during vacations.

He lent me a book the other day about Neitzsche. I can't say I like Neitzsche's philosophy. For him, the qualities that most elevate man are those of fearlessness, will to power and strength of body and mind. Charity, compassion and humility are 'slave values', obstructing his ascent. Equality is absurd: where everybody is somebody, nobody is anybody. Inequalities, he maintains, are a fact of nature and it's only fitting that the stronger is in the ascendancy and the weaker below. I feel I might be hovering near the foot of Nietzsche's edifice.

Another non-cast member I'm friendly with is one of the stage-hands. He's a curious character who broods solitarily like some modern Hamlet. We're both interested in English Literature and sometimes stand together in the wings discussing metaphysical poetry and Marlow's Dr Faustus.

Mitzi is horribly depressed after the show and, again back at the house. She is now convinced that she's in love with Bob, and nothing I say will comfort her. How easily some people fall in love! She has known him scarcely a fortnight. I wish I could introduce her to someone eligible so she'll forget this man who is, of course, MARRIED and will only break her heart.

Monday, 6 January

Another party tonight, held by one of the dancers.

Steer clear of the acrobat who, having been rejected by me, pursues Mitzi. He becomes far too ardent for her liking (out in the garden), telling her that she now is the woman of his heart.

Leave early and help Mitzi with her script. She's been asked to understudy Jill, the principal girl. She's thrilled. It might take her mind off Bob for a while, though perhaps this is too much to hope for.

Tuesday, 14 January
Lend Pat £5, Mitzi 2/6 and Chris, 2 shillings. Feel like a money-lender, except I get no interest.

No matinee today, so some of us are going to see Babes in the Wood at the Alexandra. Not impressed. It's more a variety show than a panto. Mitzi is in tears when I arrive home. Apparently, she saw Bob and his wife kissing and cuddling on the stairs. She wants to die.

Thursday, 16 January
Mitzi is getting worse and worse. Her infatuation for Bob has become an obsession, almost a disease. I'm dreading how she'll be when the show comes to an end and we go our separate ways.

She is taking to heart the line I quoted to her recently: 'one crowded hour of glorious life is worth an age without a name', and plans to invite Bob to our digs one evening to spend her crowded hour with him.

Tuesday, 21 January
A foggy day. Travelling is chaotic and there are a number of collisions.

The audience is almost non-existent, and who can wonder? It takes me two hours to arrive from Oxley which is only three miles away. The fog gets worse. There are no buses running when we leave the theatre so we have to thumb a lift.

The inconvenience suits Mitzi well. Her darling Bob, due to the fog, is unable to return to Leicester and has asked her if Mrs Bailey can put him up for the night, since he cannot find a vacancy at an hotel. She is ecstatic at the idea. Unfortunately, (or perhaps fortunately), he and Stan are later invited to stay at Ted's' place and take advantage of the offer.

Mitzi isn't too disappointed: it seems that Bob has agreed to stay with us tomorrow.

Wednesday, 22 January

Bob comes back to our lodgings with me and Mitzi. We all chat until 2 a.m. If he has any feeling for Mitzi though, he hides it very successfully, most of his attention being focussed on Mrs Bailey.

Mrs Bailey and I make up a bed for him. Later, Mitzi wanders into his bedroom to say goodnight. Later still, she wanders in again with a hot-water-bottle. This time, he suggests she 'jumps in'.

Since I can do nothing to dissuade her from seizing this opportunity, I plead with her to be careful.

Thursday, 23 January

Mitzi is ecstatic after last night, said Bob was very loving, and that it wasn't just sex. She told him she loved him and believes he feels the same way about her. I doubt this. It seems that directly he had satisfied his lust, he couldn't wait to get rid of her. He was afraid, he said, that if she stayed, her landlady would find out and talk, and it might get back to his wife.

Tonight, after the show, there are floods of tears again. I'm hoping that now Bob knows how Mitzi feels, he will be kind enough to keep out of her way.

Saturday, 25 January

Receive my Equity card. Good. Professional at last!

Pat, one of the singers, arrives late at the theatre, almost missing the opening. She's in storms of tears. It seems she had a terrible quarrel with her boy-friend, Tom, last night and thinks they might be finished. I feel sorry for her but she is a bit of a drama queen. Beryl Reid commented that her behaviour was most unprofessional and that she shouldn't let her private life interfere with her work.

Bob is avoiding Mitzi and when she asks to have her photograph taken with him, he suggests it be put off till 'sometime next week'. It appears that his wife has come to see him today.

Mitzi asks if I will speak to Bob, telling him how much she loves him. When I show reluctance, she complains that nobody ever does anything for her although she's always helping others. This sort of talk makes me cross because it's so untrue.

Thursday, 30 January

This evening we are invited to a Rugby Club dance and have a pleasant time with lots to drink.

Mitzi sings 'Give me the Moonlight' but, judging from the faces and comments made by some of the dancers, her rendering is not appreciated. Jean looks decidedly embarrassed, and I want to hide away. I hope the girls don't tease her too much tomorrow.

January slid into February, with more diary entries of parties, dances and affairs of the heart.

The show romped merrily on, each night delivering a full house and responsive audience.

Mitzi, still crazy about Bob, seized every opportunity to be with him. Bob did nothing to discourage her. Once, he arranged to borrow the room of Mike Ingham, our director, so they could make love in private. He was playing with fire, I thought, messing around with a young girl so obsessed with him she wouldn't think twice about breaking up his marriage. He was being unfair to Mitzi too. For him, this was only a fling. It was more than a fling for her.

Gossip broke out amongst the girls. Fay, a dancer, had spied Mitzi popping into the Dallas Boys dressing-room. "She's been there an hour," Fay said in a shocked voice. "She's probably having it off with all six of them."

I gave her a look. "That's a horrible thing to say!"

Gossip didn't die down when Mitzi finally appeared, hair dishevelled, make-up smudged. She ignored the cold looks greeting her. "They called me a 'good sport'," she said, smiling.

She never got the chance to be principal girl. Jill didn't get sick. Nobody did, except Yvonne, the pixie, and her place was taken by Dunia, one of the acrobats. A brash teenager with an ego the size of Wembley Stadium, Dunia was thrilled at this opportunity to show off another of her skills. Attempting a grand entrance, she took a flying leap onto the stage.

159

Unluckily, she landed on her bottom (this being quite unintentional).

The dancers laughed like drains. They resented the choice of Dunia as stand-in for the pixie, grumbling that one of them should have been chosen.

At this point Pat questioned the choice of Mitzi as understudy to Jill and said, spitefully, that it was probably because she was the only one able to fit into Jill's costumes, and that, being a singer, it was naturally assumed she could sing.

By this time the show was nearing its end. I couldn't bear the thought of leaving; of saying goodbye to the cast, the theatre crew; our motherly old landlady.

"We must buy Mrs Bailey a present," I told Mitzi, "A nice vase perhaps. Or a pot plant."

"We'll get her a poodle," Mitzi said. "She's always wanted one."

I gaped at her. Would Mrs Bailey want to look after a dog at her age, and take it out each day? I tried to make Mitzi see sense but, in the end, she had her way. She would buy Mrs Bailey a poodle, whether I chipped in or not. And I knew she couldn't afford to on her own.

We trudged round Wolverhampton seeking the ideal poodle. The weather was damp, bitingly cold, and I cursed Mitzi for being such a pain. Finally, after visiting various pet shops and kennels, we found what we wanted and returned home, complete with a little black poodle.

"The darling!" Mrs Bailey said. She looked overjoyed. I crossed my fingers she'd stay that way.

Back at the theatre, Beryl Reid sent up some bottles of wine during the show. After two glasses I felt so elated, I gave our surly director, Mike Ingham, a flirtatious smile. He'd been paying me some attention lately, ever since catching a glimpse of me in my black lace corselet. He visited our dressing-room after the show to inform me I had a tear in my finale dress.

160

Pull the other one, I thought, what you wanted was another peep.

Soon came the final company party. For fun I disguised myself, wearing a blonde wig and glasses. I fooled everyone. Jill, the principal girl, thought I was Stan's wife, while Jack Tripp was completely taken in when the Dallas Boys told him I was Shirley's sister.

I got most awfully tight. Nicky, one of the Dallas Boys, kept refilling my glass with brandy, whisky and heaven knows what else. I had no idea how I got home.

The show ended the following day, on the 22nd February. I felt bleak. Tomorrow I would be in London but where to live and what to do, I had no idea. Mitzi would be okay for a while, staying in Henley with her mother.

She was very brave for most of that last day. After the finale, though, she broke down and wept. The thought of parting from her beloved Bob was too much to bear.

The end was as I had anticipated. In spite of all her loving and giving and doting, the boys ignored her. She had to seek Bob herself to say 'goodbye'. He wished her a cool 'best of luck' and told her to look after herself. If she steers clear of characters like him, I thought, perhaps she will.

We left Wolverhampton the next day. Mrs Bailey was in tears when we said 'goodbye'.

So were we.

CHAPTER TWENTY-ONE

BUSY RESTING

Pantomime was fun. I might have been perching on only the lower rungs of the theatre-ladder but getting to the top didn't much matter to me then. The important thing was that I had achieved my goal of treading the boards and was finally doing something I enjoyed and actually getting paid for it!

I soon found though that it was a tough life in many respects. Unless you were at the top of the profession you were as often 'resting' – so called – as working. You survived these times by modelling, waitressing or demonstrating some product at Earl's Court or Olympia. You found time for auditions, but as often as not, you were turned down. The director would shake his head, smile apologetically and say, "Sorry, Sweetie but…" Then you'd be told you were too short, too tall, too fat, too thin, wrong face, wrong voice, 'not what we're looking for' and 'we'll be in touch, darling'.

After the razzmatazz of pantomime, I couldn't face going back to teaching. I survived on modelling jobs. I also got work advertising sewing patterns on Radio Caroline, a pirate radio station of the time.

I continued to train at the Roselli Academy, but by this time, I had found another agent called Mildred Challenger. Good name for a theatrical agent, I thought. She was an old woman, small and skinny, with a scrunched up face and crackly voice. "You must get a set of decent photographs," she told me. "The ones you have won't do at all."

I took her advice and went to a photographer. I can't remember who recommended me to this man but he turned out to be Lord Christopher Thynne whom I found out years later was the heir to Longleat. He was a rather scruffy young man at the time with an even scruffier car. He gave me a lift home in it one day, that's how I know.

Many photo studios as well as theatrical agencies were located in Soho, adding to its lively mix of bars, restaurants, and theatres. Back then though Soho was pretty seedy too, and crowded with strip joints and 'working girls' flats set shoulder to shoulder with the more conventional establishments.

If you visited an agent in Soho you'd often see a notice in the passage 'Model upstairs'. Model? As in fashion or photographic? Hardly. But, to get back to their notices, I remember reading a rather amusing one at that time, not in any passage, but in a phone box. It said, 'For Sale: Large chest, small drawers. Contact Lusty Linda.'

Enough about that. It's time to carry on with the story of what happened when Mitzi and I left Wolverhampton and returned to London.

Monday, 24 February

From 9 o'clock this morning until 10 this evening I've trudged around London, looking for somewhere to live. Of course, I am looking for the impossible: a largish room, nicely furnished, in one of the better parts of London, at a reasonable rent.

I miss the audition for the George Mitchell singers. Just as well. I'm not in good voice.

Tuesday, 25 February

At last, I have found somewhere to live – an address off Sloane Street. Considering it's in such a fashionable area, the rent of four guineas a week is quite reasonable. It's only a bed-sitter, of course, and not large, but it's adequate – at least twice the size of my room in Fulham. And with a few pictures on the walls and some flowers, it should look quite attractive.

Now that's sorted I'm off to Wales to stay with Cousin Joan for a few days. Doze on the train.

When I get there, an old boy-friend, Ieuan, calls and we go for a drive. At dinner, he proposes. Oh dear, how can I say no, in the kindest possible way? I evade the question.

Wednesday, 26 February
Visit my mother. She has grown wizened and old. She doesn't even try to make herself presentable. In fact, she seems to take a pride in making herself look as pathetic as possible. I hope I do not die so young for she is a kind of death-in-life. It's sad.

Meet Ieuan who proposes again. I tell him it'll be years before I start thinking about marriage.

Monday, 2 March
Back in London, move into my new room in Wilbraham Place. Norman (my photographer friend) has been so sweet. He's brought my suitcases here and left some flowers.

Attend an audition at Dineley's. No success. They liked my voice but say I'm not tall enough. I'd better get some four inch heels – or stilts!

I've done nothing else today to get work. I really must make more effort. I'll phone agents tomorrow and look through the papers.

Thursday, 5 March
Have a lesson with Michael DuBarry at the Roselli Academy. Do a duologue with Robin Phillips who – surprise, surprise – turns out to be 'Sir' Robin Phillips, a baronet.

Mildred Challenger phones. She wants me to audition for summer season rep. Fantastic. Michael sounds thrilled at my news. He's a sweetie really, even if he is queer.

Friday, 6 March
Have an appointment this morning with Mr Nieman who's useful for theatre contacts. He's a dirty old man though, so I'll need a chaperone. I take Mitzi. He's not likely to try anything with two of us there.

Says he will take me along to Wimbledon rep on Tuesday next. Shouldn't think it will come to anything. London rep companies seldom need anyone new. However, I'll go, and make an excuse to get back early.

Search for work for Mitzi but not successful. I have to pay for her phone calls and her bus fares. I wish she would take the job offered at Swan & Edgar's. It would be better than nothing till she gets a theatre job.

She's coming to stay next week, taking a room at the top of the house. How she'll pay the rent I don't know.

Monday, 9 March

I've managed to get some decent bookings for modelling jobs – one for modelling hair curlers, another for book jackets. Some months ago, before the pantomime job, I did similar work and, in order to get more bookings, I conjured up a fictitious sister called Martine. I fooled almost everyone at first, wearing a long blonde wig, paler make-up and flat shoes. I also spoke with a strong Welsh accent. But then agents and photographers began to get suspicious.

I started making mistakes, being Shirley when I should have been Martine, dropping Martine's accent. I should have worked out her character more thoroughly from the beginning and stuck to it. The solution? Either Martine or I must die. Alternatively, if we are both to survive, then we'd better not have the same contacts. It gets tedious when we are invited out together and either Martine has to make excuses for me, or I, for Martine.

Robert, a personal column acquaintance, phones, to invite me to a concert.

Friday, 13 March

What a day this has been – a complete fiasco! I postpone my appointment with Mr Nieman in the hope of getting through an audition at the Roselli Academy. I spend an age trying to make myself look like a teenager, miss lunch and my shopping, have an hour's wait, and then the blasted man doing the auditioning doesn't turn up. All that fuss and bother for nothing.

Meet Robert at Sloane Square. Enjoy the concert, particularly the Egmont Overture. I've heard it over and over, of course, but unlike Robert my love for a piece of music often grows as my familiarity grows.

Robert prefers to listen to less well-known, rarely played pieces and is inclined to look down his nose at more popular music. 'These are the favourites of the masses, and I am above the masses' is probably his personal opinion. He's such an intellectual snob.

Sunday, 15 March

Mitzi nearly sets the house on fire. She has to get the young American from next door to put it out.

This evening I go to Fulham to visit Margaret Maney, my New Zealand friend. She has finished with Alec for about the fourteenth time. She has the same problem as I – a complete inability to feel deeply romantic about anyone. Margaret though has fewer opportunities for meeting people than I have, so lacks choice. I wish I could introduce her to someone eligible. Must look up my address book.

I introduced Mitzi to Richard, an actor-friend of mine, a couple of weeks ago, hoping his company would take her mind off Bob. It seems he's done more than that. She thinks she's falling for him. I hope the feeling is mutual. Mitzi won't be safe until she's married.

Tuesday, 17 March

A photographic booking as Martine. Although this photographer met me as myself last week, he fails to realise that Martine and I are one and the same. Perhaps we can both survive a little longer.

Saturday, 21 March

Jean Clare (from pantomime) phones, telling of her success at the Tommy Trinder audition. I'm so glad she has work for the summer. Wish I had.

Saturday, 28 March

Receive letter from Richmond Rep. They have no vacancies. Perhaps my photographs put them off. They are a bit amateurish. Must find myself some work soon. It's quite pleasant being idle but I'll need more than occasional modelling jobs if I'm to increase my savings.

Sunday, 29 March

A quiet day. Write letters and listen to the wireless. Mitzi discusses her problems with me for an hour. She is worried about her complex personality – she will dramatise everything – and thinks she should see a psychiatrist. I could have suggested that ages ago.

Tuesday, 31 March

I have a hairdressing appointment which is not at all successful. It usually costs me 15/6 but because of a few extras, I find myself paying £2.10s! This is an exorbitant charge for a wash and set, particularly as I'm not at all pleased with the front bit. It's much too flat, making my silly, round face look even sillier and rounder. The back is okay, but who's going to see the back of my head in a photograph?

I've been recommended to go to Lord Christopher Thynne for my theatre photos. Afterwards, he gives me a lift in an awful old car to Oxford Circus. He's unhappy, he says, because it's his thirtieth birthday which means he'll have to be more sober and mature in the future.

Thursday, 2 April

See Christopher Thynne at 11.30 this morning. Photographs have turned out well, thank goodness. Hope they'll get me some work.

Roselli Academy – 3.30. Have a session with Michael DuBarry. Sir Robin is there. He's coming over to see me one day next week so we can rehearse our duologue.

Friday, 3 April

See Christopher Thynne again. He doesn't recognise me. Damn, I forgot I was being Martine and in disguise. I am to telephone him on Tuesday.

Get a call from Mildred Challenger. They want me to go to an audition for rep next week.

Tuesday, 7 April

Acting audition. Successful. Thank God for that. And I'm not to be assistant stage-manager-and-small-parts. I'm to be junior lead. They're sending me to Minehead for the summer season. Mitzi will be working in the same area as a dancer. What luck!

CHAPTER TWENTY-TWO

REPERTORY, APRIL TO JULY:
A SECRET LIAISON

There were twelve of us in the repertory group, mostly serious-minded graduates of RADA or one of the other established drama schools. In charge was a producer-actor-manager called Edgar, a gentle, elderly man with an air of quiet authority. Rep, I found, had none of the party-going atmosphere of pantomime. The focus was less on fun, more on hard work – hardly surprising with so many lines to learn.

We had a week to study our scripts before rehearsals began. The Forbes Russell Theatre Company did the casting as well as the auditioning. They gave me roles in five plays out of six – two murders and three comedies. When the sixth play was being performed, I would have time off.

I studied my scripts carefully. One of the murder plays, *Proof of the Poison*, was pretty awful, I thought. It had an unconvincing plot and poor characterisation. And I, alas, was the murderess, killing my victim with poison-filled chocolates. It would be one hell of a job trying to think and feel myself into this role.

Rehearsals, held in Kentish Town, London, lasted ten days, starting on the 27th April. *Rockabye Sailor*, the first play we had to tackle, was mostly froth and little else. My character, Daphne, was so bland, I wondered how I could liven her up.

One thing I noticed at rehearsals was how experienced most of the other actors appeared to be. I felt quite raw in comparison. But they seemed a nice enough bunch. One of the actors, Chris, took a fancy to me, appearing frequently in my diary during this time:

Wednesday, 29 April
Chris held my hand today and would have kissed me if I hadn't turned away. I like him, but he's married – of course. Just my luck.

Thursday, 30 April
Christopher kissed me and bought me a bar of chocolate. I let him put his arm round me. It's very naughty but I find him attractive and I love his voice. It's like a caress.

Friday, 8 May
Last day of rehearsal. When it's over, Chris walks me to the bus stop and kisses me goodbye. He says he can't wait to see me again. I can't wait to see him either. He attracts me immensely – Heaven knows why – he's plump and not at all good-looking. But he's so warm and affectionate, and I see his face light up whenever we meet.

Running parallel with the tasks of studying plays and attending rehearsals was drama of another sort. Mitzi had been seeing Richard, the actor I'd introduced to her some weeks before and fallen head over heels in love with him. One day, however, while I was busy studying my scripts, Richard phoned. "I've had it with Mitzi, I'm afraid," he said. "It's time to end things."

His words were like a punch in the stomach. "Blast you, Richard. She'll be in pieces. Why?"

He sighed. "We've nothing in common. And she's too all-over me. Too needy. I can't stand it."

"You'll have to tell her – gently mind. She doesn't deserve to be brushed aside without a word."

"I thought *you* might…" he began.

"No, Richard. I'm not doing your dirty work."

He agreed to meet her that evening.

Seeing Mitzi the following day, I was aghast at her fragile state. Wobbly on her feet, and becoming violently sick, she confessed to having taken several sleeping pills the night before.

Later that day, she became almost hysterical and threatened to cut her wrists. I managed to calm her with cups of tea, hugs, words of reassurance. Underneath, I was cursing myself for ever having introduced her to Richard.

For days afterwards she remained emotionally distraught, weeping, pacing the room, going over and over past conversations with Richard, listening to romantic records that reminded her of him. I tried to distract her, suggesting a film, walks, contacts with friends. She preferred to dream about Richard.

Towards the end of April things came to a head. "I think I might be pregnant," she said, adding "but I'd love to have Richard's baby." My throat went dry at the thought. I prayed she was mistaken.

Shortly before our move to Minehead, her doctor confirmed that she was indeed pregnant. The news sent a chill down my back. I phoned Richard. He visited us that evening, his face like a thundercloud.

"Are you sure it's mine?" he demanded, flicking through the pages of his diary. At Mitzi's indignant response, he tightened his lips. "You'll have to get rid of it," he said. "I know someone who'll help and provide the equipment so you can do it yourself."

Mitzi was left feeling shattered.

She was still pregnant when we arrived in Minehead. I worried for her, remembering my own pregnancy only two years before and the desperation I had felt.

It came as a shock when, a few days after our arrival, I heard from the Review that Mitzi had been rushed into hospital with a miscarriage. As soon as I was free, I went to visit her. She looked pale and emotionally drained but murmured that she was glad everything was over. So was I.

The next day, I received another message. Mitzi had been dismissed from the show and another girl was replacing her.

Not if I can help it, I thought. Straight away I went to see her producer, begging him to give her another chance.

He wasn't that eager but finally gave way. "If the hospital can guarantee she'll be out by Monday, I'll take her back," he said. "But I must know today, so there's time to cancel the replacement girl."

Everything turned out well, though I felt worn out by the end of the day after racing backwards and forwards to the theatre, the hospital and my digs. Still, it was worth it. Mitzi would be rejoining the show on Monday.

My heart sank though when I next saw the Review.

She danced like a half-dead thing, gazing not at the audience but at everyone's feet in her efforts to keep in step. Her spell in hospital had obviously set her back. So had her low spirits.

My romance with Chris did much to distract me from Mitzi's ups and downs. Not that it ran smoothly. At first we met regularly in my dressing-room, our chit-chat inevitably ending in kissing and cuddling. He told me I was the only woman outside his marriage he had ever wanted to make love to. I felt guilty, especially since learning he had brought his wife to Minehead and they were lodging not far from the theatre. Even so, I found him and his caresses hard to resist.

Then, quite suddenly, he began to avoid me. Thinking back, I realise he probably felt as guilty as I did about our goings-on and wanted to end them. But, sinking into melancholy, I wrote:

...He's not coming into my dressing room any more for a kiss and a cuddle. He is polite and that is all. If this sudden indifference is caused by an awakened awareness of his marital obligations, all I can say is I wish he'd thought of that before. I didn't intend having an affair, but I was so happy in his company, I couldn't help returning his affection. And now that he gives me none, I feel desolate.

171

This afternoon, have a game of table-tennis with Victor who lets me win. Later, he comes to see Proof of the Poison, a play I have a part in but he doesn't. He takes me home afterwards.

Victor was a good friend, always ready to cheer me up when I felt down. He called on me a few times at my lodgings. I got worried that he might be growing too fond of me. *'He's good-looking but very young.'* I wrote.

Whatever his attentions, he couldn't divert me from my mooning over Chris. I was getting as emotional as Mitzi. An entry for Friday, 29th May, read:

Again this evening I feel horribly depressed. Chris is still avoiding me, intent no doubt on assuring me that any past affection meant nothing. He has the misfortune to bump into me on leaving the theatre and asks, purely out of politeness, if I'd like to go for a drink. I answer coldly that I would not, thank you. Next time he asks I would like the following conversation to take place:

ME (with quiet dignity) You're not obliged to ask me, you know. I shan't feel neglected if you don't.

CHRIS (awkwardly) What do you mean?

ME: Well, it's rather strange that you should suddenly invite me for a drink, when you spend most of your time trying to avoid me. You needn't feel you owe me anything just because you couldn't keep away from me for the first few weeks.

My spirits were not lifted on receiving a letter from Jasmine, an old college friend. 'I'm so enjoying married life,' she wrote, 'and can thoroughly recommend it.' I should have felt happy for her, but could feel only envy that she was settled with a man and I wasn't.

I tried to focus less on Chris, more on acting.

Friday, 5 June
I've borrowed two books from the library: 'The Producer and the Play' and 'The Psychology of the Actor'. A lot in there about Stanislasky and method acting. Stanislasky teaches you how to immerse yourself

into a role, how, instead of assuming an emotion, you let it come from inside.

I must make a more careful study of the characters I'm playing. None of them seem that interesting but I'm sure I can make more of them. If only Edgar would correct, advise or make a suggestion now and again. He hasn't much time, of course, what with playing parts himself, and he is, I know, careful not to discourage us. But I'm so inexperienced, I could do with some constructive criticism.

Wednesday, 10 June

Practise my singing. I'm making progress. Power and range are improving. When I remember to relax my throat and drop my jaw, I can reach those top notes with ease.

Begin rehearsals for 'Flat Spin'. Don't know how we'll get it ready for Thursday.

Jackie is excellent. From the first rehearsal she knows her lines and is completely at ease in her part; movement and gesture come so naturally. I must work hard to achieve this naturalness myself.

Wednesday, 17 June

During 'Murder Delayed' this evening, there is a crisis. The murderer, Keith, forgets his gun. Luckily, the policeman manages to slide it under the scenery near where Keith is standing. Keith picks it up while pretending to stub out a cigarette. The audience doesn't seem to notice.

Thursday, 18 June

I have no role in the play being performed during the next few days so I'm off to London. I've arranged to have a lesson at the Roselli Academy with David. Hope he thinks my voice has improved.

I've also heard from Mr Nieman who says he'd like to discuss my theatrical career with me since he's had excellent reports. If he could find me a winter season engagement, it would be nice. But I need to be careful with him – pleasant, polite but very firm.

Friday, 20 June

In London, I learn about the new fashion in women's clothes: topless dresses! I saw one on display in a Chelsea shop. Two middle-aged men, having passed by, suddenly realised what they'd seen. They turned back sharply to take another look.

Back in Minehead Victor told me of a way he'd discovered for supplementing our incomes – strawberry-picking. Lovely, I thought, lots of fruit to guzzle and extra money for the piggy-bank.

Soon after my return from London, I set off to Hellecombe Farm with Frances, an elderly member of our rep group whose free time coincided with mine.

For hours we almost broke our backs in the hot sun, bending double to pick those damn strawberries. But we stuck it and managed to fill more than 100 baskets between us. By then though I was exhausted, my body stiff, my arms so burnt I couldn't bear anyone to touch them. I soon decided that the piddling reward obtained from this enterprise wasn't worth the effort and would add little to the piggy-bank.

There was always Chris to smooth away my woes. Yes, we were friends again and spending time together.

Bliss. Except that the old twinges of guilt were back. Also, I had a strong feeling that some in the group were expressing disapproval about our relationship. This made me uneasy. I didn't want a bad reputation. On the last day of June I wrote:

During the break Chris invades my dressing-room again and stays. We discuss music and literature. I leave the door wide open and talk loudly so our colleagues would rest assured we were not in fact doing anything quite wicked like having sex on the dressing-room floor.

CHAPTER TWENTY-THREE

REPERTORY, JULY TO SEPTEMBER: BOTHERSOME FEELINGS

My diary extracts of summer season rep are as much about my liaison with Chris as about acting. I'd got it bad – emotionally involved with a married man and not knowing how to control the jumble of feelings fighting inside me. I dare say that if he'd been free and had popped the question of marriage, it would have cooled me down. But he wasn't, and he didn't so I was stuck with my bothersome feelings.

I did try to disentangle myself. Sometimes when he visited my dressing-room, I'd make an excuse and head for the reading-room. One day, he followed me there, put his arm round me and told me how he wished we could spend some 'real time' together. He went on to say that his wife, Jane, would be leaving Minehead soon and it would be wonderful if I could spend some time at his place. It's a shameful admission to make but the idea thrilled me. I wouldn't do such a thing of course and risk breaking up his marriage. And I didn't want to lose my reputation altogether. If only my feeling for this man would die down.

Over the next few days I avoided him. But this made me solitary and withdrawn, especially when I saw how matey he was getting with Sally, our assistant stage-manager-and-small parts. I tried snuffing out the flames of passion by focusing on his weak points. My entry for 9th July read:

He played table-tennis with Sally today while I went alone to the reading room. What a ridiculous figure he makes in those shorts with his paunch bulging over the top! Positively embarrassing. But I feel so desolate now. Victor walks home with me after the show and tries to cheer me up.

It seemed that the more I tried to avoid Chris, the more he turned to Sally. This deepened my gloom. I wrote: *My attitude towards Chris is most immature. If he's more attracted to Sally than to me, what can I expect when I so often give him the cold shoulder? If only I could fight my stupid feelings and do what my head tells me is right. My head is by far the best guide.*

Whereas I was in emotional turmoil, Mitzi appeared to have calmed down. When I next visited the review, I found her performance much improved. She was smiling at the audience and dancing well – something at least to cheer about.

Stage-wise I, too, improved. On 7 July, I wrote triumphantly that, for the first time, I managed to *live* the character of Nina in *Proof of the Poison* and had never done so well in that part before. Perhaps my reading of Stanislasky had done the trick.

During my days off I went away now and again. I spent one weekend in Cardiff, staying with Cousin Margaret and her husband Roy in their lovely new house there. They seemed very happy together with their daughter, Pamela and the new puppy. Pamela, now twelve, made such a fuss of me, plying me with questions about the theatre, offering me lemonade and biscuits, I ended up almost in a good mood, and able to forget Chris for a while.

I travelled to London sometimes too. On Friday, 10th July, I met Norman, my photographer-friend. I felt guilty about this. How could I have anything to do with Norman while I still had this terrible passion for Chris? On the other hand, how could I end things when he'd been such a good friend? We lunched, chatted about photography, the theatre, my strawberry-picking. I didn't mention Chris.

Walking alone down the Kings Road afterwards, I spied in a shop-window, a dress to die for: pale blue, flimsy, and fitted at the waist. Chris would find me irresistible in that, I thought. Buy it!

"But he's married," the voice in my head argued, "so what's the point? Anyway, I'm saving."

I was indeed saving. Hard. My capital had already reached nearly £1,500. I hoped that one day I'd have so much money put by, I could live off the interest. Short of robbing a bank though, raking in that amount of money would take about a hundred years.

I walked on, another question confronting me: Why save for the future when I can enjoy the present? I might be dead before I'm sixty. Even if I'm not, I'll be a sad, wrinkled old thing by then, too sick and crippled to make use of my accumulated funds. I felt a shudder pass through me. Old age was scary, worse than death. Already, wrinkles were appearing around my eyes. Cousin Joan called them laughter-lines. But that was just a euphemism for crows' feet.

It must be comforting, I reflected, to believe that all the trials and tribulations of old age could be made up for in a future existence: Heaven. I wondered what God did with all his souls?

I tried not to let such personal anxieties blind me to goings-on in the world outside. My diary is full of comments about current events. As well as grumbling about the continual strikes – *If it isn't the GPO, it's the transport workers* – I also expressed strong views about affairs in America at the time:

Sunday, 19 July
I find the views of Senator Goldwater odious. He suggests that Social Security should be voluntary, since most of the poor are responsible for their lot, and people should have the freedom to spend their money as they please; with regard to foreign affairs, he points out that the war in Vietnam could be quickly ended with atomic bombs. He is against any friendship with communist countries and would try to force the Russians to surrender their atomic weapons while the Americans of course hung on to theirs. Those siding with Goldwater feel that America and all she stands for are imminently threatened by a worldwide communist

conspiracy. My own view is that if a fanatical anti-communist like him becomes president, we'd best give up all hope of world peace.

Sometime later, an article by John Crosby in The Observer got me really steamed up:

He maintains that women 'are organically, emotionally and psychologically unfit to vote intelligently on anything except maybe what colour to paint the kitchen'.

If Mr Crosby can base his judgement of all women on the stupidity of his mother's opinions and those of other equally stupid women, then he himself is lacking in reasoning ability.

Yes, there are women who are unfit to vote. Not, however, because they are women but because they are not very well-informed women. If the right to vote depended purely on a person's reasoning ability, not only would large numbers of women be excluded but great numbers of men also – the less well-informed of both sexes in fact.

I don't think journalists could express such views today without causing a rumpus. Perhaps attitudes *have* changed for the better. Whatever the case, however much I threw myself into studying the news, I couldn't distract myself from thoughts of Chris. Nor could I always resist him. I tried though to put our meetings on a more intellectual footing than an intimate one.

Tuesday, 4 August

Chris and I are talking again. We argue about birth control. Having converted to Catholicism when he married a Catholic, he is against contraception. This is the irritating thing about some people. Instead of consulting their reason, they blindly follow religious rules.

Catholics believe that contraception is contrary to Natural Law. And as Natural Law reflects the mind of God, contraception is against the law of God.

But how do we know God is against contraception? The population in biblical times was much smaller than it is now. Perhaps today he'd be glad of our assistance in keeping the population in check rather than depending solely on famines, floods and diseases to do the job.

Is it sensible, I ask Chris, to cling to rules made long ago supposedly by an invisible despot when we can see definite flesh and blood characters around who could otherwise be helped?

I can't say that our meeting on Saturday, 5 September was particularly intellectual:

Chris asks me out and I say yes. We see 'Make me a Widow' at the Queen's Theatre. It's abysmal stuff. Some actors are quite wooden and speak in a monotone. I'd be bored stiff if I didn't have Chris sitting next to me, stroking my hand.

When we leave the theatre, it's raining. Chris paddles home with me under my umbrella. We stop near the coach station and kiss, though our fleeting expressions of endearment are interrupted from time to time by the glaring headlamps of cars flashing past.

And how was Mitzi getting on during the rest of our time in Minehead? Not too well towards the end of the season. On the 22nd August, she and Jill, one of the other dancers, visited my dressing-room, looking pictures of misery. They'd spent Thursday night locked up at the police station, they said, charged with being drunk and disorderly at the Wellington Boot. Mitzi was adamant that she wasn't drunk but ill and spending most of her time in the Ladies' room. I stiffened. If there was a miscarriage of justice, then something should be done. I decided to make enquiries.

A few days later, both girls were sacked and ordered to leave straight away. Horrified by the news, I marched off to the Wellington Boot to question the bar staff. They told me that Mitzi was, as she had said, quite innocent of causing a disturbance. It was Jill who was the culprit. "She was very drunk and very disagreeable," one of the barmaids said. "She even punched a policeman."

The next day, I wrote to Mitzi's employer giving him a fairer picture of the incident. Nothing came of it, the reason being perhaps that both girls, in their struggle to avoid arrest, hadn't been above hitting out at the officers and kicking them on the shins.

Early the following month I went to London to see how Mitzi was. To my relief she seemed to have recovered from her misadventure and was bursting to tell me her news. "I've seen Richard," she squealed, her eyes shining, "and I think he's interested again."

Her second piece of news was less pleasing. Norman had taken her out and made a pass. I wonder now why this incident should have disturbed me. I wasn't after all in love with him.

Even so, I met Norman the following day and tackled him about it. At first, he denied having done anything but take Mitzi out. "I felt sorry for her, losing her job," he said. Finally, however, he admitted to accepting her later invitation to 'come in for a coffee'. While visiting the bathroom, Mitzi apparently changed into a dressing-gown. Suspecting that she had nothing on underneath and that this was a 'come-on', Norman got a little disturbed…

Later that day, Richard visited Mitzi but the evening ended with Mitzi in floods of tears. "He didn't even make a pass," she sobbed. I told her she must forget this man.

Next day I returned to Minehead. Only one week of rep. left. I wrote about it in my diary:

Friday, 18 September

Dining with Jerry and Keith (two of our rep members), we have a heated argument on how far one's behaviour is influenced by heredity and how far by social factors. I believe social factors play the greater role though their effect is probably limited by inherited temperament.

Keith, who has relatives in South Africa, believes that black people are less intelligent than white and goes to great lengths to prove his point. I argue that the intelligence of the black race could not be compared to ours with any accuracy until all had equal opportunities to develop intellectually and economically. "If they are treated as inferior beings, as they are in S. Africa," I say, "then they will act as such."

I've put Keith in a bad mood. He's scowling and has stopped speaking to me.

Wednesday, 23 September

Keith has scarcely spoken to me since that argument. It's so petty of him. He's out for revenge too. He's ruined some of my lines and deliberately spoilt my laughs.

Saturday, 26 September

Home at last. And it's a lovely day here in London, much too warm for September. It was sad saying goodbye to Chris yesterday and refusing to give him my phone number, but I know I must forget him. This will be easier now we're not working together.

I'm still undecided about what to do next. Perhaps I'll try and find a husband.

Tonight Mitzi drags me to Tooting to see 'Ben Hur'. She's got a terrible crush on Charlton Heston. He reminds her so much of Richard, she says. I can't see much of a likeness myself, but there you are.

Saturday, 10 October

Spend the afternoon at the Natural History Museum with Mr Brown, a photographer-acquaintance. He asks what's happened to Martine who shares a flat with me and whom he once took out. He's been hankering after her. He tells me finally that he prefers me. I'm smarter!

After a snack in the West End, we part, and he kisses me full on the mouth right in the middle of Leicester Square. What an idiot! I shan't go out with him again.

My diary extracts seem to fizzle out at this point. Perhaps, during the time that followed, I was too busy doing other things. I know that besides modelling and teaching I worked for a while in market research and later at VSO. At the same time I was saving frantically for a flat, studying for more GCEs and trying to find a husband, embroiling myself in disastrous relationships as a consequence.

I didn't give up my flirtation with show business. Apart from a singing engagement at the *Pink Elephant*, I landed a part in a film called *The Punch*. I was cast as a young girl in love with a boxer but pursued by a lesbian. The money was useful but the film a complete flop. No surprise there. It was the most awful trash. When I saw the rushes I gave a groan of dismay.

Then Mildred Challenger got me an audition for *The Sound of Music*, and a few weeks later off I went to Eastbourne to become a nun at the Congreve Theatre.

This might have been enjoyable if I hadn't felt so battered at the time by a love affair that didn't work out and where passion was on one side only: mine.

But that wasn't the only depressing thing. The director of this production took an instant dislike to me. It was nothing to do with my singing or acting. It was me as a person. Well, I wasn't at my best, was I? Once unrequited love stepped through my door, cheerfulness and charm flew out through the window.

I found out though from one of the girls that his dislike of me was nothing to do with my personality "It's your hair style," she said. "He can't bear women who pile their hair on top like that."

You don't believe it? Nor did I at the time, especially as he was one of those we used to call 'queer'. Why would a *queer* be interested one way or the other in how a woman styled her hair?

Nevertheless, my fellow-nun turned out to be right. At a party he threw shortly afterwards I deliberately let my hair fall down my back. Believe it or not but he was like a kind uncle to me after that. He even told Mildred Challenger he wanted me in his next show!

I didn't take up the offer. During the next few months I worked for Voluntary Service Overseas at their administration office in Paddington. The work was absorbing and helped me regain some psychological balance. I also received a proposal of marriage and was busy chewing it over.

I often wonder if I should have taken up that director's offer and carried on in show business. Who knows what might have come of it? I might have obtained a role in a west end play, in

TV, or in films that didn't flop. I might even have made a name for myself.

Some years later I saw Chris, the repertory actor, in a West End production. *He'd* made some progress. As for Richard Owens, the man who gave Mitzi such a hard time, I looked him up on the internet the other day. He's been in hundreds of films and television series.

I look up myself just for fun. There's nothing. Many of my friends are on the internet: Julian, Colin, even Wendy. But there's no sign of me. No list of achievements. Nothing. Does that mean I don't exist? We hear of people having a low profile. I don't seem to have a profile at all.

Ah, well, perhaps I don't need one. There are upsides to anonymity. I could more easily do something outrageous without anyone finding out or caring one way or the other. Perhaps that's what I should do to get a profile. Something outrageous – or so extraordinary that everyone would know about it, even though I'm not newsworthy.

Anyway, according to the internet I don't exist. But even if I don't, even if my life is no more than a dream, it continues to be an interesting one, and I don't intend to wake up just yet.

CHAPTER TWENTY-FOUR

MITZI'S METAMORPHOSIS

Soon after returning to London, Mitzi and I moved from our old rooms in Wilbraham Place and rented between us a twin-bedded studio-flat in the same building. It was Mitzi's idea. "Look at that gorgeous red carpet, Babe, and those fab curtains!" she exclaimed in ecstasy. "And we even have our own bathroom and kitchen."

"But it's nearly ten pounds a week. That's expensive," I argued, ever the old Scrooge.

"Not for a flat in Sloane Square. And we'd be sharing the rent," she said.

I gave way to her whim. Still shattered by her last meeting with Richard, she needed cheering up. Contacting him again had done her no favours.

Returning home after visiting him that day, she told me what happened.

"He's found someone else. Her name's Polly Adams. She's a terrific actress, he says." Her mouth quivered as she ended in wobbly tones, "He wants to marry her."

"You're well rid of him."

I got up and put an arm round her. She clung to me, weeping quietly against my shoulder.

"Does Polly Adams want to marry *him*?" I asked.

"She's thinking about it. I guess she will, considering she's pregnant."

"Pregnant? Well, she could always get rid of the baby as you did. She must have contacts."

"No, she's Catholic." Mitzi drew her lips together. "Anyway, Richard doesn't want her to." She broke off and covered her face with her hands, her whole body shaking with sobs. At last, she choked out, "That's what hurts: he's so damned well *over the moon* about it. He kept saying, 'I want this baby. I want this baby'." Tears of anguish turned to tears of rage as Mitzi tightened her hands into fists and said, brokenly, "Yet he couldn't wait for me to get rid of *mine*."

"Forget him. You'll find someone else." I said, feebly, wishing with all my heart that I'd never introduced her to Richard.

Some weeks later, we moved into the smart little flat on the first floor. As time passed, weeks growing into months, Mitzi grew calmer. The change of environment had done her good. Her old room at the top of the house would always remind her of Richard.

But we didn't stay there long. Mitzi decided that her mother and Aunt Beryl, her mother's sister, were unhappy living in Henley as servants to a rich family and would be better off in London.

"We can all live together in one house, and share expenses," she said, eyes shining. "It will be lovely, Babe. Absolutely fab."

Again, wanting her to be happy, I said yes.

It was a wrong move. The cheapest house we could find was in Queen's Park – a bit of a come-down after Sloane Square. I hated the place. Worse, I didn't get on with her mother.

Mrs Jones was no bundle of fun. Unlike Mitzi, she was small and slim, with a look about her mouth that spelt frustrated ambition and general discontent. She was quietly spoken and mild in manner but I suspected that underneath this sober exterior lay a mine of repressed anger.

She hadn't always been a servant. She was once a ballerina who hadn't made it to the top and was anxious that her daughter would compensate for this by getting to the top herself.

Her antagonism towards me started when I passed an audition to sing at the *Pink Elephant Club*. She was furious at my lucky break and took out her angry feelings on Mitzi. "Why aren't *you* getting somewhere," she demanded. "Look at that Cilla Black, how well she's doing, and Sandy Shaw. I'm sick of seeing them in all those TV shows, while you…" She gave a snort of frustration. "You're going to no auditions, making no connections…"

To shut her mother up, I tried to get Mitzi an audition myself. I knew a man called Malcolm who managed a group of singers and dancers. I rang him and suggested Mitzi met him for an audition. She did so soon afterwards, returning home, full of confidence, sure she'd been accepted.

But a few days later, he phoned me. "We can't take your friend on, I'm afraid. She's the wrong shape. We're looking for really slim girls."

It was the age of Twiggy, of course, the top model of the day, famed for her wraith-like figure and little-girl face. But did everyone have to ape her?

"Mitzi's an experienced dancer," I argued, "and she's not what I'd call fat."

"She's wedge-shaped," he returned, loudly. A bit too loudly as it happened. Mitzi was in the room and, realising the call was about her, strode towards me and pushed her ear to the phone. She heard this comment and snatched the receiver from my hand. A heated exchange followed. It ended with Mitzi's dropping the phone and rushing out of the room and down the stairs, where she sat near the bottom, weeping her heart out.

She was still weeping when I joined her. "He called me wedge-shaped," she sobbed.

I tried to comfort her, but Mrs Jones burst in on the scene and pushed me away, a look of sheer fury on her face. "You're ruining my daughter's life. You're nothing but a witch," she screamed at me. "You got her that audition, knowing she'd fail, so you could crow over it." She paused to get her breath, then went on, "And it was you who introduced her to a man ten years older than herself so you could crow over that when it all went wrong. You're a witch, an evil witch, and I want you out of my sight."

I seethed at the injustice of her words but I didn't argue. I moved out, finding myself a bed-sitter back in Kensington: Ennismore Gardens.

I missed Mitzi's company. It seemed strange living alone again. I think I felt more isolated during my period at Ennismore Gardens than I've ever felt before or since.

But Mitzi and I kept in contact. She came to visit me sometimes at my new place in Kensington, though, as you'll probably guess, I never again went to Queen's Park to visit her. Not with that simmering cauldron of neuroses, her mother, hanging around.

On one of her visits Mitzi had exciting news to tell. She had met Charlton Heston, talked with him, lunched with him. I thought at first she was either having me on, or had let her imagination run away with her. Guessing my scepticism, she clicked open her handbag and with a smile of triumph drew out a photograph of the two of them standing together in the lobby of some grand hotel.

"How did you manage that?" I asked her.

"I pretended to be a journalist," she said, eyes dancing with mischief, "and he gave permission for me to visit him at his hotel." She giggled. "I soon admitted this was a fib and that really I was only a fan, desperate to meet him."

"What did he say?" I gaped. The nerve of her! *I'd* never have had the guts.

"He was *fab* about it. Laughed at my cheek, and took me to lunch."

She paused and gave a secret smile. "We made love."

My mouth fell open even further. She giggled again then whispered, "But you mustn't tell anyone. He's got his reputation to keep up. And there's his *wife*."

Her eyes turned dreamy. "He's so like Richard."

I left London in 1974, and it was years before I met Mitzi again, but I shall always remember that meeting. She had changed. It wasn't so much in her thickened appearance, but in her *character*. She was older, of course so I shouldn't have been surprised at the greater stability that she showed. But, according to Mitzi, it was not age that had brought about this change. It was a spiritual awakening.

She talked about it as we sat in a cafe in Leicester Square, drinking coffee.

"It happened on a plane journey," she began. "Don't ask me to describe it because I can't... except to say that it was like a wonderful shaft of light. It sounds daft I know, but it was as if I were catching a glimpse of Heaven and receiving a revelation..." Her eyes grew misty and far away. Then she said quietly, "And suddenly I felt at peace. So at peace."

We sat in silence for a minute while drinking the rest of our coffee.

"I decided then to make some changes," she said at last. "The first thing I did was pack in my stage career."

I lifted my eyebrows. She laughed and made a face. "Career! That's a good one. I wasn't getting anywhere. And I wasn't happy. It was more important to my mother than it was to me. Anyway, she's accepted the situation now. And I'm happy."

Thank God for that, Mitzi, I thought. But I mustn't call her by that name any more. She'd buried *Mitzi Mitchell* along with her theatrical ambitions, and resurrected her old name: *Rosalind Jones*.

She'd got herself a new job too, she told me. She now worked at a theatre-ticket agency in Piccadilly and loved it. She had, evidently, not severed links with the theatre altogether.

There was yet another important change in her life.

"I married John Peed at long last," she told me.

John, I remembered, was an ordinary young man with an ordinary job. He'd been carrying a torch for her for years, despite her lack of encouragement.

"I made him change his name though," she said. "I'm damned if I was going to be Rosalind Peed. Rosalind *Reed*'s a bit more dignified, don't you think, Babe?"

For a moment, a glimpse of the old Mitzi, came back. I was glad she hadn't changed completely.

Rosalind will be in her sixties now. I wonder how she is, what she's doing, and if she's happy. I discovered an old Christmas card from her the other day with her telephone number inside. I wonder if she's at the same place and if I might try getting in touch.

CHAPTER TWENTY-FIVE

ON THE FRINGES

Thinking back, I envy Rosalind and her revelation. It gave her peace. Helped her reconcile herself to the limits of ambition, to dump it, stop searching for fame, wealth and all the other things so many search for, hoping to find happiness. She found hers by dropping the search and the rat-race of competition and becoming the best she could with what was available to her. Very wise.

Will I ever be able to do that? Resign myself to being a nonentity, part of the mass of nonentities that people the world? And not give a damn? Say to myself, okay, I'm a nonentity, I can live with that. I can forget me and my petty little failures and disappointments and focus more on the world outside and my duty to it. If I can do that, then I might be able to enjoy the present and stop obsessing about the future, with those troubling thoughts of the ultimate failure: the dying bit by bit alone and forgotten. Parting from this life, not with a quick, loud bang but with a slow, fading whimper, the sort of end which makes you wonder why you bothered to exist at all.

I unveil these bleak thoughts to Frieda at one of my sessions with her.

"Life doesn't have to end like that," she says. She gazes at me, a frown creasing her forehead.

"A heart attack would be nice and quick, I suppose. Or a fatal accident." I give a light laugh.

"What's happened to trigger off this gloom?" She gets into her wise-owl mode, hands steepled, eyes lifted to the ceiling. I hate it when she does that. It looks so studied.

I hesitate, then blurt out: "I've had one of my children's novels rejected."

She gives a sympathetic smile. "That's a pity. Can't you try another publisher?"

I carry on whinging. "What's the point? There's too much competition. I might as well give up."

She sighs. "Why don't you see things through? You gave up the theatre when you could have carried on, gave up your baby when there was a chance to keep her. And now you're giving up writing because of a rejection."

I glare at her, ready to explode. "Okay, so I'm weak and useless. Say it. It's obvious that's what you think."

She holds out a hand, palm upwards in a gesture of peace. "That's not what I think at all."

"Yes it is. And you're right. I *have* given up things. I've not been ambitious enough, tried hard enough. But what's the point when you're unlikely to get anywhere anyway? You have to know when you're beat."

I feel close to tears but pride makes me hold them back.

"Maybe it's more focus you need." She swivels round in her chair. "What was it you really wanted, more than anything, and would have worked hard to get? Was it the theatre?"

I sigh. "That's what I thought once, but I didn't want it enough, I suppose. I sometimes think it was little more than a fling, a chance to escape into a fantasy world from dull nine-to-five jobs."

"You can still have that escape. What about the U3A?"

"Yes, I can act there, and it's fun, even if it *is* only amateur." I break into a chuckle. "We've another Christmas panto coming up in a couple of months. I'm Cinderella. Not the one in the fairy story, you understand, the one who longs to go to the ball, but an older Cinderella with more modest ambitions. What *she* most wants is to join the *Country Dancing* group at the U3A."

I feel my mood lighten as I ramble on. "It should produce a few laughs. I love entertaining and interacting with the audience. That's what I liked about my old theatre days…"

On the way home from therapy, I think back to those days. There were two productions I took part in that I haven't written about. One was a comic opera by Benjamin Britten – *Albert Herring*. Although this would be classified as an *amateur* production – the singers received no salaries – most of them, even so, were professionals. One had sung at Covent Garden.

The opera was performed at the Curtain Theatre, London, in March 1973, some months before I auditioned for *The Sound of Music*. My day-time job was no handicap since rehearsals were in the evenings.

For the audition, I sang *Musetta's Waltz Song*, and subsequently acquired the part of Emmy, one of the child characters. It wasn't a big part but at least I had a chance to sing and act on my own.

I still squirm though when I think back to the first rehearsal. We were expected to sing through our parts straight away. While this was no problem for any of the others, it was a hell of a problem for me: I couldn't read music. The skill hadn't been necessary for the shows I'd taken part in. But this was opera. And Benjamin Britten to boot! A bit different from the stuff I'd sung at the *Pink Elephant*.

Panic set in. How on earth was I going to cope when it came to my turn?

All too soon that moment arrived.

"Emmy?" the musical director looked across at me, eyebrows raised, waiting for me to start singing.

I sat there as if paralyzed. This was the ultimate nightmare. Should I own up? Admit I couldn't sight read? Suggest they found someone else? Damn, no. I'd die of embarrassment. Anyway, I wanted this part. I'd have to think up an excuse.

I gave a loud, rasping cough. Oh dear, it didn't sound that authentic. I tried again, hand clutching my throat as if trying to stop it. Still not right.

"Sorry," I began, my voice a croak, "but I think I'll have to give singing a miss tonight. I seem to have developed a sore throat." I gave an apologetic smile. "I should be okay by next week."

To my relief, they let it pass, no questions asked.

The following day I made a dash for the public library. And you know what? That lovely librarian found for me a full recording of *Albert Herring*. I could have kissed her.

I have a good ear and in just a few days I learned my part thoroughly. And it wasn't long before I knew everyone else's part too.

Rehearsals went well. This was in spite of the odd tussle between the producer and musical director. The problem was, the musical director could never seem to arrive on time. This made Andrew, the producer, tear his hair in frustration. "He's got too many irons in the fire, that's the trouble," he'd say to us, gritting his teeth. "It's about time he sorted out his priorities."

Fortunately for everyone, once they were both there, things usually ran smoothly.

I soon began to enjoy *Albert Herring*. It's a very funny opera, the story being all about a young man who is chosen, against his will, to be King of the May. Why chose a King, not a Queen, you might ask? The answer is that Albert is reputed to be a virgin, whereas there's no girl in his village thought to possess this essential qualification.

There's plenty of action in the opera and lots of stage business to entertain the audience. I found this particularly enjoyable.

As well as enjoying the story, I soon grew to love Britten's music and the qualities of atmosphere and drama in his work.

The Stage gave us a good write-up. I am happy to say I was one of the few minor characters to get a mention. The reviewer described me as a 'pert Emmy'.

The other production took place years later, long after I'd given up professional acting (or thought I had) and when I was past sixty.

It was around 1998 when I got this sudden urge to act again. It started in a newsagent's. While searching for the *Radio Times* I caught sight of *The Stage*. I had almost forgotten its existence but now, curiously, I picked it up, glanced through, and finally bought it.

On the bus home, I turned to the advertisements page. One in particular attracted my notice.

Witches needed for Macbeth. Auditions at the Two Way Mirror Theatre, Alexandra Park. Apply with photo and CV to Amanda Ling, Director by 15th November.

A little shiver of excitement ran through me. Why not? It was only Fringe, of course, so I'd hardly make a fortune. You were lucky to get expenses or even a token payment at the end of the run. Still, I'd always wanted to be one of the witches in Macbeth. And it had been such a long time since I'd done anything in the theatre that wasn't purely amateur. Twenty-five years at least, if you discounted the walk-on I got in *Eastenders*.

I wrote to Miss Ling the following day, enclosing a photograph which made me look about eighty (What a good thing I hadn't binned it!) and apologising for the gaps in my CV. I didn't think I'd hear from her but a couple of days later, she phoned, asking me to come for an audition on Monday of the following week.

Over the next few days I read through Macbeth and worked like mad on the witches' speeches. In my mind's eye I saw myself transported to a desolate Scottish heath, old, hunched up and wrinkled, plotting calamities with my weird sisters. Conjuring up feelings of menace, I strived to express them through voice and gesture.

By the time of the audition I was more or less satisfied. I had added one or two sinister little touches to the part, which I thought would go down well with the director.

Perhaps though I should do something about my appearance, make myself look older. Not that I didn't look pretty old already. But I could make my face look gaunter. And if I darkened those circles under my eyes and added a few more wrinkles to my chin, I'd look the ideal witch.

The audition was at 12.30. I set off in good time, my pulse racing more than usual, but determined to be the last word in evil old crones.

Miss Ling turned out to be a pleasant, middle-aged woman with red hair and an easy manner. To my relief, she asked me little about my background before inviting me onstage to perform my piece.

It went without a hitch. Time and place melted away until I saw myself again plotting in the Scottish mists with my sisters.

At the end of it all, almost overcome with euphoria, I waited eagerly for the director's response.

"That was fine," she said at last. "Yes. You should be excellent as Aunt Julie in our production of *Hedda Gabler*."

I gasped. "Aunt Julie but... I wanted to be a witch in Macbeth. Wasn't I any good?"

"Hmm." She frowned and gave a little cough. "There is one snag, and when I tell you what that is, you might be less keen to have the part." She paused and looked across at me, her eyes seeming to rest on the wrinkles round my chin. "The witches are going to be *young* women for this production."

Damn, I thought, after taking all that trouble to look as decrepit as possible.

"Not only that," she went on, "but they're going to be naked."

"Naked?" I gaped at her.

"Naked," she repeated. "Not my idea, I assure you. It's the other director, Chris. He thinks it will bring in the audiences." She gave an apologetic smile.

"I see," I said, sadly.

She passed me a script. "Perhaps we can give this a run through?"

"Okay."

And that's how I got the part of Aunt Julie in Hedda Gabler.

A couple of days later I got a call from the White Bear, a theatre I'd also been in touch with. It was more up-market than the Two-Way Mirror but I still had to turn down their offer of a part. I'd already committed myself, and both productions were on at near enough the same time.

Sad to say, Fringe was about all there was available to an old has-been who'd been out of the business for years. For anything more ambitious, there were plenty of established actors to fill the gap.

I think back to my therapy session, Frieda's question scrabbling round my head, "What was it you wanted more than anything else in life?"

What indeed?

I wanted many things: to educate myself, to act, to write, to have a home of my own...

I set about achieving them. But I realise now that not one of them was my most important need.

What I wanted most in life was the thing nearly everyone wants: Love – good, old-fashioned love. It might sound sentimental, even cringe-making, but it's a basic need. Yet, for me, this basic need seemed harder to attain than anything else and there were times when I wondered if I would ever attain it.

HEARTACHES, HOMES AND HELPERS

1966–1974

CHAPTER TWENTY-SIX

OBSESSION

My need for love reached fever pitch during the late sixties when I had parted from Rosalind.

Living alone, I seemed to enter a world of emptiness, an emptiness which lasted at least two years, those years being perhaps the worse in my life. I missed having my scatty friend around, listening to her chatter, sharing in her ups and downs. Without her, my new apartment in Ennismore Gardens seemed unbearably bleak.

I tried to throw myself into my work, to socialise more. But it wasn't enough. It didn't fill the gap in my life. What I wanted now, more than anything, to fill that gap was romantic love, and I wanted it fast. I'd had no luck waiting for the gods to work their magic. Either I fell for a man and he didn't reciprocate or he fell for me and I didn't feel the same way. I'd met kind, loving, well educated men who wanted to marry me, but my feeling for them seldom rose above luke-warm. I was picky, I know, and hard to suit. That's why finally and desperately I prayed to God.

Now I don't really believe in the power of prayer, or in the power of God for that matter, but this was urgent so I decided to give it a go. My plea wasn't so much a prayer as a bribe and it's a wonder the Good Lord didn't strike me dead for my insolence. "Please God, send me a charming man whom I can fall madly in love with," I begged, adding, "Then I'll believe in you."

Well, how could God resist such a challenge, I thought, or such an offer?

God sent me a man. He arrived from a personal column. And he seemed just what I wanted.

Six feet tall, thick set with greying hair, he had the warmest brown eyes I had ever seen. They shone with affection and sincerity and I could almost feel myself sinking into those liquid depths.

His name was Peter Weston, his age 40 and his address Gayton Road, Hampstead. He was a molecular biologist, he said, busy with research, but not too busy to start a relationship.

"Let's meet again," he suggested, after our first lunch. "When is the best time to phone you?" He smiled a smile that would have charmed the rattle off a rattlesnake.

I returned home that day in a state of bliss. "Thank you, God," I murmured. "He'll definitely do."

By the end of our second meeting, I realised that I'd fallen madly, passionately and hopelessly in love with him. Did he feel the same way about me? It was early days yet but I couldn't help fantasizing. I started having crazy day-dreams about our setting up home together, about holidaying in the Caribbean, running, hand-in-hand on a solitary beach, just the two of us...

I must have given him a clue of my feelings when we next met, especially when I suggested we met more often. "We see each other only every two or three weeks," I said, "I can't even ring you for a chat because I don't have your number. And you're not in the phone book."

He paused. "No, I'm ex-directory. And I can't give you my number, I'm afraid. My wife or one of my daughters might answer the phone."

"Your wife?" The words came out in a whisper. I felt as if a lump of ice had got stuck in my lungs and was freezing up my whole body.

He gave a light laugh. "Oh don't worry. We have an 'open' relationship. She doesn't mind my having girl friends. So there's nothing to feel guilty about. Mind you, we both value discretion."

I stayed silent, trying to take in these unwelcome new details. It all sounded so casual. He was, I thought, just toying with me then. That wasn't what I wanted, a no-hope relationship. I should finish things, I thought, now, before it goes any further. The trouble is, I'm forever giving myself good advice, and then not carrying it out, following my heart rather than my head. And what filled my heart at this moment was the utter desolation that awaited me, if I didn't see him again.

"You have my address. You can always write," he said, softly. He had such a soft, soothing voice, the sort that could persuade, seduce, lull you into submission.

"I know," I said. "But you'll call me? Soon?"

He stood up. "Not soon, I'm afraid. We're very busy in the lab just now."

And off he went, leaving me alone again. No euphoric feelings this time. Only an aching sense of insecurity. I was drowning in it. Not knowing when or even if I would see him again, I avoided going out most evenings in case he rang and I missed his call. Night after night I sat close to the telephone, pathetically clinging to the hope he would contact me, unable to focus on anything else.

This, I knew, wasn't love, not in its true sense. It was *obsession*, an obsession that was growing into a disease. I began to lose my appetite, surviving each day on glasses of milk and the odd apple or orange. This went on for weeks, my weight plummeting to six stone. At the same time I was in a constant state of anxiety, finding it impossible to sleep without the aid of sedatives. On top of that I developed a skin disorder, ugly patches of red appearing on my face in response to the slightest heat or tension. My skin began to flake. Soon, I felt so ugly I wanted to hide away. But I couldn't. I had to work. And this I did, dragging myself, zombie-like, from one job to another.

One day, posing with others for a TV commercial, the director asked me to move from the front of the set to the back. The make-up artist wasn't able to cover adequately the red patches on my face. I felt my throat tighten. Clearly, I wasn't fit to be seen. If this went on, I would become unemployable.

Meanwhile, a month had gone by, and still no Peter. I had written but there was no response. I finally persuaded Directory Enquiries to give me the phone number for his address. I'd phone him. I could always pretend I'd dialled a wrong number if his wife or a daughter answered.

It was a man's voice that came over the line. "Could I speak to Peter Weston?" I asked.

"He doesn't live here," he answered. "This is a newsagent's. He uses us to receive his mail."

My shoulders sagged at the hopelessness of my quest. So, Gayton Road was an accommodation address. Peter was obviously playing safe. Perhaps his wife wasn't as easy-going as he'd made out.

At last, I received a postcard from him. He was in Wales, at a conference. But he would be back soon and would call me. I gave a long sigh of relief.

We met a couple of days later. Before he came, I got busy with my powder puff, covering the red blotches on my face as best I could. If you're red with tension, or come across as shy, or too eager to please, he'll guess how needy you are, I warned myself. So act casual. Nothing puts a man off more than a needy woman.

Little shivers raced up and down my spine as the doorbell rang and I rushed to let him in. I flung myself into his arms, clinging tighter and tighter, until gently he pulled away. So much for the casual act, I thought. If he didn't know before, he knows now how besotted I am.

I stood facing him, fiddling with my hair, rubbing my forehead. "Well, it's nice to see you at last. How have you been? How did the conference go?" The inane questions came tumbling out. "Did you have a good journey? Would you like a coffee?" Damn it. I was gabbling.

He lay back in the shabby armchair, legs stretched out, observing my awkwardness, a smile of amusement on his face. "I've been well. The conference went much as expected. I had a decent journey, thank you. And, yes, I would like a coffee."

He was laughing at me, I could tell. I rushed to fill the kettle. You're acting like a moron, I told myself. When you're not gabbling, you're tongue-tied. Why can't you behave like a normal human being when he's around. He's not the Prime Minister, for God's sake.

I heard a rustle of paper. Peter was taking something out of his bag.

"I've brought you a present – a souvenir from Wales."

"A present? For me?" My spirits rose. He must care a little, I thought, if he's bought me a present.

He handed me a woollen shawl, bright yellow. It felt rough to the touch. That didn't matter. Coming from Peter made it a gift beyond price. My heart sang: he cares for me.

My cheerful spirits didn't last long. While we sat drinking coffee, he took something else out of his bag – a magazine. It appeared to be full of personal ads.

"There are some interesting get-togethers advertised here," he said. "I thought we might try one or two."

"What sorts of get-togethers?" I asked.

"Most intriguing ones. Why not take a look?"

I felt a shiver go through me as I flicked over the pages. "But this is a sex magazine," I faltered. "The advertisements are for wife-swapping, orgies, that sort of thing."

"Well?"

"No. I'm not interested. Definitely not."

"Pity. I'm really keen. Think about it anyway."

When he left, I slumped down on the sofa and wept all over my new shawl. Had his gift been only a bribe then? And was his plan all along to get some vulnerable idiot like me so hooked on him that she'd do anything he wanted?

I had to end it. I was on an emotional roller-coaster. And the ride was becoming a nightmare.

I heaved a sigh. The snag was, even if I did summon up the strength to say goodbye, how could I then cope with the hell of never seeing him again. Such a prospect seemed worse than death itself.

But perhaps I was over-dramatising. Maybe he'd drop the wife-swapping idea. It was gross. He must know that it was only *him* I wanted, no one else. I wiped my eyes. Perhaps he wouldn't mention it again.

And perhaps I was living in Cloud Cuckoo Land. "I've been in touch with a very nice couple," he told me at our next meeting. "You're sure to like them. Stephen's a psychiatrist, his partner, Mary, a speech therapist." His smile oozed charm. "They're anxious to meet us. What do you say?"

"If it's one of those sexy get-togethers, no."

"Oh, come on, try it. It should be fun. They're providing drinks, food…"

"No. Take your wife. Or go on your own."

"My wife isn't interested. And I can't go without a girl."

So, he couldn't go without a girl. My feeling of self worth, or what remained of it, shrivelled to a fragment. Clearly, I was nothing special to him – just a girl who might be persuaded to serve as an entry ticket into sex parties and fun with other girls.

But even facing this stark reality didn't cure me of my obsession. I still went on longing for a glimpse of his smile, for the smooth timbre of his voice. Where's your pride, I asked myself.

I confided in Rosalind, telling her of my obsession. "You must stop seeing him," she urged. "He'll ruin your life. Remember what happened to me?"

I also confided in Wendy, my old college friend, who'd recently come back into my life. "The man's a monster," she exclaimed. "Promise me you'll finish with him. Please."

"I can't," I replied, choking on my misery. "I can't not see him again."

How pathetic I must have sounded. How lacking in will power and self-respect.

A few more meetings followed, but Peter's manner towards me had changed, becoming decidedly cool. He began to insult me. I was too thin, he said. As for my being thirty-two, that was nonsense – I looked so much older. He jeered at the books on my shelf, saying, "I don't suppose you've read any of them. You're not the academic type." And when I suggested he invite one or two of his friends over for drinks, he said "I couldn't possibly bring them here. They're used to elegant surroundings, antique furniture and so on." He eyed with contempt my shabby bits and pieces. I felt humiliated, like a lowly insect crawling about in his presence.

In spite of his cool treatment, he hadn't given up on the subject of sex parties. He continued to cajole and persuade, sometimes by letter. Perhaps he thought that in time I'd succumb, if only to try and sweeten his mood towards me. He finally gave me an ultimatum: "I'm a busy man," he said, "I can't come hopping down here time after time, unless there's something exciting in the offing. Either you come with me to these hedonistic events, or we finish."

I winced. He was bribing me as I'd tried to bribe God. Only if I acceded to his demands would he give me my reward – the chance to see him again.

But by now *I* was changing too. My obsessive love became mixed with hate until it reached a point where hate and anger fused and formed the bigger part of it.

When he left that last evening, I made a note of his car number and later passed it on to Tony, a man I knew, with contacts. Tony offered to do some detective work.

And guess what? I found there was scarcely a grain of truth in any of the personal details he had given me. Not only was his address false, but his name, profession, even his age. His real name was Claude Wedeles, not Peter Weston, and he was not a molecular biologist but a psycho-analyst. As for his age, he wasn't forty but fifty. He'd lopped off ten years!

He'd covered himself pretty well, I thought. He could play around to his heart's content and use people as he liked without any fear of comeback.

But now and again, your sins will find you out. And I had found him out.

Once more, he phoned me. "Well, have you decided?"

This time, voice trembling, I let rip my anger."Yes. We're finished, so don't call again. You're a lying, manipulative bastard, utterly selfish, using people for your own ends…"

Unruffled by my outburst, he gave a light laugh and said soothingly, "Feeling better now?"

I said nothing, too afraid I would break into sobs. So he went on, "Perhaps I am selfish. But be realistic. We *all* are, aren't we? It's human nature, a fact of life."

I slammed down the phone. Damn! I'd let him trump me again, exposing my anger and hurt like that, while he simply laughed at my feelings, his own emotions intact. He had won.

But had he? Not if I could help it. His laugh echoing through my brain, I thought up a plan.

What he didn't know was that, through Tony's detective work, I now had his address.

The following day I sent a letter to his wife. Not a letter from me but a letter from him to me, written in his own hand and inviting me to an evening of group sex. I put no note of my own with it. His own letter, I thought, would suffice. His wife would recognise his hand and know what he'd been up to, if she hadn't known already. And *he* would realise it was I who had sent it. Perhaps it would open both their eyes to the seriousness and even danger that could arise from his manipulative and casual treatment of women. After all, the next one might be more ruthless than I and resort to blackmail or worse.

Sometime later, I discovered he'd given up his post of senior registrar at the Tavistock Clinic and also his assistant lectureship at UCL. Had he done this out of fear, I wondered. Was he concerned I might report him, kick up a rumpus, blacken his name?

He needn't have worried. I wasn't trying to ruin him, just frighten him a bit, and discourage him from using other people the way he'd used me. I suppose I also wanted to show him that he couldn't treat me as he liked, and get away with it.

I'm not proud of what I did. My act sounds too much like the 'fury of a woman scorned'. I was not after all without blame. He was an opportunist, true, but he didn't *force* me into anything. And though my loneliness made me vulnerable, a vulnerability he was eager to exploit, it was still my responsibility, no one else's, to combat my obsession and stop seeing him. It can have been only a temptation to a man choc a block full of testosterone and perhaps in a mid-life-crisis.

It was years before I could forgive myself for losing my head over this man; for letting him take hold of my life and squeeze from it every drop of self-esteem I'd had.

There were though one or two positive effects of the liaison. It was after this episode that I turned to studying again, gaining enough qualifications to get into university. How dare he assume that I didn't read my books and that I wasn't the academic type! I also started looking at properties and set about buying myself an attractive, three-bedroom maisonette in Earls Court and furnishing it with taste. How dare he imply that my room in Ennismore Gardens was too shabby to receive guests! From now on, I would see that no such comment could be made about my accommodation.

But almost everything I did, I did in anger, feeding on it. And there were times when I wondered if that anger would ever subside and leave me some space to enjoy life again.

CHAPTER TWENTY-SEVEN

MOVING ON

Still angry and wounded following my affair with Claude Wedeles, I finally shook away my tears, dumped the yellow shawl he'd given me, and set about buying a property.

Get moving, I told myself. A place of your own will give you purpose, security – even an income, if you rent part of it. You'll probably never marry, but with rents coming in, you'll at least be able to support yourself in times of difficulty. To top it all, you'll have achieved another of your goals: setting down roots in London.

By 1968 I had saved more than three thousand pounds, an amount sufficient for a deposit. I finally bought a maisonette covering the two top floors of a house in Philbeach Gardens. It comprised a spacious living-room, kitchen and cloakroom on the lower floor and three bedrooms plus bathroom on the upper floor. It cost £6,750, at least half of which I paid with cash, the rest being a loan from the National Westminster.

I didn't move in right away. I let it for a few months, rent free, to my old college friend, Wendy who, in return for my help, did some painting and decorating. I decided that, in the meantime, I would work hard, save more money and start furnishing it.

Wendy badly needed help. She had recently married, and her husband, Peter, was in a critical state, dying of spinal cancer. She had married him, knowing of his illness, knowing she would have to support him both physically and financially, and aware he would never be able to give her children. Her sacrifice impressed me.

What a brick, I thought. That's real love.

Peter had already had an operation to remove his cancer but it was only partially successful and the process had damaged other organs. While staying at Philbeach Gardens, he visited his consultant at the Westminster Hospital to see if more could be done. There was nothing. "You haven't much time left, I'm afraid," his consultant said. "Weeks at the most."

But there was still hope: Peter had heard from Dr Issel's Clinic in Bavaria. Issels was treating cancer patients with some success. He had heard about Peter and offered him free treatment there.

His treatment was greeted here with scepticism. Nevertheless, Peter and Wendy made a grab for what seemed to be the one straw left and stayed at his clinic for four months. Peter, moving with Wendy to a flat in Hampstead on their return, survived another five years. He spent much of that time writing a book called 'A Time to Heal' (published 1971) which vindicated Dr Issel's treatment. Wendy herself wrote a story of their life together for *Woman's Own* magazine.

My friends' problems made my own seem very trivial. Even so, I couldn't get Claude Wedeles out of my system. I raged at myself for my folly. Never again would I lose control and give way to passion.

Having had Peter and Wendy around did help, if only to focus my mind on other people from time to time rather than narrowly on myself.

There were other things that helped too.

For a time, Margaret Maney, who'd been a tenant with me at Kenyon Street, rented a room at my new place. I liked having my New Zealand friend around again. It was she who introduced me to another friend and helper: Tigger.

Tigger was a tabby tom-kitten whom she'd found wandering in the street before foisting him onto me. "Poor little thing," she said, "He's got no home."

"But I don't have a garden or even a patio for him to run around in," I protested.

"Oh I'm sure he'll manage," Margaret replied. "You've got a nice big sitting room."

Grudgingly, I took him in. But he soon won my heart. He was actually able to make me laugh – a great feat, for I didn't laugh much these days. Every morning at about seven o'clock, he would jump onto my bed and give my face a series of pats to wake me up. And whenever I left the house, he would jump onto the window sill, glare down at me as I walked into the street below and give vent to a storm of angry meows through the open window, as if to say, "Out again? What about me?" He was very possessive and I was flattered to think he liked having me around.

Now and again, while at Earls Court, I took him to Holland Park for a treat. I carried him there in his basket, letting him out for a run, once we arrived. One day he climbed a tree and wouldn't come down again. It wasn't long before a crowd of people was standing in a circle around the tree, holding out shopping bags and other receptacles for him to jump into. But they couldn't coax him down. He sat on a branch observing them haughtily while washing his face, his whole manner suggesting that he'd climb down in his own good time, thank you very much.

Take my advice: if you want to make new friends quickly, don't walk your dog in the park, walk your cat.

I had other friends and helpers besides Tigger, in particular, Eileen and Roy. They both stayed at my place, after Peter and Wendy left. Eileen stayed only a short time, though we became good friends and have remained so.

She was a single mother, in her early forties, with a five-year-old daughter called Selene. She must find it tough, I thought, journeying backwards and forwards between Southend and the City each day, struggling to make a typist's income cover rent, child care and travel costs. Selene's father, it appeared, contributed nothing.

Eileen was great as a companion, witty and well-informed. She never grumbled about her difficulties though I knew she was hard up. I tried to help out now and again.

Though not university educated, she read a great deal, usually magazines or books on science or philosophy. I used to call her jokingly 'an intellectual snob' since she seemed to turn her nose up at anything that could be described as 'low brow'. She would drag Selene to museums and art galleries, hoping her own cultural tastes would rub off onto her daughter. I think they did eventually, but at that early age Selene showed little interest in such pursuits.

Every night, Eileen would escape into her books. She sometimes retired at ten, one tucked under her arm and say, "I'm going to bed with Einstein tonight." Then on would go the bedside lamp as she opened Einstein's 'Theory of Relativity'. Rather her than me, I thought.

Though slim, attractive, and not short of men friends, she had no ambition to marry. "I'm damned if I'm going to lose my freedom," she told me.

I wondered what freedom she thought she had, tied to a job she disliked, with a child to support, and always having to pinch and scrape her way through life. Selene wanted her to marry. She sometimes ran up to young men and asked "Would you like to be my daddy?" This embarrassed her mother no end as well as the young men in question.

Eileen's friend, Roy, was foreign editor for *The Times*. He became a good friend and companion until he died in the 1990s. Though not at all handsome, he was funny, lovable and knew just what to do and what to say to cheer you up when you were down.

He owned a boat called *Sheer Delight* and often invited one or another of us onto it. Even Tigger came on one occasion. Tigger didn't care for water, or travel for that matter. On the other hand, he seemed to like my going off without him even less.

But in spite of such distractions, I was still a captive of my past, specifically my past with Dr Wedeles. Put it behind you, I kept telling myself. Move forward. You have good friends *and* your studies. Forget Wedeles.

But the feeling of bleakness and insecurity so reminiscent of that time kept coming back, interfering with my studies and everything else. My appetite had improved, but sleep remained a problem.

I took a wonderful sleeping aid for a while called Mandrax which always worked. However, teenagers got hold of it and gave it the thumbs-up. You can guess the rest. Goodbye Mandrax.

Worst of all, I still had my skin problem. My doctor diagnosed it as *acne rosacea* and said it was rare in women who hadn't reached the menopause. "Avoid heat, alcohol and spices," he told me.

In wintertime it got particularly bad. My skin couldn't cope with moving from the cold outside to the heat inside a building. To counteract this problem, I wore a cotton frock under my winter coat in the middle of January. Immediately I got inside a building I'd take the coat off. I must have raised many an eyebrow when I walked into John Lewis' on a freezing cold day, carrying my coat and exposing a skimpy summer garment underneath.

The condition lingered right to the end of my year at UCL. It distressed me and again served as a reminder of my episode with Wedeles, when it had begun.

No medication appeared to help. Doctors did their best but sometimes the creams they prescribed made things worse.

My cure came about in an unexpected way.

Wandering around Foyles bookshop one day, I spied a paperback called *How to stop Worrying and Start Living* by Dale Carnegie. I flicked through the pages. Before long, hope began to stir. That's just the book for me, I thought. I bought it.

Once home, I began to read. I read chapter after chapter. The stories were all about people in dire straits, people suffering such misfortune or danger they were ready to kill themselves rather than carry on. Each time, however, they came through their difficulties, and recovered the strength to live again, realising that worry by itself was unhelpful and a waste of valuable time.

Before I was half way through, I began to see things in perspective. These people had real problems I thought, not pseudo-problems like mine.

Three-quarters of the way through, and a feeling of euphoria swept through me. Suddenly I knew, knew with certainty that I was on the mend: my skin would clear up and even the memory of Claude Wedeles would eventually fade.

I was right. It sounds like a miracle. Perhaps it was. All I know is that I finally gave a great sigh of relief and relaxed. Really relaxed. My face cleared up, not gradually but rapidly and without the aid of medication. Soon, hate and anger against Claude Wedeles and against my own foolish self began to diminish. I was even able to sleep again.

CHAPTER TWENTY-EIGHT

TONY

Before moving into my new flat, I met Tony. I was waiting for a bus at the time and it was pouring with rain, bucketing down. He stopped his car, asked where I was going and offered me a lift.

Dripping wet, miserable, and tired of waiting for the bus, I accepted his offer and hopped in.

Not the thing to do, accepting lifts from strange men? Suppose he was a weirdo, drove me to a lonely place, and there brandished a knife or strangled me?

Given the mood I was in, I didn't much care. It was just days after my last meeting with the man whom I knew as Peter Weston and whom I had more or less decided never to meet again.

As we drove into London, I soon found myself confiding in this total stranger as if he were a kindly uncle. I told him how fed up I was and what a rotten time I'd had with a man who'd lied to me and messed with my feelings till they were in tatters. He listened attentively, asking the occasional question and making a comment here and there.

By this time, I must appear not only a risk-taker but utterly lacking in reserve. The trouble is I'd reached such a low point in my life following my disastrous affair with that psychiatrist I became not simply reckless but unable to think or talk about *anything* else. Perhaps I hoped that some wise listener would be able to magic me out of the pit I had unwittingly dug for myself.

This man was elderly, late fifties at least, slim, smartly dressed and well spoken. Although he was a stranger, there was something safe, something fatherly about him. Before dropping me off, he clasped my hand warmly and asked if he might take me for a meal some time.

I met him again and found that my instincts about him were correct. He exuded warmth and compassion. It was he who pushed me into ending my unhealthy liaison; he who took from me the car number I'd noted, and found out who Peter Weston really was. Mind you, he was dead against further contact with him. "Leave it alone," he said, "Far better to forget the whole thing."

If I hadn't been so browned off with life at the time, I might have been impressed by Tony's connections. The son of a general, he came from an aristocratic family in Ireland, was educated at Eton, after which he trained at Sandhurst to become an army officer. Of his two brothers-in-law, one was the Earl of Shrewsbury, married to Tony's sister, Nadine. The other, husband of his sister, Sylvia, was John Chandos-Pole, Lord Lieutenant of Northamptonshire and equerry to the Queen.

If you valued introductions to the upper echelons of Society, I suppose Tony was a useful friend to have. But that wasn't what I was looking for just then. What I needed was Tony's company and support, someone who could guide me back to stability.

At the same time, I did gain some experience of how the other half lives.

Tony introduced me to members of his family. Sometimes we stayed at Newnham Hall, the house of the Chandos-Poles in Daventry, Northamptonshire. There, we even dressed for dinner. Princess Ann had stayed on occasion. In the drawing room hung beautiful pictures painted by eighteenth century artists. Tony photographed me gazing up at one of them – a lady in a flowing blue gown.

Other times we spent weekends at Basmore Lodge in Berkshire with Lady Shrewsbury. They were both rather splendid places, I thought, though Nadine described Basmore

215

Lodge as 'horribly suburban'. She'd come down in the world since her divorce from the earl and no longer had even one live-in servant. Tragic! She talked nostalgically of her old place with its ballroom and Great Hall. In that more spacious house, she and her ex-husband, had been able to entertain their guests with concerts and operas. The countess herself had a strong operatic voice. On one occasion she had sung at the Wigmore Hall under the name of Nadine Credy. She sometimes tried to persuade me to sing when we stayed with her, but I always declined. My sweet little soprano would have sounded pathetically weak compared with her strong mezzo.

Nadine Shrewsbury was red-haired, outgoing and full of life. She had four daughters and two sons. Her three older girls were married and had married well. One had become the Princess Borghesi. The youngest was only just 'out'.

Marguerite's coming out was apparently a bone of contention between Nadine and the earl. "He's such an old meany," she grumbled. "The least he could do is finance a ball for his youngest daughter. Poor Marguerite!"

I smiled to myself. What? No coming-out ball? How heart-bleedingly sad!

But Nadine was warm, kind, and a good hostess. She still looked after her old nanny who had in the past attended to the needs of Nadine's children as well as Nadine herself. Tony said with a laugh that though now pushing eighty, Nanny would still boss them around, given half a chance.

I stayed friends with Tony until he died. You could describe our relationship as a father-daughter type, I suppose. He would call me his 'Squirrel-Minx' and address me as such in his letters. He would sometimes couple me with his daughter, Alicia, and say things like, "I must buy you and Alicia a nice pair of boots each for the winter."

Eileen's little girl, Selene, adored Tony. One day she clasped him tightly round the waist and said "I do love you, Tony." And Tony was so touched by her words that his eyes filled with tears.

He had no place of his own. He stayed with one or another of his sisters. In Daventry he helped his brother in law with the administration of his estate. Sometimes, he went trout fishing in Ireland staying with friends there who owned a trout stream.

Since retiring from the army, he had no profession to speak of. His downfall was a liking for whisky which he began to drink directly he got up in the morning.

He wasn't a rich man, and when he died I believe he left only debts. Perhaps in his life he was too generous to his friends. He'd take me to theatres, concerts, sometimes to dine at the most expensive restaurants, such as the Ritz where I enjoyed my first taste of caviar. Often though the venue would be the more reasonable Cavalry Club. It never occurred to me at the time that he might not be able to afford some of these places. If it had, I would have declined his more generous invitations.

Once, he took me to the House of Lords for the opening of Parliament. The Duke of Norfolk was officiating and appeared to be making guests comfortable and showing them to their seats. Before the Queen's Speech, a parade of Royals walked by. The Queen, in her forties at the time, looked exquisite, I thought, and almost sylph-like. Princess Margaret walking behind was something of a contrast, appearing quite dumpy in comparison. What surprised me was the thick, rather orangey make-up she wore. It made her look – dare I say it? Tarty. I felt a twinge of pity. Gone was the famed sparkle in her eyes. What showed instead was a kind of world-weariness.

Things didn't always run smoothly between me and Tony. Sometimes he drank too much and that led to unreasonable behaviour such as knocking on my front door at one o'clock in the morning. Sometimes too we had heated arguments about the ethics of fox hunting and pheasant shooting. I hate blood sports and continued to preach. "Sport? You call that sport? How would you like to be chased by a load of hounds and then torn to pieces till you're dead?"

Of course, I'd get the usual clap-trap back: how blood sports are a natural tradition of the countryside; how it was necessary to keep down numbers; what a nuisance the fox is to farmers. And so on and so on.

"I love animals," Tony said, cross that I implied he didn't. And indeed, he showed plenty of affection for the domestic sort, being quick to pet dogs, cats and horses whenever he got the chance.

One evening, he proposed to me. I said, jokingly, "But Tony, you haven't got a title. I couldn't possibly marry a man without a title."

He laughed and said, "You're such a squirrel-minx," adding, "It's probably not a good idea anyway, considering I'm old enough to be your father."

But it wasn't his age that put me off. I knew he loved me. And I was fond of him. But my fondness never amounted to anything more. I hadn't yet got over my obsession with the psycho-analyst or my anger with the male sex in general.

Nevertheless, Tony helped me greatly and I don't know how I would have coped without his support. He came into my life at just the right time. Sadly, he died scarcely more than two years later. I met Nadine a few times afterwards and we sent each other birthday and Christmas cards but eventually we lost touch.

CHAPTER TWENTY-NINE

THE UNHAPPY DUCHESS

When I think back to that black period between my affair with Dr Wedeles and the move into my new home, my emotional state felt very close to madness. Hatred and anger mixed uneasily with a feeling of worthlessness. My moods swung from rage to despair.

Meeting Tony helped – I felt no anger against him. At the same time, I reached a stage when I'd given up all thought of any serious relationship with men. Marriage had become a no-no. I would cope on my own. I was, after all, independent now. I had my own property. And perhaps one day, I would buy another, and another. I would then live off the rents.

As for my earlier view that a father was essential in rearing a child, a view that had prompted me to give up my daughter, it was a load of rubbish. A father wasn't essential at all. Perhaps one day, I'd find a man with really good genes, get a child by him, then send him packing. A man, once he'd delivered his seed, I decided, was surplus to requirements. An independent woman could be mother and father to her child. No problem.

It was this rather screwy attitude that led to my fifteen minutes of fame and the set of screwy events that followed. With the help of Tom Banks, a journalist I knew, I wrote an article for *The People*, expressing my unconventional views – unconventional, that is, for that time. My emphasis on good genes though caused as much of a stir as the rest of my article. The word *Eugenics* comes to mind and harks back to the twenties and thirties. Hitler had been keen on the subject. So had a lot of other people, including many Americans.

Some of those unfortunates whose genes were thought to be not up to scratch were sterilised so they wouldn't burden the community with inadequate offspring.

I knew nothing about any of that, but I decided that if I wanted a clever, intelligent child, then genetics was as important as upbringing.

"Is that what you plan to do?" the journalist asked, "Find a man with the right genes for procreation, then bid him goodbye and look after the child yourself? And you'll write about this?"

"Yes."

It was a crazy thing to do, an act of impulse, triggered off by my venomous feeling towards men.

A week later, there was my picture in the paper together with my controversial article.

I seemed to have opened a Pandora's box. All sorts of things came flying out: cameramen, magazine editors, a TV producer wanting my story, mail from everywhere – some approving, others condemning my ideas.

I was stunned at the reaction and soon wanted to run away from the rumpus generated. "You're unhinged," I told myself.

There were consequences. Some of them I wrote about weeks later in a letter to my friend Wendy. She and her husband were staying with her parents in Norfolk at the time. I had moved to Earl's Court.

Dear Wendy

Two weeks ago I had a most surprising caller who came uninvited to my Earl's Court flat. Margaret met her first. It seems she had called before but I was out. Margaret described her as 'a poor, harassed looking creature in her fifties'. She felt sorry for her and offered her a cup of tea.

Well, my dear, two days later she called again. It must have been no more than ten in the morning and I was still slopping around in that frightful old dressing-gown of mine, you know, the one with the marmalade stain that won't come off.

Anyway, the doorbell went and there she was standing at the top of the stairs outside my flat. She did look a bit worn-out. But then most people do, after trudging up three flights of stairs to get to 61a.

She was actually smartly dressed, not at all shabby-looking as Margaret had led me to expect.

"Good morning, are you Miss Stephens?" she asked in a thin, tired sort of voice.

I nodded. I had no idea who she was but she soon put me in the picture.

She clapped open her handbag and took out her passport. "I'm the Duchess of Lienster," she informed me, thrusting it under my nose. "I'm sorry to come unannounced, but you're not in the phone book and I really must speak to you."

Well, honestly, Wendy, you could have knocked me down with the proverbial feather. I don't normally have real live duchesses call on me on Saturday mornings. I move in much humbler circles. I did meet the Duke of Norfolk on one occasion but only so he might inspect my pass before entering the Royal Enclosure at Ascot. Hardly a tete-a-tete.

Anyway, I invited her into the drawing-room. Luckily, the place was reasonably tidy. That's more than I can say for myself with that awful old dressing-gown on and my hair in tangles.

But to get on with the story. The first thing she said when she sat down was: "Tell me, who got you to put that message into the personal column of The Times, the one headed Duke?"

Her words nearly took my breath away. My message was the follow-up to a response I'd got from The People article by someone calling himself 'Duke'. Could it have been her husband?

She looked a bit shame-faced. "I'm afraid I had to resort to some arm-twisting at the Times office to find out who you were," she explained. "However, when I told them of my strong suspicion that the person behind it all was no duke but a dangerous character who'd been persecuting me and my husband for months and would be likely to harm you too, they were prepared to give way."

I almost choked over my coffee. Dangerous?

She gave me a searching look. "Tell me, what were the circumstances that led him to contact you?"

I said nothing for a moment. Well, really, Wendy, what could I say? She obviously hadn't read that shocking article I wrote in The People, the one that started it all. And I wasn't that keen to go into detail.

I should never have written it, of course, but I was in such an angry, man-hating mood after my affair with that psychiatrist, I was ready to do any crazy thing. Of course, as Margaret says, doing crazy things is only to be expected when you have dealings with psychiatrists.

Luckily, the photograph they published wasn't a good likeness so no one recognised me. I also changed my first name to Julie – I can't bear Shirley. Not that I needed to worry. None of my friends read that sort of paper anyway.

The funny thing was I got loads of fan-mail as a result, offers by magazines to serialise my life story, to say nothing of a chance to go on television. One of the letters sent me was from someone in South Africa who addressed her envelope: Miss Julie Stephens, Much in the News Lately, Somewhere in England. And would you believe it? It got to me – through the paper of course. My home address was kept private. Still, pretty amazing, don't you think?

Then there were all those proposals of marriage. I can't think why they wrote, since I wasn't looking for a husband anyway, simply for a man with good genes who could provide me with healthy, handsome brilliant offspring, and be content to shove off afterwards and leave me in peace.

And now we come to the Duke business. At least, I assumed he was a duke from the letter he wrote. There was no address or telephone number on it, just a brief message which said, 'I am rich, titled, and might be of help. However, secrecy is essential. If interested, please place message in the personal column of The Times which reads – Duke. Meet me soon – Julie. We'll take it from there.'

Well, I have to admit, I was sufficiently intrigued to do as he asked.

And now to get back to the Duchess.

She sat there, poor dear, anxiously awaiting an explanation.

I said finally, "He responded to a short article I wrote in the press, and got me to insert that message."

That seemed to satisfy her, so I hurried on, "but I haven't met him or anyone posing as a duke."

She pursed her lips and frowned. *"I know it's him. And he's got something up his sleeve, some plan for ruining us, you may be sure of that."*

She clasped her hands tightly together till her knuckles showed white. *"My husband is seventy years old and getting frail,"* she said, plaintively. *"He can do without this worry. Are you sure you haven't had a stranger call? A thin, weazily-looking fellow, for instance, fair-haired, about thirty?"*

It hit me then. Do you remember, Wendy, that awful man I told you about who called last week, said he was a journalist and wanted to write a book about me? Well, it was him. I was sure of it. Goodness knows how he got hold of my address. Not from the paper surely?

"Is his name Peter Selby by any chance," I asked.

The Duchess took a sharp intake of breath. *"That's the one."* She sat, grimly alert in her chair.

"Don't worry, I sent him packing," I said. *"Didn't trust him."*

She gave a great sigh of relief and leaned back.

At last, I asked her the question that most puzzled me. *"But why is this man persecuting you?"*

"It's a long story." She passed a hand wearily across her forehead. *"The fellow insinuated himself into our circle. He seemed pleasant enough at first and often amusing. We were kind to him and began to treat him as one of the family. Then everything changed. As time went by he became more and more obnoxious. He began to slight me, mocking my preferences in music and art, criticising and laughing at me in front of my husband and our friends. He would say things like 'you'll never learn, will you?' and 'Dear, oh dear, what plebeian tastes!' Finally, of course, we dropped him. He's never forgiven us. He's threatened, lied about us, vowed to get even. And now, we suspect, from our last confrontation with him, he's going to fabricate a scandal and resort to blackmail."*

She gazed across at me, her eyes fearful. *"He'll drag you into it too, my dear. I doubt if you've seen the last of him. Be very careful."*

"Don't worry, if he calls again, I'll phone the police," I told her, *"which is what you should do."*

She gave a bitter laugh and rose. *"Police? Oh, he's much too subtle for them. And for us."*

I showed her out. And that was the last I saw of her.

Well, Wendy, wasn't that a strange encounter? Like something out of a novel. I must say I felt sorry for the poor thing. Still do, in a way, in spite of Tony's comments. You'll guess, of course, that the first thing I did after she left was to ring him up.

"You're not having anything to do with her, I hope?" he asked, sounding shocked. "She's an awful type. Has no idea how to behave. Nobody bothers with her, you know. Can't imagine what old Lienster was thinking of, marrying a woman like that. Poor chap must have got soft in the head."

Same old Tony.

I hope that frightful Selby man doesn't contact me again. It just shows, doesn't it, how careful you have to be when writing articles in downmarket newspapers.

However, there's one good thing that's come out of it all. Having accepted various offers from magazines here and abroad, I should have enough money to pay off my bank loan soon. We'll see.

I must stop here and prepare to meet Tony. We're spending the weekend at Netherlypiat Manor in Gloucestershire. He and his partner are trying to sell it but can't get any offers above £80,000. It's probably due to all those rumours about its being haunted. Such a shame. It's a lovely old place too, with magnificent front gates and a super ballroom. You and Peter must stay with us there some time. You'd love it.

Glad to hear Peter is feeling so much better. Wish him good luck with the book

Lots of Love

Shirley

Looking back at this letter, I find it so full of snobbery and name-dropping, I'm quite ashamed of myself. I suppose I couldn't resist it when writing to Wendy. Until I met Tony, it was she who had the grand acquaintances, Bertrand Russell and Yehudi Menhuin to name only two. I had none to speak of. I had talked with Yehudi once over the phone but only to say, "Sorry, but Wendy's not here just now."

But showing off about your grand friends is a bit pathetic really. Does knowing people of worth make *you* a person of worth? Of course it doesn't. You have to do things yourself to

224

achieve that acclaim, though what you count as 'worthy' will depend on your own definition of the word. In any case, it's no use hoping that someone's fame will brush onto you simply by standing beside him.

With regard to my newspaper article, I didn't start meeting any of those men boasting of superior genes. The newspaper did set up some interviews, hoping I would make a choice from the men they selected. This would have created a satisfactory sequel to the first article.

But it was an odd, far from superior bunch they selected. One, I remember, was a retired vicar, a wizened little man who looked as if he'd never see seventy again.

I made sure that nothing went further than the interview. As already stated, the whole thing was an act of impulse. And I soon went right off the idea. I decided that having a child by a stranger, whatever the quality of his genes, would never compensate for the child I had lost, any more than it would for the rejection I had suffered.

CHAPTER THIRTY

TROUBLESOME TENANTS

I continued to let rooms. The rents were a useful addition to my income, especially during those periods when I spent more time studying than earning. But the business had its ups and downs.

Reading about smooth running *ups* can be a big yawn so I won't bore you with accounts of nice tidy tenants who caused no trouble. I'll focus on the *downs* – those who did.

I could divide those tenants into categories: 'bad', 'very bad' and 'even worse'. I'll skim over the bad: There was, for instance, a Spaniard who smoked pot and ruined my carpet in the process. He also drew complaints from the clean, civilised South American, Claudio, in the room next door. The Spaniard kept pestering him for supplies of cannabis or any other drugs he could lay hands on the next time he journeyed home. Claudio was appalled at his cheek. "He's trouble, that one," he told me.

I had to get rid of him. I got rid of the carpet at the same time.

Then there was the Australian who stayed a month, paid no rent and vanished, taking my best Indian silk bedspread with him. Well before that, I had expressed my unease about him to Eileen. "I don't trust that man," I said. "And he'll never pay his rent. He'll have to go."

"Oh, don't get rid of him," Eileen said, "He's so interesting."

I clicked my tongue. "I can't live off *that* sort of interest."

I was a bit naive for this business, I suppose, and a bit too easy-going.

But I did have strong instincts about people. The pity is that more often than not I ignored them.

This was certainly the case with Danny.

Danny was Chinese. Now I've nothing against Chinese or any other nationality. But my gut feeling when meeting this man was so strongly negative it was like a shout of NO through my system. It wasn't that he was over-large or displayed aggressive behaviour. On the contrary, his manner was quiet and polite. But there was something secretive about him, a worrying reserve. There was, I suspected, underneath that polite exterior, a character that might prove troublesome.

He wanted the small, single room, and he seemed determined, in his quiet, polite way, to have it. I tried to pretend that I'd more or less promised it to someone else. But he wasn't having that. "This room will really suit me," he said, "and here's my first week's rent."

He shoved a five pound note into my hand.

So why did I allow him to push me into giving him the room when my gut instinct was warning me against it? I suppose it was partly that he was foreign. If I turned him away, I might appear racist. And I wasn't. So I took his money and gave him the room.

Things went reasonably well the first week. Danny was clean, tidy, didn't take drugs or play loud music. What was worrying was that he appeared to have no regular job. He told me he was a salesman. Occasionally, I did see him go out with a kind of basket holding plastic bottles of something or other. Was selling stuff in the street what he meant by 'salesman'?

But at the end of that first week something occurred to turn my niggling unease into utter dismay. Returning from work one afternoon, I was startled by strange noises coming from his room. I listened carefully. Very odd. It sounded like a baby crying. Did he have a radio on or what?

I went upstairs and knocked on his door.

Danny opened it and let me in.

There, sitting on the bed, was a beautiful young woman, European, with dark shoulder-length hair. She was holding a baby.

Danny didn't seem the least put-out by my walking in on them. "This is Cathrine, my wife, and our little boy, Emile," he said, proudly. "They're staying with me."

Cathrine greeted me with a smile. "It's very good of you to have us here." She spoke with a slight French accent but her English was perfect.

I gaped at them. What the hell was I to do now? I couldn't throw a couple with a baby out onto the street.

"You can stay till the end of next week," I said, "but you must find somewhere else. There are three of you. You can't all live in a small, single room." I turned to Danny. "You should have told me about this, Danny."

He shrugged. "I needed the room. And I needed my wife and baby with me."

They stayed for more than another week. During this time I had long chats with Cathrine. It appeared she came from a middle class family in Brittany. I can't remember where she said she had met Danny, but he had fascinated her. "He's had such an exciting life," she told me, her eyes shining. "He survived poverty as a child on the streets of Hong Kong; later, he went to live in America; even worked for the Mafia." This fact seemed to thrill her no end.

It didn't thrill me.

"Weren't you frightened?"

"A little. But I couldn't resist him. I've always longed for excitement. And I knew that life would be exciting with him."

"What are you both doing for money?"

"We're not doing very well. Danny goes round selling Kimbo. It's a washing up liquid." She sighed. "It doesn't bring in much."

That didn't surprise me.

"What about you? Can you work – with a baby?"

"Danny's got me a job at a night-club"

"What will you do there?"

"I'm going to be a night-club hostess."

"Is that wise? I'm told you're expected to entertain the men at these places, even go home with them. Wouldn't Danny object to that?"

"Oh Danny wouldn't allow me to go off with any man. He's very – how you say – possessive."

My God, I thought, what a job for the wife of a possessive man to do!

Even 'possessive' was an understatement in Danny's case. He was devilishly jealous. I'd seen him look daggers at a man who so much as glanced at his wife. And if the look suggested more than polite interest, Danny's face would darken with rage.

You could understand it in a way. Cathrine was beautiful and charming. She was bound to attract notice. As a result, Danny felt jealous and insecure, even paranoid. He suspected mischief on her part when there was none. This often led to quarrelling and fighting.

I began to feel afraid for her.

My fears came to a head when one day, I heard a medley of noises coming from their room: Danny shouting, the baby crying; Cathrine giving a sudden scream; finally, the shattering of glass.

This was too much. I ran upstairs, banged on their door, and stormed in. And there was Danny standing menacingly over Cathrine, a broken drinking-glass clutched in his hand. He looked as if he were going to smash the jagged remains in her face. He was so preoccupied in this act, he seemed hardly aware of my presence.

"Stop this at once, or I'll call the police," I bellowed.

He came to then, but his face was red, his jaw tight.

I glared at him. "You've already overstayed your time. I'm giving you two more days to find another place, and this time I mean it. And attack your wife like that again and I really will call the police."

229

The following day, Cathrine came down to talk to me. "It's no use," she said. "I'm going to have to leave Danny." She shook her head helplessly. "But where will I and the baby live? And suppose Danny finds me?"

I pondered on the problem. Finally, I phoned two friends of mine, Nina and Helen and explained Cathrine's situation. They had a large flat between them in Great Portland Street. To my relief, they offered to take Cathrine and the baby and give them shelter for a few weeks.

"You can stay with them till you sort things out," I told her. "Nina might help you get a job."

Cathrine left later that day, taking Emile with her. Danny was out selling Kimbo.

Now *I* was the one in danger.

On his return, Danny soon realised that the birds had flown. He burst into my room, fists clenched. "Where is she?"

"I've no idea," I lied.

He pursed his lips. "I don't believe you. But I'll tell you now, if you're at the bottom of this, there'll be hell to pay."

He walked to the door and stood there a moment. Then he turned to face me, a look of menace in his eyes. "I shall find her. If I don't, I'll be back, and I'll smash your head in."

Danny didn't come back that night, or the next, or the one after that. But he still had my front door key. I went to bed each night with a hammer under my pillow together with a toy gun Tony had given me. It looked very real. If he burst into my room in the middle of the night, I'd be prepared.

But by now I was sick with worry. Like it or not, I'd have to change the locks, damn the expense.

Before I had a chance to do so, Danny returned. Hearing his key in the lock, I grabbed my toy gun and, legs like jelly, stepped forward to meet him.

"Is that real?" He took a pace backwards.

"Why don't I try it and see?" Brave words but I was shaking all over.

He attempted a smile. "Don't worry. I've found her. We've sorted things out."

Almost collapsing with relief, I lowered my toy.

He glanced warily at it. "I'd be careful with that if I were you. It looks real, even if it isn't."

He drew my door key from his pocket and slung it over. Then he marched out.

That was the last I saw of him. How he managed to find Cathrine is a mystery. But find her he did.

Nina and Helen told me how he had visited them and taken her away, and how she'd gone like a lamb. What's happened to them since I have no idea.

All I know is that I got rid of my 'very bad' tenants. I felt sorry for them, particularly for Cathrine. It must be awful, struggling to exist without a roof over your head and with a baby plus a violent husband in tow. Not a situation conducive to happy marriage.

As for myself, I decided that in future I would pay more attention to my instincts. At the same time I put away the hammer and the toy gun and began to relax.

CHAPTER THIRTY-ONE

A HOUSE FOR TIGGER

I felt that Tigger was getting a raw deal living in an apartment without a garden. Poor thing, I thought, stuck inside the whole time with only an occasional outing to the park or visit to the vet. Something must be done.

I had paid off my loan by this time and with the help of rents coming in, had more money in my piggy-bank. I doubted though if there was enough for a deposit on a second property – one with a garden.

But help was at hand. Eileen introduced me to Andrew – a man she had temped for in the City. He was an insurance broker and a Member of Lloyds.

Eileen had told him some sob-story about my having a wardrobe that needed painting and, poor me, I had no one to do the job. She suggested to him that, since he was keen on DIY he might like to help out. The truth was, I suspect, that she had tired of this latest boy-friend and thought she'd pass him on to me as a kind of consolation prize. She might also have hoped I'd appreciate his company. Tony had died not long before.

Meeting Andrew for the first time almost took my breath away. He was – I'm not joking – the living image of that old devil, Wedeles. The likeness between them should have put me off. Instead, it heightened my interest.

Andrew might have looked like Wedeles, but his character was totally different. He was honest, kind, good natured and, in short, a bit of a softie – someone whom a ruthless sort of person could easily take advantage of. I liked him straight away and we became friends. Before too long we became more than friends.

When I told him of my longing to buy a place with a garden for Tigger, he immediately said, "I'll go halves, if you wish."

In a short time we purchased between us a house with a garden in Trevor Place, Knightsbridge. We didn't tell anyone we were moving to this fashionable area for the sake of a cat.

We bought the house for the absurdly low price of £5,600. This was due to the short lease of seven years.

It was already part furnished, had five bedrooms, three of which could be rented out and, if I remember rightly, two bathrooms and a cloakroom, plus a large eat-in kitchen and a utility room in the basement. Most important, it had a patio and garden at the back of the house with a little garden-seat. Some people might have described it as 'pocket-handkerchief' size. But it was better than nothing. At least, Tigger would be able to enjoy some fresh air now and again and sniff at the grass. And Andrew had promised to get him a tree so he could have some exercise climbing.

We fixed a cat-flap into the back-door so he could go in and out as he pleased.

For the next two years I rented my maisonette in Earl's Court to a pleasant, civilised French family who gave not an iota of trouble.

In the meantime, Andrew, I and Tigger moved into the new house in Knightsbridge.

I crossed my fingers that Tigger would like his new garden. He was a fastidious sort of cat.

To our disappointment, he turned up his nose at it. He condescended to go out when nature called, occasionally sharpening his claws on the bark of the new tree. But he soon got bored.

What he liked best was the front of the house. The cars parked there fascinated him and he spent a good deal of time sniffing at the tyres. I couldn't understand this new interest of his and wondered whether, if he'd been born human, he'd have become a glue-sniffer or addicted to sniffing coke.

Luckily, there was little traffic in Trevor Place to make it much of a danger. Even so, I discouraged him from roaming the street by keeping the front door always shut. Imagine my surprise therefore, when, having used his cat-flap to visit the garden, he would mysteriously appear at the front of the house. I couldn't figure out how he managed this since, after investigating the back of our terrace, we could see no way that a cat could move from the back to the front.

But one day, I discovered his secret. Walking down Trevor Place on my way to the Supermarket, I caught sight of Tigger running down someone's fire escape at the end of the street. So that's how he solved the problem, I thought, by visiting the end back garden and using the fire escape to get into the front. As usual, he'd found a way of doing what he wanted.

He developed another unusual interest while at Trevor Place: an interest in accompanying me whenever I left the house. He'd trot at my side like a guardian angel or chaperone protecting me from kidnap or other mischief.

On one occasion, he escorted me to the doctor whose surgery stood in a square at the upper end of the street.

On arrival, Tigger settled himself near the front steps and waited.

My consultation with the doctor coming to an end, I said to him, "Thank you, doctor. I'd better dash off now. My cat's ouside, waiting."

"I don't believe it." Wide-eyed, my doctor jumped up. "This I must see."

He followed me to the door.

And there was Tigger, climbing up the surgery steps and meowing furiously at having been kept waiting so long. My doctor shook his head in amazement.

I had bought Tigger a collar from which hung a disc. On it was written his name and phone number. One evening, after returning from a singing lesson, I felt a twinge of unease. My cat wasn't waiting for me in his usual place. This was a street round the corner from Knightsbridge. He was wise enough never to accompany me to a busy road, but to wait in a quiet street nearby. Today he wasn't there. He wasn't at home either. I began to fear he'd been knocked down by a car or stolen by some cat-thief.

Later that evening, the phone rang. "We've got your cat here," a woman told me. "He was standing in the street, meowing his heart out. He's okay now. I've given him a saucer of cream to cheer him up."

Incidentally, on the subject of singing, Tigger didn't like my voice. Whenever I started to sing, he'd immediately walk out of the room with his nose in the air. I found this rather offensive. One day, therefore, while practising a song with some rather high notes, I shut him in the room with me so he couldn't walk out.

His first reaction was to make a beeline for the door.

He stood there a moment, glaring at me, the look in his eyes saying, "Open it, Dumhead. Can't you see I'm waiting?" I ignored him and carried on singing.

This was too much for Tigger. His tail started waving in all directions as he stepped towards me with a warning growl. His whole manner signalled "Stop. Or else…"

I went on trilling.

Wrong move. Tigger came closer, raised his paw and gave me a cuff across the face. He didn't stick out his claws at the same time, thank goodness. But what a cheek. A mere cat!

You might be wondering what Andrew's thoughts were about Tigger and the way I spoilt him. I'm not sure about his *thoughts* but he and Tigger appeared to get along perfectly well. Andrew sometimes hinted though that I regarded him as a poor second to my cat. Underneath, he might have resented this.

He invited us both to his mother's house a couple of times. It was in Suffolk, a longish journey from London for a cat. But Tigger, like a good sport, put up with it. At least, he enjoyed the garden there. It was a lot bigger and more interesting than his own.

At Trevor Place, we made friends with some of the neighbours. One of them was a little old woman called Mrs Fowler who lived near the bottom end of the street. Mrs Fowler was the proud owner of six small terriers. You would see her every morning taking them for their walk, three at each side of her.

She knew I was an animal lover and, like Margaret, started foisting stray kittens on me. "I can't keep cats myself," she explained, "not with six dogs to care for." It was the usual plea to my better nature: "Poor little thing. He needs someone to take care of him."

So, at Trevor Place, I acquired two more cats: a ginger tom I named *Figaro*, and a female tabby I called *Mimi*. To my relief Tigger accepted Figaro into the household without so much as a growl of complaint. In fact he was quite paternal towards the kitten, washing him, letting him snuggle up and play with his whiskers, showing him around and becoming altogether his friend and protector.

Mimi came later. I introduced her to Tigger and Figaro. Neither made any protest, though it was Figaro who took possession of this kitten, washing her and generally looking after her as Tigger had him. And Mimi followed Figaro everywhere as if he were her dad.

She had little interest in me. I think she disliked humans in general, though she never scratched or growled at them. She simply avoided them whenever possible.

I soon learned what different characters cats have from each other. It irritates me when people say that all cats are independent or that cat-love is always cupboard-love. They are over-generalisations.

My cats had their own unique characteristics. Tigger was bossy, self-willed and possessive; Figaro, loving, affectionate and easy-going; Mimi, timid, frightened of her own shadow and always, it seemed, expecting the worst.

I could probably write a whole book about my cats. However, since this is supposed to be a story about *my* life, not theirs, I'd better bring my cat-narrative to a close and start writing about what else happened while living with Andrew at Trevor Place.

CHAPTER THIRTY-TWO

LOST LOVES

A comfortable feeling of contentment permeated my life at Trevor Place. We make a nice little family, I decided: Andrew, I and the three cats. From time to time memories of Claude Wedeles intervened to disturb my peace, but less often nowadays and with less pain.

Then Andrew asked me to marry him. He set out his proposal in a letter, adding to it a long list of his financial assets as if to reassure me that he was well able to support a wife.

Not very romantic, I thought. Did he think I was interested only in his money. And how curiously old-fashioned, listing his assets like that! What was even more curious was the fact that Andrew was in no position to marry. He had a wife.

True, he and Pam, didn't get on and were more or less separated. She sounded a real bitch. I bet she made mincemeat of poor Andrew. But he hadn't severed ties altogether. They weren't divorced.

"So, will you marry me?" Andrew asked.

"You're still married."

"I can get a divorce. Will you marry me then?"

"Hm, I'll think about it."

It was after his proposal that I started finding fault with him. He was a bit slow, wasn't he? A bit ponderous. Not quick enough on the uptake. This irritated me. And he was too easy-going, too ready to give me my own way. I wanted a gentle, warm, affectionate man. But I also wanted one who would take charge – a father-figure who would be the guiding light in my life, taking the place of the father I never had.

Andrew had started divorce proceedings. His wife, the wronged party, cited me as the co-respondent, or 'other woman'.

But I still hadn't made up my mind. He kept asking me the marriage question and I kept answering, "I'm thinking about it." I wondered why we couldn't carry on in the same old way.

However, Andrew wanted marriage, and I couldn't go on stringing him along.

"Perhaps we ought to spend some time meeting other people," I suggested.

"Okay, if that's how you want it."

Andrew started going out on his own, and so did I.

He had joined some club called 'London Village'. One night, he returned home all dewy-eyed, his voice as gooey as melted chocolate. "I've met a wonderful girl called Gill," he told me. "We've fallen in love."

I forced a smile. "That's nice."

A flash in the pan, I thought. They've met only once.

It's a shameful admission to make, but though I wasn't sure I wanted Andrew myself for a husband, I was positive I didn't want anyone else to have him. He was my friend and partner. I didn't want to lose him.

About a week later, he brought Gill along to the house and introduced her to me. Younger than I and about twenty years younger than Andrew, Gill was somebody's secretary, not particularly pretty, but reasonable, I suppose, and nicely spoken. I wished though that she'd disappear.

I should have been happy for Andrew. He was a good, kind sort of person and deserved some luck in his life. Instead, I kept hoping that he and Gill would fall out and that the love affair would collapse. I decided that, if it did, I would definitely marry him.

No catastrophe happened. Soon the couple started planning their marriage, where the honeymoon would be, where they would live. They agreed to settle in Suffolk.

I would be alone again. I couldn't bear it.

I *wouldn't* bear it. I'd find someone else.

I moaned about my status to Helen. It was she and Nina who had sheltered Cathrine that time. "I'm thirty-seven and without a partner," I said, my voice sounding like the whine of a chained-up dog. "I'm fed up."

"Perhaps you should meet my friend, Peter Bauer," she said. "He's single. And a professor of Economics at LSE. He fancies me but knows I'm not interested in anything serious. I'll introduce you, if you like."

He sounded just the sort of medicine to perk me up and help me get over the loss of Andrew.

I met him. He wasn't my type to look at, being short and stocky. I prefer tall men. But he had an interesting face with strong features. He was, besides, a vibrant, dominant sort of character who knew how to take charge. That he was around twenty years older than I was an added advantage. It made him an ideal father-figure.

He had a spacious flat in Montague Square and a housekeeper to look after him. I sometimes visited. His housekeeper would cook us dinner and serve champagne.

So, while Andrew and Gill were engrossed in their love life and happily preparing their wedding, I went dining and theatre-going with my new man, Peter Bauer.

We didn't meet that often. He was very much tied to his work at the university and focused on his subject. He had written several books, one of which I read. It was all about the uselessness of giving overseas aid. A country would never thrive economically, he argued, when it had aid to rely on. I wasn't sure I agreed with many of his arguments though in some respects he was probably right.

He found economics absorbing and was filled with excitement when a new idea came into his head. He said to me once, in rhapsodic tones, "This morning, I conceived – in my bath." Like Archimedes, I thought, and his shout of 'Eureka!' on discovering the principle of the upthrust on a floating body.

Though a workaholic, he did suggest using some of his valuable time to take me to Leningrad (as St Petersburg was then called). "I must show you the wonderful Hermitage Gallery," he said. "It's a sight worth seeing."

The idea came to nothing. I can't remember why. It might have been something to do with the weather in Russia at the time.

I could have wept with disappointment. I'd have endured any sort of weather to be with Peter.

He then suggested Madrid and a visit to the Prado museum. I was less enthusiastic about this. However, the fact that Peter would be taking me there more than made up for any lack of interest in visiting Spain.

That suggestion too came to nothing. This time something had cropped up connected to work. And work, of course, had to come first.

"I shall never get married, I'm afraid," he told me, as if to warn me off any such dangerous idea. "No woman would put up with me, and my devotion to work."

That certainly put me in my place.

I had begun to feel in myself that uncomfortable mixture of yearning and insecurity, the kind I had so often felt during my time with Wedeles. Not that Peter Bauer was at all like that man. He was straight-forward and by no means insulting or exploitative as the psychiatrist had been.

But it was obvious he wasn't in love with me. In the circumstances therefore, I would have to blot out those romantic feelings that had developed and look elsewhere for a partner. I couldn't go through all that pain again. Next time he contacted me I would be ruthless with myself and give him the brush off. Politely, of course.

At the same time, I'd have to ignore the sinking heart and pangs of distress that would inevitably follow.

I find that when you are trying to get over a failed love affair, the best plan is to distract yourself and turn to other things, such as an all-absorbing occupation. In my case it was a new job. I started work at Voluntary Service Overseas, a charity based in Paddington. It recruited volunteer-teachers, engineers and other professionals prepared to work for a period in undeveloped parts of the world.

Having taken a short course in typing and worked out my own system of shorthand, I applied for a job as secretary in their Paddington office. I was accepted.

But my typing skills left much to be desired. Not only was I slow but I made errors – loads of them. And in those days there were no computers to correct your mistakes. You had to manage with Tippex. And if Tippex didn't do a good enough job, you were stuck with the task of typing a letter or report all over again.

As for my shorthand, half the time I couldn't read back what I had written.

As it turned out, my incompetence as a secretary did me a favour. Instead of typing letters, I was given the task of advertising VSO on posters and leaflets and of creating literature encouraging people to work in unpopular areas such as Algeria. To help me in this, I would rifle through letters from volunteers and find positive things to quote.

I was also asked to join the panel of interviewers who met recruits and afterwards discussed their suitability. I found these new tasks much more interesting than shorthand and typing. So interesting in fact that when Mildred Challenger, my theatre agent phoned, offering me a role in a new musical, I turned it down.

Added to my work at VSO was my Saturday job. This entailed travelling to Hertfordshire to help an elderly man sort out his correspondence and keep his study in order.

But in spite of these distractions, my self-esteem remained low. I was alone. There was no man in my life. Though I'd scoffed at marriage some years before, I now felt that for a woman in her late thirties to be still husbandless was pathetic. I was becoming what used to be called 'an old maid'. Someone left on the shelf, a poor, plain thing that nobody wanted. I had to find a solution.

And what happened to my two old beaux, Andrew and Peter Bauer during the years ahead?

Peter Bauer, I learned, was made a peer by Margaret Thatcher. He became Lord Bauer, and was much respected at the Institute of Economic Affairs.

I met him again years later. He had never married and had become a shrunken little man who had suffered two strokes. He didn't remember me. Not very flattering. Nor did he remember Helen who had introduced us. But he liked my visiting him and I did so several times before he died. His housekeeper gave us champagne even if my visit was in the morning, and prepared us smoked salmon sandwiches.

I got to know more about him during these visits than I had ever known before. I learned he was a Hungarian Jew, whose father, a bookie, sent him to Oxford to study. Though unable to speak English initially Peter still managed to get a First in Economics. I found the stories of his life fascinating Sadly, he died about a year after this second contact with him.

I met Andrew again too and his wife, Gill. They weren't getting on. Andrew had long chats with me sometimes in the evenings over the phone, while Gill went line-dancing with her friends. The last thing I heard was that Andrew, at the age of eighty, had left Gill and run off with another woman.

But I'm getting ahead of myself. Back to 1974 then and the niggling worries about my status.

LOVE, MARRIAGE, DEATH ~

CHAPTER THIRTY-THREE

MARRIAGE AT LAST

(1974–1978)

By this time, marriage had become the most important of my life goals. I'd got myself a decent education, been on the stage, bought properties in London. But I was still without a husband. I had dropped the goal of motherhood, pretty sure that by now I'd reached my sell-by date. Again I cursed myself for giving up Juliet Amanda.

More than once I had contacted the adoption agency, hoping they'd give me a clue of her whereabouts. I might as well have asked for the secret of the universe. "We never release such information to birth-parents," they said. I sighed. No hope of tracing her then.

I pushed the unhappy memory away and focused on the marriage question.

I won't wait for love, I decided. If I do, I'll wait forever. I'll find someone who's reasonably this-that-and-the-other and manage the best I can.

After all, in those cultures where they have arranged marriages, the couples don't love each other straight away. They start off cool and then get hot. Is that any worse than our own system where couples start off hot and end up cool?

I'd thrown away my chance with Andrew, a nice, easy-going man. And Peter Bauer was never going to marry me. Still, there'd be other chances. And I wouldn't turn my back on them anymore. I'd marry the next man who asked me.

The next man turned out to be the man I worked for on Saturdays, Sir Frederic Osborn. He was a retired town planner who'd been knighted by the Queen. He'd played an important part in planning his own neighbourhood, Welwyn Garden City. The local comprehensive school was named after him.

Friends and acquaintances called him FJ or Sir Fred, and when they asked him how he was, he'd answer, cheerfully, "Same as usual: Crumbling." He was, as you'll guess, a good bit older than I. Oh dear, another father-figure? Worse. A grandfather-figure.

Well, at least he's got a sense of humor, I told myself, and a multiplicity of interests. And there was the title. That wasn't to be sneezed at. It might be rather fun to be addressed as 'your ladyship' now and again. Besides, I *had* decided to marry the next man who asked me.

"All right," I told him, "I'll marry you."

Once home, I clapped a hand to my forehead and groaned, "My God, what have I done?"

A cartload of complications attending such a marriage crashed through my mind.

One by one I squashed them. You're thirty-nine, I told myself. Do you want to be an old maid forever? Suppose no one else asks you?

But the alarming implications of such a move were further magnified at our very next meeting. Frederic arranged lunch at a restaurant with me and his two children, Tom and Margaret. They were both tall and thin like their father. Tom was in medical research, a little older than I. Margaret was about my age, worked for the BBC World Service, and had a formidable frowning face which people less than kind might describe as 'sour'. Neither had children.

There was nothing wrong with the restaurant. However, this lunch date was the worse I'd had in my life. To my horror, Sir Fred announced to his children, "We are going to get married."

Their reaction could hardly have been worse had there been an explosion at the next table or the sudden entry of a gunman with the shout, "Hands up!"

After a stunned intake of breath accompanied by staring eyes and gaping mouths, Tom shook his head helplessly while Margaret almost choked over her soup.

There followed a five second silence.

It was Margaret who spoke first. She leaned over the table and gave me a long hard glare, saying through clenched teeth, "You'll not get the house anyway. That's held in trust for me and Tom." She turned to her father, grimly. "Thank heavens our mother saw to that before she died. She knew all about you and your women." She swiveled away and muttered into her napkin, "Dirty old man!"

Wow, I thought, I certainly hadn't prepared for this.

"You needn't worry about the house," I said, sounding, I hoped, coolly polite. "I have my own properties."

Shaking inside, I left them. What a daft thing for Sir Fred to do. He must have known that bad-tempered daughter of his would start tearing me to shreds. He should have talked to them on his own first.

Back home, I put the kettle on to boil and sat down with a sigh. This wasn't going to work. Marrying Sir Fred was a mad idea. Now that I'd met his children it seemed even madder.

That night I phoned him. "I'm sorry but I can't go ahead with the marriage after all."

"But you've given me your promise."

Oh dear, he sounded angry. He went on, "Don't worry about Tom and Margaret. They're already getting used to the idea. I've promised it won't hurt them financially."

"Sorry, but I've decided. No."

There was a pause. Then he said, his voice breaking, "If that's the case, I'll cut my throat."

My God, was he blackmailing me into marrying him? Probably. But suppose he really did mean to kill himself because I'd broken my word?

I went ahead and married him in August 1974. As well as changing my surname, I also added Catherine to my Christian name. A good opportunity, I thought, for getting rid of Shirley.

When we emerged from the Westminster registry, we found ourselves surrounded by cameramen and news reporters.

"Don't talk to them, whatever you do," his children warned. "You don't want to make any further exhibition of yourself."

But Frederic did. "I'm getting married again before it's too late, and I pop off," he told them.

His words got into the papers, scandalizing his son and daughter.

We were front page news.

After the reception, my new husband and I flew off to Vienna to enjoy our honeymoon. Margaret's parting words to me were, "Be sure not to allow Father to carry his suitcase himself."

I didn't see much of him in Vienna. He had timed the wedding and honeymoon to coincide with a Town Planning conference taking place there. He wanted to kill two birds with one stone.

I didn't mind. I hadn't been to Vienna before and had a pleasant time wandering round parks and visiting historic buildings. We met for lunch, often eating Escalope of Veal Holstein which I loved.

We were married in name only. I was more housekeeper, nurse and escort than I was wife.

He was a good man: kindly, tolerant, sociable and not the least bit snobbish. He had one weakness: he was over-frugal. Some would say, stingy. I believe he thought that a wife would be cheaper to keep than a housekeeper. I thought I'd better rid him of that illusion as soon as possible. I don't think anyone would accuse me of being a gold-digger. On the other hand, I wasn't a push-over either. Fair is fair. If I was going to cook and clean for him, then I would expect my housekeeping money to match that of his last housekeeper.

My years with Frederic were not easy ones but nor were they for him. I'd get impatient, even disagreeable at times. Then I'd be cross with myself for not being a nicer, kinder person.

Some aspects of the marriage were enjoyable. It was fun at first being Lady Osborn. But you quickly adjust to the novelty. And very soon the novelty wears off and you cease to notice your change in status. I suppose a similar thing happens if you marry a billionaire. You adjust to spacious rooms; the yacht on the river; the power to buy almost anything you want. It all becomes the normal way of life. If you get discontented, it's about the things you can't have, things money can't buy.

Apart from the snob value of my new title, there were the invites to grand parties to meet grand or important people. We were sometimes invited to dinner at the House of Commons or the House of Lords where we'd meet and chat with people like Anthony Crossland, Lord Green or Duncan Sandys.

Once, we attended a reception at St James' Palace and met the Queen. She seemed quite pleased to talk to me. "Your husband says he actually met Queen Victoria," she said, her voice full of awe. "Isn't that amazing?"

We were invited to her Silver Jubilee Ceremony held at St Paul's in 1977. Crowds lining the pavements outside waved as we paraded into the cathedral. I felt terribly important, I must admit. Once inside though, I can't say there was much to see other than all the hats in front of us. We would have done better watching it on television. Nevertheless, it was an honor being invited to the ceremony.

Frederic did his best to keep amused a spouse so much younger than himself. And he put up with my three cats without a murmur of protest.

Tigger still followed me around from time to time. And when Frederic and I were invited to have tea with Gladys, the retired doctor who lived round the corner, he stood with us on the doorstep, expecting to come too.

"You can't, I'm afraid," Gladys said firmly. "Humans only. Sorry."

Tigger must have been most offended to have her front door shut in his face.

Gladys, was ninety years old and still with her full set of marbles. During the summer she would drive me to the open-air swimming pool some afternoons. The water was very cold, and, being allergic to cold water, I would make my way to the shallow end and immerse myself gradually. Not Gladys. She would dive straight into the deep end, no problem.

Frederic had loads of friends and acquaintances. Amongst them was the actress, Flora Robson, who came to tea on occasion. Though an established actress, she had started out as an amateur and been a member of the Barn Theatre in Welwyn Garden City. I felt a momentary pang when I remembered the excitement of the theatre and the casual way I'd abandoned it.

Another interesting friend of his was a retired concert pianist called Dorothea. Dorothea was German and had met Hitler in her early life. She had been a guest at some retreat at which Hitler was either the host or a guest himself. Whatever the case, Dorothea described him as a very odd man who would turn up for breakfast dressed in a kind of raincoat. She herself had been married to a Jew. What happened as a consequence of this I do not know. Perhaps, when things became too difficult, they both fled Germany.

Not far away lived a nice, elderly couple, the Herons. I used to visit them sometimes and they always made me welcome. They had been friends with Frederic for many years. Tom Heron liked to write poetry, as did Frederic. They had a son called Patrick who was an artist. I'd seen some of his pictures at the Tate. I didn't care for them much, I must confess. I find that four blobs of colour dabbed on a canvas with no apparent sense or connection between them is a bit boring. But then I'm no connoisseur of art, and I have yet to discover if the Emperor is wearing clothes.

In one way and another there were things to interest and occupy me at Welwyn Garden City.

But poor Sir Frederic could not be a husband to me in the true sense, and I still hungered for love and romance. This made me vulnerable to opportunities.

CHAPTER THIRTY-FOUR

LOVE AT LAST

Though living now in Welwyn Garden City I still had the London properties to sort out.

The Knightsbridge house had to go. Andrew, moving to the country with Gill, needed his share of the proceeds – and fast. Pity. Property prices had slumped in the seventies. Not a good time to sell. Anyway, I loved the house set in the sedate little street – bang in the middle of Knightsbridge. But when the piggy-bank is empty, what can you do? I couldn't sell my Earl's Court maisonette yet. That had problems to tackle first.

The Knightsbridge house sold for £26,000. Having bought a longer lease, we made no profit.

The maisonette went around three years later. The tenants there came under the 'even worse' category, and I didn't know how to get rid of them. Again, I had felt from the beginning that they were unsuitable, but I was in a hurry and easy to bend under pressure. Besides, the main tenant, Stephen, who had been there some months before the others, seemed reasonable enough and capable of handling his co-tenants.

After a couple of years, however, he moved out. That's when the trouble started. The two remaining tenants were by no means reasonable. They stopped paying rent, manufacturing an excuse for non-payment by deliberately vandalizing the place. I phoned them, sent letters of notice, to no avail. They decided to stay.

I finally went over, taking a suitcase, and leaving my husband in the hands of a temporary housekeeper. My moving in, he agreed, might encourage my 'tenants' to move out.

No such luck. It is at times like these that I wish I were a tall, formidable person, able by a mere raising of an eyebrow to put the fear of God into my adversaries. But, however tall I try to make myself, however commanding a pose, they take one look at me and decide I'm a pushover. And it doesn't take them long to start pushing.

If I said I wasn't afraid of confronting my 'even worse' tenants, I'd be lying. This young man and his partner were bullies. They saw politeness as weakness and were not open to reason, argument or compromise. Their aim was to throw me out of my property, even to change the locks if necessary.

I went to the police and to the local council for advice. In both cases, they said their hands were tied. Their only advice was to change the locks.

It finally cost me £400 in lawyers' fees to get rid of them and goodness knows how much in painting, and refurbishing to repair the damage they had done.

In the meantime, there was my new friend, Patrick, to watch over me there. My tenants didn't treat him as a walkover. He didn't need to utter a word. His very presence was sufficient. Why is it, I wonder, that some people command respect even while silent whereas others are pushed around and treated with indifference? Is it size, sex, posture, tone of voice? Or is it an inner confidence that somehow exudes outwards, making an enemy step back and think twice before acting?

A strongly-worded solicitor's letter plus Pat's presence had the desired effect. They finally left.

And who was this good Samaritan, Patrick?

I'd better start at the beginning.

While living with Sir Fred, I thought I'd missed the boat so far as romance was concerned. And now it was too late. I was in my forties and married.

Then I met Patrick. He was a tall, slim aeronautical engineer in his fifties with refined features and hair a distinguished grey. He owned a part-share in a glider kept at Dunstable.

I met him through his daughter, Pauline, during a short stay in hospital. I warmed to this highly strung young girl with her enthusiasms for yoga and eastern philosophy and we became friends. When her parents visited I became friends with them too. We met regularly after I left hospital.

Her father attracted me from the first. Though often gentle in manner, especially towards Pauline, he had a virile energy that set my body tingling. It showed in his decisive walk, in the firm edge to his voice. I didn't expect our meetings to end in an affair. He was married after all, and I was friendly with his wife and their children. The last thing I wanted was to break up a marriage. But I couldn't help having romantic fantasies about him. He's so manly, so clever, I thought.

The affair began when, on driving me home from his house one night, Pat confessed he had fallen in love with me. Instead of turning away in horror, I sat silent a moment, letting the thrill of his words sink in and sweep over me. A struggle with my conscience followed: This was *wrong*. But then Patrick kissed me, and all thoughts of right and wrong flew from my mind. I wrapped my arms around his neck and kissed him back. Parked in a lay-by with moonlight filtering through the trees into the car window, we clung together, unwilling to break away. I knew then I was hooked.

Patsy doesn't need to find out, I told myself. Nor does Frederic. What they don't know won't hurt them. I gave little thought to the question that adultery might be wrong in itself, involving deceit, lies, broken promises...

The truth is, I had such a deep yearning for love I felt I would wither and die without it.

I tried to reassure myself: okay, he's married, but aren't most men over forty? Anyway, you can't *choose* whom you fall in love with.

Besides, he and Patsy were not hitting it off. They had constant rows, usually about money. Sometimes, Patsy told me, she hated her husband and wouldn't care if they divorced.

But am I rationalizing, I asked myself, exaggerating the conflicts, to put myself in a better light?

Whatever the case, Patrick and I began to meet in secret. He took me to restaurants, concerts, once to a dinner and dance at the Whitehouse Hotel in London.

Then came the reckoning:

Patsy paid me a visit. I can see her now in that elegant, fur-trimmed coat of hers, not a strand of blonde hair out of place, confronting me in Frederic's sitting-room. Though calm in manner, the accusation in her eyes was unmistakable as she asked the dreaded question, "Are you having an affair with my husband?"

I could have brazened it out, lied. Instead, I squirmed in shame. "How did you find out?"

She gave a crooked smile. "The way he looked at you; his unexplained absences…"

"I'm so sorry," I faltered. "But I won't see him again, I promise. I don't want to break up your marriage."

I kept my word and, leaving Frederick with a housekeeper again, went off to Wales to stay with Cousin Joan. I knew I could never forget Patrick, but perhaps he would forget me if I stayed away a while.

When I returned, however, Patsy phoned, saying, "You'd better carry on seeing Patrick. Without you, he's become impossible. I'm getting a divorce."

Oh God. Guilt gnawed at me. I'd broken up a marriage, and there were three children affected. True, the girls were in their late teens, and Pauline would be going to college soon. But the boy, Nick, was only fifteen. I could hear him yelling in the background while his mother talked. He was clearly devastated by what was happening.

The divorce went ahead. Nothing I can do now, I thought, the damage is done. I've achieved my happiness at the cost of destroying someone else's. It wasn't a comforting thought.

After a while, I resumed my secret meetings with Pat, secret, that is, to Frederic.

During this time I managed to lick the maisonette into shape and finally sell it for £18,000. This, together with my share of the proceeds from the Knightsbridge place, paid for a house in Hendon. I would need somewhere to live if Sir Fred died. There was no way I would stay in his house and pay rent to his children.

Sir Frederic died in 1978 following a spell in hospital.

Sometime after the funeral, I moved to Hendon. Eventually, Patrick moved in with me. His house in Caldicot was sold. He continued to support Patsy until she remarried soon after the divorce. She wedded an old school friend, David Robson, a nephew of the actress, Flora.

Their son, Nick, now sixteen, became an apprentice thatcher with digs in Bedfordshire. Their daughter, Debbie went to university to study psychology; Pauline went to Northern Ireland to study Art. She stayed there with Patrick's first wife, Joan and Joan's second husband, Hilary Frost-Smith.

Patrick and I didn't marry for some years. He journeyed backwards and forwards to Stevenage each day, while I worked at ordinary nine-to-five jobs in London, busy accumulating more capital.

I didn't care for Hendon. *Dullsville*, I thought. And Pat's grand piano hardly fitted into our sitting-room.

"We ought to move to a larger house, nearer your work," I suggested. "Then you won't have that long journey each day." The look of pain on Pat's face showed what he thought of that idea. In the end I offered a bribe. "If we move, I'll marry you."

He consented. I kept my word and a year or two after we moved, I married him. I retained my previous name, Osborn, adding to it Patrick's surname, Boyer.

Our new house was situated in Chipperfield near King's Langley. It had quinces growing over the front wall, and a black, wrought iron gate for entry, with the name *Silvertrees* written on it. It lay in a private lane called *Wayside*, a quarter of a mile from the village. In the front garden grew silver birches and at the bottom of the drive was a double garage standing next to the house. The house itself was spacious with a drawing room more than large enough for a grand piano.

The place boasted a garden of just under an acre. It was divided into front and back gardens, kitchen garden and fruit garden. In the back garden were two ponds: an upper one from which a waterfall splashed down into the lower pond. A wooded area lay near the bottom, and a beautiful cherry tree grew outside our bedroom window. On rising in springtime, it was a delight to open the curtains and see it standing there in the morning sun, shedding its blossom everywhere.

Patrick was in his element. He was a keen gardener, if not an expert one. Neither of us had green fingers. Whatever we did, things seemed to wither and die under our hands: plants, frogs, fish, even the lovely cherry tree outside our window. The only things that really flourished were weeds. But whatever the difficulties, we enjoyed our garden, especially on summer days. Squirrels frisked there, competing for nuts with blue tits and finches. We also had a visiting toad and, in winter, roe deer.

We kept in touch with Patsy and her third husband, David. They sometimes joined us for dinner and spent Christmas day with us. Patrick introduced me to Joan, his first ex-wife, now living in Cumbria, following the death of her second husband. Sometimes Patrick and I and his two ex-wives would spend time together there.

Our relationship had its ups and downs. Patrick had a short fuse. I was a sulker. But I was pretty well content with the way things were. I stopped yearning for love and romance. I had it right there at Silvertrees. I still had hopes and dreams, and Patrick encouraged me to realise them. It was while I was with him that I studied for my degree, and started writing my children's novels. But my dreams no longer included finding love. I had finally achieved that most difficult goal.

CHAPTER THIRTY-FIVE

THE PIANO TEACHER

We settled peacefully into Silvertrees and made our acquaintance with the neighbours. Next door lived Betty and Gordon Percival, an elderly couple who presented us with a bunch of flowers on our arrival. Then there was Jenny, on the other side. She was older than the Percivals, with a husband who suffered from Alzheimer's. Opposite, in a tumbledown house, lived a gentle, middle-aged couple who greeted us shyly from their gate. It was a while though before we got to know their names. All we learned was that they were both animal-lovers. We saw dogs, cats and pet chickens running around their garden.

Before we had been there long, a new neighbour arrived, settling herself in the house on the other side of Betty and Gordon's. Her name was Mary.

Though well into her forties, Mary looked a real man-eater: glossy black hair, eye-lashes to die for, and curves in all the right places. On top of that, she was unattached, and drove a Porsche.

"She's not short of a bob or two," Betty next door told me with a confidential wink. "No wonder. She's a funeral director. Can't lose with a job like that."

I didn't see much of her for the first couple of weeks. Then one day, without warning, she appeared on our doorstep.

"Hullo, I'm Mary, just moved into the house two doors down." She spoke in a breathy voice and flashed me a smile, revealing a set of dazzling-white teeth.

261

I thought she'd come merely to introduce herself or ask about the village.

"We've not lived in Chipperfield long ourselves," I said. "And we don't know many people yet, apart from Betty and Gordon and the people across the road, who keep all those chickens…"

She gave a polite cough. "Actually, I'm looking for someone called Patrick."

I grew wary. "That's my husband."

"Ah, I've come to the right house then. Your next-door neighbour tells me he gives piano-lessons."

"News to me," I said.

Strains of the Appassionata came pounding out from the sitting-room. Pat, at the piano again, murdering Beethoven.

"You'd better come in and see him," I sighed.

Pat, full of smiles, rose from the piano-stool to greet her. "I'll be delighted to teach you," he said. I tightened my lips. Talk about eager!

Warning bells rang. It's not that I don't trust my husband. He loves me, I know. But the thought of this woman, with her plunging neckline and sexy chain-belt, cosily installed in our drawing-room with him, for an hour-long lesson… Anyway, what did *he* know about teaching music?

She turned up the following evening for her first lesson. I stayed in the kitchen, washing dishes. From what I could make out, they spent more time nattering than working on chords or scales. Pat *did* play a couple of piano pieces to show off his skill. But, apart from that, all I could hear was the odd rumble of conversation mixed with shrieks of laughter from Mary.

I've never known anyone laugh so much. Perhaps, I thought, I'd better enter the funeral business myself. It might lighten me up a bit. Just now, I felt like some lightening up. I'm not normally a jealous person but it made me seethe to find myself stuck with the dishes, while those two had a great time, laughing and joking. What the hell were they up to?

"Nice girl," Pat commented, after seeing her out. "Good sense of humour. And she likes my playing." He smiled in a self-satisfied sort of way.

She came for another lesson later in the week, and again, on Wednesday of the week following. This time, after the lesson had ended, Pat invited me into the sitting-room for a drink with them. Big deal, I thought. I did my best to be polite and chatty but found it hard to disguise the chill in my mood. I could tell she didn't feel at ease with me. I wasn't too comfortable with her either. What do you talk about to a funeral director? What questions do you ask? How many corpses have you had in today?

"I'm taking Mary into Chesham on Saturday to find a piano," Pat told me later. "Want to come?"

"Sure I won't be in the way?" I asked, my voice heavy with sarcasm.

"Don't be silly. I *want* you to come." He put an arm round me. "Let me play my new Chopin piece to you. It's one of your favourites."

"No thanks. I've heard enough thumping on the piano for one evening."

He dropped his arm and turned away.

I shouldn't have said that. He didn't always thump. There were times when I loved his playing. But I wasn't in the mood for dishing out compliments.

I decided I *would* go piano-hunting with them. I didn't trust that woman.

I'd heard from Betty lurid details about her sexual proclivities. Betty had heard about them from George, the postman, who never missed the chance of a gossip. Mary had apparently opened the door to him one morning, clad only in a transparent nightdress. "You could see *everything*," he told Betty, drooling.

Betty told me she and Gordon had once spotted her, dressed in nothing but a pair of shorts, mowing her back lawn. "Good thing my Gordon's so unobservant," she giggled. "All he said was, 'She shouldn't be gardening in bare feet like that. She might step on a thorn'."

You can see what I was up against. A real siren. And fancy starting piano lessons without having a piano!

The following Saturday, Mary went with Pat to buy one. And, of course, I tagged along too, feeling more like a gooseberry in this threesome than anything else. I yawned and sighed, like a sulky ten-year-old, as we searched for the music-shop.

They didn't seem to notice. Too busy jawing. Pat was airing his views on modern composers such as Michael Tippet, and rattling on about the merits of a Bluthner Grand as opposed to a Steinway. Mary listened attentively, responding now and then with cries of "Really?" and, "How marvellous!" Each utterance followed, of course, by her usual trills of laughter. She knew next to nothing about music, I could tell. She'd had probably thought Michael Tippet was a footballer, or a politician.

At the music-shop, Mary flitted from piano to piano, admiring this one, then that one, Pat, close at her side, acting the connoisseur. I heard him run his hands along the keys of each one, to make sure it had an acceptable tone. I watched, eyes glazing, as he peered at the woodwork and questioned the salesman about its condition. After more than an hour, he gave Amy his advice on the best choice. She took it.

I breathed a sigh of relief. At last!

"I hope you're charging for her piano lessons," I said, after we arrived home.

"Oh no. I couldn't possibly."

"Why not? You've spent enough time on her. And you're always complaining about what little time you've got. Anyway, she's not exactly hard-up."

"Don't be mercenary. I do it because I enjoy it. Besides, I could hardly *charge*. I'm not qualified."

I wondered about that. What the hell had made Betty recommend Pat in the first place? I'd have to have it out with her.

It was what happened the following day that finally decided me. Pat had gone to the Garden Centre and spent ages there. When he got back, he announced, "I've just had a chat with Mary in her garden."

"I hope she had more than shorts on," I snapped.

He ignored my sarcasm. "I thought it would be nice to take her to that Mahler concert with us on Thursday evening. I could easily get an extra ticket."

I almost burst a blood-vessel.

"You don't mind, do you? She's all on her own. She needs a few friends."

"I'll *bet*." I shot him a filthy look, banged the sitting-room door, and stalked out into the kitchen. There, I started crashing saucepans about.

He followed me in. "What's the matter with you? Don't you like Mary?"

"No, I don't bloody well like her. And she doesn't like me." I plonked myself down on a kitchen chair, arms folded, lips pursed. "And if *she's* going to the concert on Thursday, you can count me out. *I'll* go into London and have some fun on my own."

Patrick lifted his eyes to heaven. "You're acting like a spoilt child. And it's ridiculous to say Mary doesn't like you. She *does*. She thinks you're – sweet."

I winced. *Sweet*!

"Anyway, I've already invited her."

"Then uninvite her."

"No. I can't do that." It was his turn to bang the door and stalk out.

I gritted my teeth. I'd put a stop to this liaison somehow.

Later that day, I popped next door to see Betty.

She was pottering in the kitchen, making lemon-tarts. "For my grandchildren," she explained. "Have one. Can't touch them myself, not with my figure." She spread out her arms. "Look at me. Size of a house. And I eat like a bird."

I came quickly to the point. "It's about Mary. I wondered why you recommended *Patrick* to give her piano lessons."

She frowned. "Why not? He's a professional piano-teacher."

"You've got it wrong, Betty. He plays the piano, yes, but he'd never given a lesson in his *life*, before Mary came…"

I stopped. Betty, who'd been frowning and gaping at me in turn, broke into a gale of laughter.

"I don't believe it!" she finally gasped. "Do you mean to say, she's coming to *your* Patrick for her piano lessons?"

I nodded.

"The daft ha'porth. I suggested Patrick Bryant opposite you. I even pointed out the house."

"Oh, I didn't realise… I thought they just kept chickens." My heart lifted. "I'd better explain to Mary. I'm sure Patrick – *my* Patrick, I mean – wouldn't want to give her lessons under false pretences."

I stepped into my own house, feeling several pounds lighter. I couldn't wait to phone Mary.

Before I could do so, *she* phoned us. "I'll have to abandon my lessons for the time being," she said. "There's a lot of work coming in. I'm going to be terribly busy. And I can't make Thursday, after all, I'm afraid. Sorry to mess you about."

Perhaps she'd heard from Betty about her blunder, and was too embarrassed to face us again. Or perhaps she really *was* busy. Maybe the current heat wave had caused an increase in fatalities.

Whatever the case, the news suited me fine. As for Pat, his only reaction was to say, "Piano teaching isn't really my thing anyway. I've too much else to do with my time."

We saw little of Mary after that, other than to glimpse her red Porsche disappearing up the lane.

A few months later, she disappeared from the village altogether. Betty told me she'd left for Switzerland, at midnight. Nobody knew why, or what she was doing about her funeral business.

"A bit fishy, isn't it?" I said, "leaving like that in the middle of the night?" I had a gratifying vision of the police on her trail for some hideous crime such as nicking gold rings from her dead clients and melting them down for profit. "D'you think the police were after her?"

"Of course not," Betty answered in shocked tones. She lowered her voice. "More like she's fleeing from her ex. He's been pestering her again, and there's an injunction against him." She shook her head, gravely. "He used to beat her, you know. Gave her hell, for years."

I shooed away my unkind fantasy and murmured, "Poor Mary!"

I told Patrick the news.

He said, "I guessed she was hiding a problem or two, behind all that laughter."

"She was very attractive," I ventured.

He shrugged. "I didn't really notice. She was nice, though. And she liked my playing."

So that's what it was about, I thought. She'd shown an interest in his piano-playing. Something I'd seldom done. And we all like a bit of appreciation now and again.

"She had good taste," I said. I clasped his hand, a feeling of tenderness welling up inside me. "Play some Schubert. I loved that piece you played this morning."

His eyes began to glisten. "Did you? Honestly?" He squeezed my hand, and something like joy crossed his face as he sat on the piano-stool and began to play.

CHAPTER THIRTY-SIX

DROPPING OUT

Our time together at Chipperfield, though mostly blissful, wasn't entirely without conflict. We had heated arguments about science, religion, politics and sometimes, wait for it, money.

I had started teaching again. I didn't much want to but I needed the cash. I had used up most of my capital on the purchase of Silvertrees as well as on the renovations incurred. Patrick, at the same time, inherited money from his father and spent the lot on a prestigious new glider. He couldn't wait to impress his friends with it at the Gliding Club.

I was furious. "I'm all for you enjoying yourself, Pat," I said. "But when are you going to pay me your half share for the house? I've contributed most of the capital. It's left me short."

He gritted his teeth and muttered, "Don't worry. You'll get it."

I did get it, and sooner than expected. Pat decided to take early retirement. British Aerospace gave him a pension together with a lump sum. He handed part of this to me to pay off his debt.

After a few years my capital reached £75,000.

When I told Pat, his eyes nearly popped out. "How did you manage to save all that?"

"Just wise investing," I said with a casual flap of the hand. "You know, buying when the market's down; selling when it's up."

This was, of course, a load of codswallop. I was merely showing off. As for wise investing, I had come a cropper more than once dabbling on the stock market. Most of my money was in the building society, and my astuteness amounted to nothing more than reliance on the sky-high interest rates of the day, increasing my savings.

Pat wasn't used to a wife who was financially independent and it took him a time to adjust. I was certainly not going to be the dependent little woman. Pleasant as it is to be coddled and given presents, the thought of having to rely on a man for my very survival was anathema to me.

Once retired, Pat had time to pursue his many interests. There was the garden, piano, books, computer and, of course, visits to the gliding club. I sometimes went with him, though I found hanging about for 'lift' tedious in the extreme. "How about some aerobatics?" I'd say, when finally up in the glider. He'd laugh, and off we'd go, spinning, diving and looping the loop.

The thrill we both felt gave me the idea of a really exciting gift for his sixtieth birthday: a parachute drop. I would drop with him. It would be an adventure.

When I told Mac, our glider-pilot friend, that we'd signed up for a parachuting course, he gaped. "Parachuting? At your age? Planning to kill yourselves, are you?" A grin started at the corners of his mouth. "Anyway, how will you cope with jumping from a plane? I'm told you freak out even at the thought of driving a car."

I gave him a dirty look. "You can get killed driving a car." With a shudder I remembered my last driving-lesson when I'd almost knocked down a cyclist and very nearly killed myself and my driving-instructor at the same time. Confidence shattered, I'd cancelled my next lesson. At least, with parachuting, I thought, I was risking only my own life, not everyone else's as well.

Mac heaved a sigh. "You can get killed all sorts of ways," he agreed. "But anyone jumping from a plane by choice wants his head read. It's a hell of a dangerous sport."

I rolled that over in my mind. If anyone knew about danger Mac did. Time after time he'd taken risks with his glider and his powered aircraft. It seemed though he drew the line at parachuting.

I choked back the flutter of nervousness rising to my throat. Damn it! I wasn't going to back out now. Not when it was all arranged and paid for. And Pat was crazy on the idea. I did have a more personal motive. I wanted to prove to myself that for once in my life I'd do something that took guts. And who knows? If I dared to jump from an aircraft, I might eventually dare to drive a car again. I'd show that Mac I wasn't some ageing wimp.

When the time came, we stayed at the Shobden Parachute Club overnight, so we could turn up on the dot for our one-day crash course the following morning. It was a beginners' course, starting at 8.30 in the morning and ending with the jump at 5.00 in the afternoon.

Pat and I exchanged wry smiles as we scanned the rest of the group. We were the only senior citizens there. And I was the only woman. The others were all lads, sturdy, and ready for anything.

The morning's events started off with a lecture and discussion on the mechanics of parachuting. Not knowing the mechanics of *anything*, I surprised myself by asking a couple of intelligent questions. At least, that's what the instructor called them.

After this, things became more physical, with a long session of exercises such as press-ups, followed by intensive training in the techniques of parachute landing. One after another, we practised falling, landing and rolling under the scrutiny of the coach.

"How much longer is this going on for?" Pat asked me with a sigh. "I'm puffed out. And I feel like a geriatric, trying to keep pace with these youngsters."

"Look on the bright side," I said. "There's no time to get in a flap about the actual jump while we're so busy practising it."

But as the day wore on, I could feel myself getting more and more jittery. This feeling approached fever pitch when, in the middle of the afternoon, we had a lesson on emergency procedures – what to do, for example, if the parachute proved faulty. "In this case," the coach said, "you'll have to abandon it and pull the rip-cord to release your spare one."

"Suppose that's faulty too, or the rip-cord gets stuck and you can't pull it?" I whispered to Pat.

"Listen, and maybe you'll find out!" he whispered back.

The coach went on. "Again, there's the problem of an unexpected wind springing up and blowing you into a tree. The important thing here is to shield the face."

At this point I really began to lose nerve. The possibility of having a faulty parachute or of crashing into a tree set my whole body trembling. I began to pray that the drizzle that had started up would develop into a thunderstorm so that our jump would have to be postponed. I'd be spared then the shame of having to chicken out.

But the drizzle stopped. The sun came out, and at five o'clock Pat and I, rigged out in our parachute gear were standing with three others from our group, ready to step into the small plane awaiting us.

My inside felt like jelly. So far, I had won the battle with my nerves. There was still time to disgrace myself, but I knew that, once on the plane, there was no backing out. If, at the last moment, I refused to jump, not only would I be letting myself and my sex down, I would also be letting down the group. Being the lightest, it was my job to jump first. If I didn't, no one else could either, for I'd be blocking their way to the exit-hatch. In my mind's eye I could see three disappointed young men fuming over their bad luck at being placed in a group with an elderly female who, predictably, copped out at the last moment.

"Feeling okay?" Pat asked, squeezing my hand as he helped me into the plane.

"Fine," I lied, making an effort to keep my voice steady. "Happy birthday."

There was very little room on the plane. We were huddled together like factory-farm chickens. I, being the first to exit, knelt near the doorway. At a signal from the coach I was to sit facing it, legs splayed out, a foot on each side of the opening, waiting for the order, "Jump!"

My teeth were chattering now as, through the exit-hatch, I could see the ground getting further and further away until soon only clouds were visible below me. I began to feel physically sick. "Give me a push when the time comes," I urged the pilot.

It's funny, but I can't seem to remember if I was pushed, or if I jumped. When I try to recall that crucial moment of dropping out, my mind remains a blank.

What is clear to me is the interval between that moment and the moment my parachute opened. It should have been the most nerve-shattering point in the course. But it wasn't. I was still nervous, of course, but now my anxiety was mingled with a kind of exhilaration. I felt not so much the sensation of hurtling down to earth, more the feeling of swimming through space.

At the same time, I had to follow instructions. First, I had to manoeuvre my body into the correct spread-eagle position. This wasn't easy, with the wind buffeting me about. Also, I had to yell out the seconds: ten, nine, eight…

On the seventh count, the parachute opened. I breathed a sigh of relief. So far, so good. All I had to do now was grasp the wooden toggles and steer myself towards the landing place marked with an orange cross.

It was at this point that I faced my first hitch. I couldn't *see* the landing place. A voice came over my radio: "Face the cross, number one!"

I desperately scanned the panorama of fields and hills spread below but could recognise nothing, let alone the cross.

Over the radio the voice repeated the instruction. I began to sweat. Then, in dismay, I realised what was wrong. In my haste, I had put on my reading-glasses instead of my distance ones. No wonder everything below looked so hazy. The instructor tried a different tactic. "Pull your right toggle."

I did so but, although I was getting nearer and nearer the ground, I still couldn't make out in any detail what was below me. There was no sign of the orange cross and, whether it was a field of corn or a forest that was rushing up to meet me, I could not tell.

I got into the correct position for landing, closed my eyes and prepared for the crash which would surely knock me senseless, if it didn't kill me.

To my amazement, I met the ground with a gentle bump and sustained not even a graze. I had landed in a field of corn. I lay there a moment, elated. I'd done something dangerous, extravagant, rash. And I was still alive to tell the tale. After this, I thought, what are driving lessons? I would take them in my stride.

Admittedly, I'd bungled the landing. Not that I was the only one. I later learned that one unlucky young man had dropped on the runway and broken his ankle. Another had fallen amongst a herd of cows who tried to eat his parachute! Pat, of course, landed bang in the middle of the cross. He would!

A few weeks after our return home we phoned Mac. I was eager to tell him that, having participated in 'a hell of a dangerous sport' without mishap, I now felt quite relaxed about driving.

Sadly, we were never to chat or joke with Mac again. We later learned from the Gliding Club that he had been *killed* – in a car crash.

The irony of his death stunned us. That Mac, so keen to point out the dangers of parachuting, should himself be killed – driving his *car*, seemed as unlikely an outcome as the contrived twist at the end of a tale.

Except that it was true.

We haven't repeated our parachuting adventure. For me, once is enough. Pat says he'd like another shot, but adds, "So long as I don't have to go through all those exercises again."

Yet, even if it turns out to be our last as well as our first experience, I'm glad I plucked up the courage to do it. It's done wonders for my ego.

I have to confess though that I still haven't learnt to drive. After hearing about Mac's accident, I cancelled the lesson I'd arranged, and I've yet to arrange another.

CHAPTER THIRTY-SEVEN

TRAVELLERS' TALES

Hard though it was to drag Pat away from his beloved garden, I did manage to push him into touring the country with me now and again, even into taking trips abroad. This was easier now he was retired and I was teaching part-time.

Betty and Gordon volunteered to water the garden in our absence, while Christopher, a nice, reliable schoolboy from the other side of the lane, offered to feed the cats.

I had a preference for the exotic. And our tours abroad included Tunisia, Thailand, Singapore, Jamaica and Bali as well as less far-flung places such as Italy and Crete. I'd like to write about all of them. However, since this is a life story, not a travelogue, I'll confine myself to two areas only and a single incident experienced in each.

The first was an incident we met with in Jamaica in 1981.

We were strolling along the sea front, past a row of banana trees when Pat spotted a boathouse. "Let's hire a boat," he said.

"But we're not dressed for a boat trip." I looked down at my high-heeled shoes and smart new sun frock.

He shrugged and went ahead anyway.

Typical Pat. If, all of a sudden, there was something he wanted to do, and a chance to do it, then do it he would. No stopping to consider if we were suitably prepared. Or bothering about possible consequences.

That's how we came to be sitting in the little red sailing-boat, drifting further and further away from the shores of Jamaica. My husband, dressed in his new tropical suit, was busy attending to the sail. I, clutching my sun-hat with one hand, my handbag with the other, was trying to maintain the boat's balance by constantly changing my sitting position. That's when I wasn't ducking my head to avoid being struck by the boom.

The trouble started when we sailed into a rough patch of water where gentle little waves gave way to big bold ones. They slapped aggressively against the sides of the boat and sometimes spat into it.

I had to keep really busy, shifting my weight from one side of the boat to the other in an effort to keep it the right way up. Pat, a worried frown on his face now, was trying to turn it round so we could make for the shore again.

But the boat was unpredictable and didn't seem to want to turn round. It was I who got the blame.

"Isn't it about time you did your share of the work?" Pat demanded. "It's obvious you're more interested in trivia, like that handbag of yours, than in keeping us afloat."

"Well, I like that!" Flames of indignation shot up inside me. "We'd both be overboard by now, if it wasn't for me." I was about to give him another mouthful, when the boom gave me a whack across the head. I swore at it, furious, forgetting for a moment my job of keeping the boat the right way up.

It was at that moment that the bow rose from the water and I found myself sitting below in the stern.

We were about to capsize.

There was an ominous splash. A second later, Pat was nowhere to be seen.

Still clutching my handbag, I threw my weight towards the toppling bow. Instantly, it dropped, and the boat was the right way up again.

But where was Pat?

My heart began to pound.

There was a splashing and a floundering nearby. Suddenly, an arm appeared above the waves. A grim face followed. I let out a gasp of relief and held out a helpful arm. He ignored it, and dragged himself over the stern. I raced to the bow and sat down hard.

Pat, coughing and spluttering, was dripping sea-water from his sad, tropical suit. It was clear he'd never be able to wear it again. On top of everything else, he had lost a shoe. Tight-lipped, he ignored such trivia, focussing his whole attention on turning the boat into calm waters. This time he managed it, and soon we were sailing for the shore again.

"If you'd been concentrating more on the boat, and less on your handbag and that ridiculous sun-hat, we'd have been all right," he growled.

I suggested, unnecessarily perhaps, that next time we went sailing we'd dress for the occasion and leave behind air-tickets, dollars, travellers cheques, camera and other such trivia I kept in my handbag.

"How was I to know you were going to hire a boat?" I demanded.

Pat, still wet and minus a shoe, said nothing. But if looks could have killed...

Following our week in Jamaica, we travel on to Haiti where Papa Doc's son, Baby Doc, is in power.

One evening we take a trip to the backwoods in a battered looking taxi. Rattling along mile after mile we watch the sun sink into the horizon leaving us steeped in darkness. It's startling how swift and sudden night falls here. It seems to drop like a black curtain, shutting out all signs of life.

I lean forward in the taxi. "How much further, Pierre? Are you sure we're on the right road?"

Our driver laughs. "Don't worry, Madame. I not lose the way. We arrive soon. Okay?"

Patrick sighs. "He told us that half an hour ago."

I'm growing uneasy. We seem to have driven for miles in the setting sun, along the bumpy roads of Haiti, way past Port au Prince. We've covered remote villages, hills and barren plains. Now, in the darkness, it's hard to tell where we are. We seem to be driving into a forest.

I nudge Patrick. "This is scary. Let's go back."

I sense his lips tightening in the darkness, the stubborn gleam in his eyes. "Turn back? When we've got this far? You're joking."

He's been cross with me all day for arranging this trip.

"You didn't even bother to consult me," he grumbles. "What I wanted was to do something normal for a change. Like go out to dinner."

Pierre hears us bickering. He grounds the car to a halt and turns to face us.

"Be calm, Madame. You will enjoy it. There will be dancing and singing. It will be – how you say? – the bright light of your vacation. Okay?" He opens the car-door, his chocolate-brown face beaming with enthusiasm. "Me? I will enjoy it also." He jumps out. "Come. We arrive."

What? Here?

We clamber out, glancing around us. We are in some sort of clearing, surrounded by trees. From the light of the moon breaking through the clouds, we see at the far end, a raised courtyard or stage with a ceremonial altar at the back. It looks like a temple. In front is a scattering of chairs.

We follow Pierre to the courtyard and grab two of them. Pierre grabs another.

We sit silent in the darkness, waiting. Before us is the temple, pillared, roofed and empty. And out of the stillness, from behind it, comes the croaking of a thousand frogs, harsh and unceasing.

I chew at my fingers, still wishing we hadn't come. But it's too late now. In this solitary shanty-town at the edge of the forest, we are far from the lights of Port au Prince. There's no going back yet. Patrick I know will not be persuaded. As for our driver, he can't wait for the thing to begin.

Already though, I'm feeling queasy. Annoyed with myself too, at having made such a blunder.

It was I who had wanted to come, threatening to go alone, if Pat wouldn't come with me.

In my ignorance, I'd expected a drive to some lush hotel where we'd see dancing girls going into trances to the sound of Voodoo drums. A synthetic entertainment for the tourists – such tourists as existed. Our own hotel was empty apart from ourselves and a couple of Americans.

We chatted with one of them tonight while waiting for Pierre. He was quick to confirm Pat's fears about the 'entertainment' I'd arranged. "I doubt if it's a floor show," he said, with a chuckle, "or some fake ritual. But everyone to his taste, I guess."

A tremor of dismay rose to my throat. I shook it off. It's an assumption, I told myself, not fact.

So far, Pierre had not let us down. We enjoyed our trip to Kenscoff up in the mountains to visit the Friday market; our drive through the main streets of the capital, to see its art galleries and restaurants.

We'd had glimpses of the Tonton Macoute, of course, the president's loyal and sinister militia men. Pierre told us that the name in English was *Mr Knapsack* and that it stemmed from an African legend in which a scary old man grabbed children unawares and carried them off in his sack.

From what I've heard of the Tonton Macoute, it's an apt name.

And tonight, on the way here, Pierre showed us the rest of Port au Prince, eager to point out prisons and palaces, a famous brothel, and, of course, the presidential building of Baby Doc. We saw grimmer sights: a legless man, crossing the road, like a crab; barefoot children rummaging in the dirt.

Leaving the capital, we passed through squalid shanty-towns. Then on and on through bare darkness, where poverty is sensed rather than seen. No hotels now. No music. Nothing except the chorus of frogs and the occasional screech of a cockerel.

A stirring from behind the courtyard forces me back to the present. Beams of torchlight, a murmur of voices, then footsteps coming closer in an even stride. Soon a massive woman, turbaned, and dark as night, strides up the steps and onto the courtyard. She is bedecked with candles.

"That's the Mambo," Pierre whispers.

She sets up the candles, arranges them into groups and lights them one by one, slowly and carefully. After that, she kneels down and, in the flickering light, chalks upon the floor the required signs and symbols in preparation for the ceremony.

Having performed these initial rites, she rises and disappears into the darkness.

Now the Voodoo drums begin to beat. A shrill chanting breaks out. And devotees of the Voodoo faith dressed in a riot of colour, snake their way to the candlelit floor, moving and singing in rhythm to the drum-beat.

The ritual dance has begun.

The music is monotonous, but hypnotic. There are three drums. The largest is the *mamman*. The leader-drummer beats this fiercely with one stick and a hand. The drums are for summoning the spirits to come and possess the performers' bodies.

Once the music starts the mambo takes a kind of rattle from the altar and joins the others.

The songs, like the drum-beats, are hypnotic, the voices piercing. The dancers are tireless. On and on they go, like bright, tropical birds flitting across the stage until, one after another, swooning and trembling, they drop to the floor in a trance.

As the dance approaches its end the drumbeat quickens.

Soon I see a young man fetch a chicken on to the stage. The poor thing looks half-dead already. He swings it backwards and forwards as he dances round and round on the temple floor.

I close my eyes to shut out the sight. But I can guess what is happening. The man is killing the chicken, biting through its neck until it's dead. The chicken lets out not a single squawk.

This marks the end of the ritual.

There is an outburst of appreciative shouts and claps from Pierre, and some gentler clapping from me and Patrick in a show of politeness.

We rise slowly and soon we are hobbling along behind Pierre to his taxi. It's late and we're half asleep. As Pierre drives us back to our hotel, I fall into an uneasy doze. I see again the young man dancing round the stage with the sacrificial chicken. Only this time, *I* am the chicken. I feel helpless and giddy as I'm swung backwards, forwards, round and round. Suddenly, the dancer stops. I see his jaws open and gleaming white teeth ready to strike at my neck…

I wake with a jump.

As we drive on, I try to rationalise the ritual killing of the bird. It is, I'm told, a humane way of despatching an animal. Maybe. I doubt, anyway, if the sacrificial chickens here are any worse off than the battery hens we have at home. As for our horror of violence to animals, we are both prepared to eat meat, so what are we but hypocrites?

Pat is hungry. It's a long time since we've eaten. I expect we'll have a snack at the hotel before going to bed. Some sandwiches perhaps.

Hopefully, not chicken.

CHAPTER THIRTY-EIGHT

THE CHOCOHOLIC

I loved Christmases with Pat. We got loads of presents, including gifts from his ex-wives. We kept them up in the loft till Christmas day. When that day arrived, I'd bring them down and we'd spend the morning unwrapping them in bed. Thinking of this routine, I'm reminded of one particular Christmas when we found more than we bargained for in our spacious loft.

It was ten days before Christmas when I made the discovery. I'd gone up to hunt for an old coat, one I'd worn in my mini-skirted days and had a sudden urge to wear again.

Not that it would do as a *coat* any more, I thought, unless mutton-dressed-as-lamb was to be my new fashion statement. A white leather coat, trimmed with fur, and cut well above the knee, was hardly the in-thing for the mature woman. Still, worn as a jacket, over a sensible skirt or trousers, who knows?

I clambered from the top rung of the ladder to the loft floor and straightened. You could do this in our loft. It was huge, like a barn. It was also *packed* with stuff. We were hoarders, Patrick and I. Dismembered toys, torn bedding, scribbled-on books, up they came. There were lines of clothes on hangers, in boxes and sacks. "You never know," I'd tell myself, "they might come back into fashion."

It was going to take time and patience to find that coat.

I glanced to my left. As I did so, my mouth started watering. A stack of chocolates all ready for my Christmas binge were piled up there, together with early gifts from friends and relatives, probably chocolates too. Daft place to keep them, I suppose. On the other hand, up here in the loft, they were out of the way, less easy to get at. The truth is, I'm a chocoholic. I've been trying to curb my addiction, especially as waistbands get tighter, and bulges develop in so many places. "Don't ask me if your bum looks big in those trousers," Pat warned. "You might not like the answer."

Like it or not, I could *smell* those chocolates, and *taste* them. An imaginary piece filled with soft caramel lay on my tongue, waiting to be rolled around.

I felt my will power crumble. Perhaps, I thought, if I just check on the pile…

I stepped to my left, knelt down and peered into the open box displaying the chocolates.

That's when I let out a gasp. Every bar and box had been vandalised: wrappings torn off, boxes bitten into, half-eaten chocolate liqueurs, spilling their sticky contents over everything. A giant chocolate Santa had its silver tunic ripped to shreds, while its head was nowhere to be seen. Not a single item had remained untouched.

Forgetting all about the coat, I sprang to my feet and clumped down the loft-ladder, uttering threats of violence at every step.

Patrick, was working at his computer in the study.

"Who's been after my chocolates?" I demanded. "They're half-eaten."

"Don't look at me. I wouldn't dare." He got up. "Sure you haven't eaten them yourself?"

"Don't be stupid. I wouldn't eat my Christmas stuff."

"Must be mice then." He heaved a sigh. "That's *all* we need. We'll have to get the council in."

Mice. So *they* were the intruders. I should have guessed. I pulled a face. I was partial to most animals, but not at all sure about mice. I didn't care for their pointy faces or worm-like tails.

"How will they get rid of them?" I asked.

Pat shrugged. "Poison, I expect."

"That's horrible. "I don't want the poor things suffering, thieves or no."

Pat put on his thinking look. "There are humane traps," he said at last. "You stick in something tasty. Mouse makes a dive for it, and, wham, door shuts, and you've got him."

"Then *I* come to the rescue. That sounds better."

Pat frowned. "It'll be hard work. You can't let them into the garden. They'll only find their way back to the loft again."

"That's okay. I'll take them to the woods and free them there."

"If you don't mind traipsing half a mile every morning."

He stepped into the passage. "I'd better get rid of those chocolates. They won't be any good now."

"No." I followed him out. "There are bits the mice haven't got at: Santa's feet, for example."

He shook his head. "You're mad. They'll be full of germs, even mouse-droppings, I shouldn't wonder."

My heart sank, but the thought of mouse-droppings did take the edge off my appetite.

"It's crazy anyway, storing chocolates in the loft. Bound to attract mice."

I watched him climb the loft-ladder, thinking of my chocolate feast, or what was left of it, being flung without mercy into the bin.

"You'd better keep *some*," I called up, "to put in the mouse-trap."

Pat bought the trap later that day. "Not much room for a mouse to move in," I said.

I found a transparent box, roomier than the trap, with air-holes in it. I'll transfer each mouse into that, I thought, then I'll take it to the woods and set it free.

That night, Pat took the trap to the loft and put some chocolate in it. The next morning when I went up to investigate, I found a small brown mouse sitting inside, a look of surprise on its face.

I felt a flutter of nervousness as I picked up the trap. I'd never seen a mouse up close before. I took it downstairs, setting it carefully on the kitchen table. I felt sorry for the poor thing. It was anxious to get out and trying to climb the walls. I opened the trap and dropped the mouse carefully into the box lying beside it. I quickly jammed down the lid. It sniffed around, then began to wash its face.

"Come on, I'll give you a lift," Pat said, his face appearing at the kitchen-door. "But don't expect it every morning. About time you learnt to drive."

When we arrived at the fringe of the woods, I lay the box on the grass, and opened it. The mouse peered around him, seeming in no hurry to go. At last he placed his front paws at the top edge of the box and peeped over. Finally, he jumped out and scampered away till all you could see was the whisk of his tail.

Every morning, it was the same routine. I grew quite fond of the creatures. "Look how they wash themselves: the backs of their necks, behind their ears," I told Patrick.

One little mouse let me stroke its head while it washed. It felt soft, delicate. I stopped worrying about their long tails and pointy faces. "They're pretty," I said.

Pat gave me a stern look. "They might be pretty," he said, "but they harbour germs. We should have got the council in. God knows how many more mice are up there."

Freud would have found Pat an interesting case. He's obsessed about germs. If a can falls out of the fridge, he'll wash it before putting it back. And if he offers to do the dishes, he sees they're thoroughly hand-washed first, before being popped in the dish-washer.

You can guess, therefore, what a flap I was in when, one morning, an unusually clever and athletic little mouse refused to be dispatched from the trap to the box but leapt down to the floor instead.

He scuttled through the kitchen seeking a way out. I tried to catch him but he vanished behind one of the units.

Pat threw a fit at the news. "I knew something like this would happen." He flung up his hands. "It was stark staring mad, dropping a mouse from a trap into a box."

He took the trap from the loft, put chocolate in it and shoved it behind the wall-unit nearest the kitchen-door.

That night, taking a peep in the trap, I found that the chocolate had gone. So had the mouse.

"That's one clever mouse," I exclaimed.

Tight-lipped, Pat adjusted the spring, put in more chocolate, and placed it behind the unit again.

The same thing happened. In the morning, the chocolate was gone, along with the mouse.

"It's a Mensa mouse," I gasped.

"Mensa nothing. It's that useless trap." He flung it in the bin in disgust. "I'll get a new one."

I felt sad to find the plucky little mouse imprisoned in the new trap the following morning. When I looked at him sitting forlornly in his glass prison, he turned away, as if embarrassed, and hurriedly washed his face.

That morning I took him, still in his trap, into the woods. Pat drove me there. He wanted to make sure that it was the last he'd see of this bold mouse.

We kept the new trap in the loft for the next few days, but no more mice got caught in it. I was relieved. Pat had threatened to call the council.

However, the day before Christmas, I came across something else up there. A mass of white stuff spilling out of a dust-bag which I'd thought was full of old toys.

I pulled it out. It was the white coat I'd come up to find in the first place – at least, what was left of it. Leather and fur had been nibbled away. It wasn't even fit for a jumble-sale.

Sadly, I held out the remains and scanned them. I shook my head. I must have been crazy to imagine it would still fit, even as a jacket. Had I really been that slim those years ago?

I carried it down the loft ladder, to shove in the bin.

Perhaps the mice had done me a favour. They'd found my coat, reminding me how much weight I'd put on over the years. And they'd stolen my chocolates, helping me start on my new year's resolution.

But it's not the New Year yet and I'm off to do some last minute Christmas shopping. I shan't go mad, but I'm a strong believer in the old saying: *A little of what you fancy does you good.*

CHAPTER THIRTY-NINE

AN ECHO FROM THE PAST

It's months since I've visited Frieda. She's been ill and unable to practise therapy.

But she's back now, and today I'm visiting her again. This visit, I've decided, will be the last. I've learned to accept myself and my undistinguished past. In the greater scheme of things what does it matter? I'll make the most of the time left.

As soon as I step into her consulting room, I have to suppress a gasp. She seems to have aged by ten years. Her clothes are hanging, scarecrow-like from her body – she's lost weight – and her face has faded to a pale grey. I notice her hand tremble as she reaches for her notebook on the table. What's been wrong with her? Has she had something really awful like the Big C?

We exchange polite greetings. "So sorry to hear you were ill," I say. "I hope you're okay now."

She gives a faint smile and murmurs, "Thank you. I'm fine." Then, slowly, she opens her notebook, ready to get down to business.

I'm silent as she turns the pages, thinking, she doesn't *look* fine. I'm wondering if she has family or friends to help her, but don't like to ask. It seems impolite somehow for a client to ask a therapist about her domestic arrangements.

She coughs. "You were going to tell me about your daughter and if you managed to trace her. We didn't get round to discussing it at our last session." Her voice sounds weak and wavery like water-weeds.

"No, I didn't manage to trace her." I pause. "But that doesn't mean it was the end of things."

I pull off my scarf and hang it on the back of my chair, cross my legs, and start thinking back. Then, taking a deep breath, I plunge into my story.

Not long after our move to Silvertrees, I received an unexpected call from my cousin, Mair in Wales. "An old acquaintance wants to contact you," she said, "She sounded genuine enough so I gave her your number and new name."

"Did she say who she was?"

"Hm. Something Bennet – I think."

An old school friend, I thought, or someone from college.

The following evening the phone rang. I was busy fixing dinner. With a groan, I snatched the receiver from its cradle and barked into it, "Yes?"

The caller sounded young, hesitant. "Hullo. Is that Catherine Osborn? My name's Amanda Bennet. Is it okay to talk?" I uttered a grudging 'yes' and she went on, "I'm – your daughter. Could we meet some time?"

In an instant the spluttering of steak frying and smell of onions faded from my consciousness. My daughter?

I sank into a chair, struggling to maintain my grip on the telephone. My head spun. More than twenty-five years, I thought, since I lost my child. I'd given up hope of ever finding her. Now, *she* had found *me*. She must have got my details from the Adoption Agency – my maiden name, place of birth…

My voice came out faint, quavery, as I replied, "I'd love to, Amanda."

I remember that meeting as though it were yesterday. Remember standing outside Romano's at the corner of Baker Street. It's close to Amanda's work, and not too out-of-the-way for me.

Pat knows my secret. He wanted to come too. But I decided to meet Amanda alone this first time.

While I'm waiting, fumes from a noisy stream of traffic assault my nose and mingle with the smell of coffee drifting out of Romano's each time the door opens and shuts.

My heart is racing as I scan each young woman who passes by, wondering if it can be this one or that one. 'Small and slim' is all I have by way of description.

Anyway, she's bound to see me standing here. I've told her what I look like and what I'll be wearing. Once she glimpses my beige outfit she'll guess it's me. We'll exchange smiles, and go for a bite to eat. It will be lovely.

At least, I hope so.

I can't help having qualms. How will we get on? Will she like me? Will I like her?

The questions buzzing in my head make my pulse race, my palms feel clammy. She'll quiz me perhaps. Demand answers to awkward questions. And how shall I respond? Honesty is the best policy, they say. But sometimes the truth can be too brutal. I'll play it by ear.

My thoughts scatter. Someone is stopping, trying to catch my eye. A young woman in a maroon jacket. Is it her? She's slim and about my height, with dark hair, cascading down her back. And her eyes are blue, like mine, though bigger and brighter. She gives a tentative smile.

It *is* her. My heartbeat starts to quicken.

"Hullo, you must be Catherine. Good to meet you." She holds out her hand.

We go into Romano's and grab a table in a corner.

I can't stop staring at her. She's quite good-looking with her peachy skin, and dark, curling eye-lashes. Not that looks matter. Still, I'm glad she's attractive.

"I often come here in my lunch break," she says. Her tone is soft, lilting.

I'm suddenly at a loss for words, and I can feel my face getting hot. I put on my busy, taking-charge voice. "What will you have, Amanda?"

"An orange juice, please, and some salad. I'm vegetarian."

"For health reasons?"

She shakes her head. "I just hate the thought of animals being killed."

I look up from my menu in surprise. "That's just how I feel. I couldn't become vegetarian, though. If I did, I'd probably starve. I *hate* vegetables." I give a self-conscious laugh before plying her with anecdotes about my beloved cats, Mimi and Lulu.

Oh dear. I pause. I'm beginning to gabble. And I so much wanted to make a good impression.

The waitress comes to take our order.

When she goes, I'm tongue-tied again.

Amanda helps me out, chatting about her home in Surrey with her adoptive parents, her plan to move into a flat. "Not that I'm unhappy at home," she assures me. "The family's great. But I'm twenty-six. It's time I moved."

She goes on to talk about her work. "I've been illustrating children's books since leaving university," she says. "I love it."

She got that from me perhaps. I was good at art once.

She turns to the subject of her boy-friend and her eyes begin to sparkle. "John's an accountant. He came with me to the Adoption Agency for information and helped me trace you. He's clever at things like that."

She's done well. Good education, clever boy-friend, work she enjoys. How well would she have done, I wonder, with a lone mother struggling to bring her up?

I can't take my eyes off her. It sounds daft, I know, but the idea that I'd actually produced another human being who could walk, talk, paint pictures and be a vegetarian struck me as amazing.

She looks anxious a moment. "I hope it's not a problem, meeting me like this? I'm not needing help or anything. It's just…" She pauses, searching for words. "I've had this urge to find my birth-parents, discover my roots. I kept dreaming about it."

Then comes the dreaded question, "Didn't you *want* to have me?"

She's frowning now, leaning forward, her eyes flickering over my face. I feel my cheeks beginning to burn again.

No, I didn't, the voice in my head answers. If abortions had been legal then, I'd have had one like a shot. As it was, I did my best to drown you with gin, poison you with obnoxious powders and blast you to smithereens through deliberate tumbles downstairs. Nothing worked. I was stuck with you.

I toy with my napkin. "I didn't at first." I say. "Soon after you were born, though, I was desperate to *keep* you. But I had no means. I was alone, you see. It was difficult for single mothers in those days."

She smooths back her hair, breaks into a smile. "I realise that. And there was the stigma, too."

I nod, remembering the raised eyebrows and frowns of disapproval. Although it was 1962, the 'swinging sixties' was yet to come. Waves of half-forgotten shame flow in again, like the returning tide. I'll lose my teaching job, I wailed, once they find out. How will I cope? Run to my parents? No way. They had enough problems. And I'd sooner die than meet the father again.

In mounting panic, I pretended I'd got married, and became Mrs Barclay. Six months passed before the education authority caught on and demanded an interview. It made me squirm, having finally to spill out the truth.

Then came the horror of putting myself in the hands of social services, and moving to a mother-and-baby home. And, finally, the hospital stay, when the baby was due. I was the only one on the ward with no visiting husband.

The waitress bustles up with the omelette I've ordered, and my daughter's salad.

Amanda adjusts her napkin. "What about my father? Do you know where he is?"

My mouthful of omelette acquires a sour taste. Here comes the creative part. I haven't decided what to say about *him*. "He's dead," I mumble at last. I look away. Well, perhaps he is by now.

A frown puckers her forehead. She looks disappointed. "Dead?"

"Well, not exactly." I shift in my chair. No use going along that route. One lie will only lead to another. "He's just dead to *me*, that's all." My voice crackles, sounds false. "And I don't know where he is. It happened at a party, you see. There was too much to drink and…" I shrug.

She can see I'm embarrassed. "It's okay. Stuff happens." She picks at her lettuce. "I've found you anyway. That's the main thing."

I smile at her, relieved. She's making things so easy. I've told her she's the end-product of a one-night stand. And she takes it in her stride.

What if I'd told her the *truth*, though, the whole truth?

What if I told her I'd stupidly gone out to lunch with a man, not because I liked him but because his constant pestering wore me down; that even more stupidly, I went to his flat afterwards and let him ply me with drinks? What if I told her how when staggering to the door later, intending to leave, I found he'd locked it? Or how he dragged me back, clapping his hands over my mouth to stop me shouting.

I couldn't have told her that. Any more than I could have told how I'd tried to abort her. Or how I wouldn't even *look* at her for two days after she was born. Some truths are better left untold.

She finishes her salad. "At least, you didn't get an abortion. I'm dead against abortions."

I wince. I can see she feels strongly about this. She's tossing back her hair, and her eyes are flashing. I can't agree with her, though. Much depends on the circumstances.

"I did want to keep you," I say, trying to steady my voice. "Not straight away, but once we got… attached. I even tried

293

to get you back after your adoption. But it was too late then. And it wouldn't have been fair to you or your adoptive parents."

She nods her agreement.

I feel happier now. The hard part is over. I finish my omelette and order a lemon mousse for Amanda and an ice cream for me.

We chat about other things, about Patrick, our village in Hertfordshire, and my hobby: amateur dramatics. "I used to be professional," I tell her.

Our talk becomes more animated. "I like acting too," she says. "John and I belong to the local drama society. We'll soon be rehearsing for the Christmas pantomime. Perhaps you and Patrick would like to come?" She pauses, eyebrows raised in question. "He does know about me?"

"Of course. And he's dying to meet you."

We seem to have much in common. Maybe there's more to heredity than meets the eye.

Anyway, things go with a swing after that. Our mutual love of the theatre has broken the ice.

We shall meet again, I know. My inhibitions have gone. So have my regrets. It hadn't been easy being unmarried and pregnant those years ago. Still, I'm glad now I failed to get that abortion. I'd had a child, a living, feeling human being. The thought fills me with an inner glow.

"Let's meet again. Soon," I say.

She takes out her diary.

"And did you go on meeting her?" Frieda asks, her voice transporting me to the present again.

"Yes indeed. She finished with John and married a charming man called Ian. They live in Bournemouth." I add proudly, "I've two little granddaughters now, Rachel and Amy. I stayed with them last Christmas."

A smile lights up her face. "So you're not alone. You have a family. And you're keeping in touch with them."

Her expression changes. She looks awkward a moment. "I'm sorry I've not been here for your therapy sessions. How have you been coping the last few months?"

"Fine," I say, "I've been busy writing my life story."

Her eyes snap open. "Your life story? That sounds like quite a task. Will you get it published, do you think?"

I give a disgruntled laugh. "Writing's a competitive field. Anyway, who'd want to read the life story of someone they've never heard of?"

"Have you had nothing published?"

"Several short stories, in various magazines, that's all."

"Several short stories? But that's success. Many people get nothing published, however hard they try." She leans forward, an earnest look on her face. "Why not focus more on your successes instead of always on your failures?"

"I'll try and remember that." I smile and feel for my scarf at the back of the chair. It's almost time to go.

She closes her notebook and looks at me thoughtfully, a hand propped under her chin. "You seem to be much better. Are you ready yet to manage without therapy?"

She takes a sip of water from the glass on the table and pops a pill into her mouth. "I'm retiring soon and moving to the country to live with my sister. I can pass you on to one of my colleagues if…"

"No, please don't," I say, hastily. "I shall miss my sessions with you, but I'm okay now. I can cope. I dare say I'll still get into dark moods from time to time, but moods change, don't they, whether you have therapy or not? I think mine are as much down to nature as nurture. I've inherited my mother's depressive trait and my father's instability. There's still room for manoeuvre, I know. There are also limitations."

"Perhaps. But psychotherapy has been helpful, I hope?"

I pause. "It's given me a chance to get things off my chest and to put things into perspective," I say, at last.

"I'm glad of that. What you need, as I've said, is to focus less on your failures, more on your successes. It helps too to cultivate friendships."

I wish her well. She gets up a little unsteadily to see me to the door. "I'm thrilled about your meeting with Amanda, by the way. " She takes my hand, squeezes it and adds quietly, "Have you thought that, when you die, you'll be leaving something behind? A part of yourself – not a book or a film-clip – but a *person*, your daughter. That's something to be happy about, isn't it?"

I smile. I shall remember that.

CHAPTER FORTY

LIFE WITH LULU

Thrilling though it was to meet Amanda and to go on meeting her, it saddened me that I had missed out on the joy of watching her grow up.

The only outlet for my maternal instincts was caring for my cats. They were, I suppose, my child-substitutes.

But there were only two left by the time I moved to Hendon with Pat. Poor Figaro, having suffered a pancreatic disorder, was already dead, and buried in Sir Fred's garden. Later, at Hendon, Tigger too died. He was fourteen years old so I suppose he'd had a decent innings for a cat. But during that last year he had lost all his panache. Even the birds in the garden were quick to catch on. They hopped and tweeted around him as if telling each other, "Don't worry about him, mates. He's past it."

There was only Mimi left.

Soon I was longing for another cat.

I finally bought a pretty Persian kitten, calling her Lulu. She was ginger all over and utterly charming. As a kitten, she followed me all round the house and garden but, unlike Tigger, never strayed further than the garden gate. Loving and affectionate, she seemed to like nothing better than to lie in my lap or sit on my Thesaurus while I typed away in my study. Sometimes, she would put her paws round my neck and try to wash my face. At other times, if feeling boisterous, she would spring out at me from behind a chair or a cupboard as if I were a mouse or bird.

Mimi didn't like her. When I introduced the new kitten, she spat at her and ran off. Lulu looked surprised. She tried to be friendly. But Mimi snubbed her advances by growling and scuttling away as though fearful of this new arrival. Why was it, I wondered, that the two males, Tigger and Figaro, had welcomed the arrival of a kitten, whereas Mimi, a female, treated kittens as aliens? Perhaps she was devoid of a maternal instinct.

You soon noticed the contrast in personality between the two.

Lulu was friendly, confident and trusting, Mimi, timid, wary, always expecting the worse.

One day, Lulu jumped on the grand piano. I gave a gasp. Patrick would have a heart attack if he saw her on his precious piano. I gave her a sharp smack. She jumped down but seemed not much bothered by her punishment. It was Mimi who was bothered. She dived under a chair and cowered there for several minutes. Was she afraid she was going to be next, I wonder?

Then there were their different reactions to the hoover. This piece of equipment terrified Mimi. Even while it rested against the wall, she would spit at it and growl before hurrying past, head down, ears back, till well out of its way. And once it was switched on, she'd dash for the cat-door as if a pack of wolf hounds were chasing her.

Not so, Lulu. She adored the hoover, trotting behind it lovingly whenever I switched it on and started cleaning. At the same time she would give out plaintive meows. I knew what she was after. She wanted me to vacuum her coat. I had tried it once for fun. She loved it.

Lulu was an attention-seeker. When we moved to Chipperfield, she developed a habit of climbing onto the roof, then crying for me to get her down again. This meant climbing a ladder and holding out a basket for her to jump into. She was so confident and trusting that she never shied away from jumping. She seemed to enjoy it.

"She can get down perfectly well on her own," Pat said with a laugh. "I've seen her. She just likes the fuss and attention. That's why she goes up in the first place."

He was right. Lulu soon stopped calling for my help once I began to ignore her calls.

She became friendly with the black and white tom in the next lane. He used to appear in the kitchen garden, and Lulu never chased him away. Soon, the inevitable happened. She got pregnant and produced a litter of kittens. Giving birth took her hours and terrified her so much she yowled if I left her alone for only a second.

The kittens were adorable balls of fluff and I spent hours fondling the little beauties. We invited Amanda and John over to see them. Amanda's face lit up with pleasure. "I shall definitely get a cat when I'm settled in my own place," she said.

That heart-warming day ended with a trip in Pat's glider. How lucky I am, I thought, to have a family!

It was sad to see the kittens go to their new owners when they were eight weeks old. Still, I earned myself fifty or sixty pounds from their sale.

"I'd have got much more if they were pure-breds," I told Pat. "Perhaps next time she's on heat, I'll take her to a breeder."

I did. But it turned out to be a great disappointment.

"She rejected my male," the breeder said. "He's a handsome fellow too."

The next time Lulu was on heat, we found her rampaging about with the black and white moggie again. "Just look at that," I grumbled. "She spurns a well-bred Persian for that bit of rough down the lane."

Lulu wasn't the cleverest of cats but she was the cutest and dearest, and loyal and trusting as a dog. There was a close bond between us. I remember falling awkwardly in the garden and dislocating my shoulder. While I lay on the grass moaning, Lulu displayed great distress. She ran in circles around me, meowing frantically as if she knew I was in difficulty but helpless to do anything about it.

The cleverest cat I knew was *Pussy Willow*. Such a silly name to give a self-respecting tom cat, I thought. He belonged to Patrick's ex-wife, Patsy and her husband, David. He was the apple of David's eye.

One night, while having a pleasant drink with them at their flat in Wembley and chatting non-stop, the drawing-room door shuddered open, and in walked Pussy Willow. For a moment, this handsome black male stood majestically at the door, swishing his tail and eyeing us each in turn.

"Meet Pussy Willow," David said proudly.

We continued our chat. But not for long. Pussy Willow, perhaps annoyed at such scant attention, advanced towards us in a determined manner. Reaching the coffee-table between me and Patsy, he sprang upon it, stood on his hind legs and, raising a paw, pulled at the switch-cord attached to the standard lamp, and switched off the light.

All chatter was brought to an abrupt end as Patsy, in the darkness, fumbled for the switch-cord, and flicked it on again. "He wants his supper," she sighed, "but it's too early yet. He'll have to wait."

Pussy Willow, however, had no intention of waiting.

He hovered expectantly at the door for another moment or two, then, receiving no response to his meowing or tail-swishing, he once again advanced upon the coffee-table, leapt up and repeated his performance with the light switch. It was clear that no further conversation would be permitted until he had his supper.

"We have a master-servant relationship," David said with a laugh. "Guess who's the servant."

Some weeks later, he gave me a photograph of his cat in the act of switching off the light. It has pride of place in my special album of cat photographs.

But all good things come to an end, even cats. By the time Lulu had her second litter, Mimi died. She was seventeen, and died of heart failure. Some years later, at the age of fifteen, Lulu, too, died. I was more affected by her death than I was by the death of any of my other cats. She was a companion, and had looked up to me as if to her mother. I wept on and off for three days afterwards. Pat had a lot of consoling to do.

CHAPTER FORTY-ONE

ENTER THE GRIM REAPER

I'm writing this chapter on the 8th April, 2013, a day when one piece of news is dominating our screens. Margaret Thatcher is dead. She died yesterday of a stroke.

Here in the UK feelings about her are mixed. Some see her as a national hero who solved Britain's problems and made her great again. Others see her as a villain who destroyed the manufacturing industries and the communities dependent on them. She also, people say, set off the 'greed is good' ideology, an ideology continued under 'New Labour' and leading to the widening gap between rich and poor.

In my view Margaret Thatcher, though admirable for her courage and determination, was no national hero. But nor, on the other hand, was she a Hitler or a Stalin.

Patrick admired her. Unlike me he veered to the right in his politics. Our opposing views were no problem. They added spice to the conversation helping us to have a better understanding of the other side and sometimes even to modify our views.

I'm writing of Patrick in the past tense because, he too is now dead. He was the same age as Margaret Thatcher but whereas she died yesterday, Pat died thirteen years ago at the age of 75. Our life together lasted twenty-two years and came to an end in the year 2000. Three years before, he had been diagnosed with prostate cancer.

The news sent a pang of alarm rippling through me. But soon a grain of hope intervened. Perhaps they'd got it wrong. Perhaps he'd been misdiagnosed. Possibly his medical details had got muddled with someone else's. Maybe it was all a mistake and he wasn't going to die after all.

Wishful thinking of course. But it wasn't until the last three months that he showed all the signs and symptoms of a life approaching its end. There was no whinging or self-pity but I noticed his pace weaken and his eyes take on a dazed, unfocussed look. He gave up gardening, driving, playing the piano. Instead he shuffled about in his slippers, a pale ghost of his former self. Soon, he lost interest in food and the ability to keep it down.

It was time for me to accept reality.

I believe I wept every day during the last month of his life and not only when I was alone. I wept at the hospice where he lay unconscious. I wept in the middle of shopping or waiting for a bus. Once, a driver, seeing me at a bus stop with tears trickling down my face, stopped his car. "Can I help at all?" he asked. "Drop you somewhere?" He finally drove me from Chipperfield to the hospice in Berkhamstead. Just another instance of the kindness of strangers.

Perhaps I should have felt ashamed of such loss of control, such inability to maintain a stiff upper lip. What would people think? But sometimes you are beyond caring how people judge you.

"I feel I'm losing an arm or leg, losing Pat," I told Betty next door. "I don't know how I can survive without him." She gave me a hug and murmured, "You will."

She was right. Strangely enough, at the funeral, I was dry-eyed. There seemed no tears left to shed.

Many of Pat's work colleagues and friends from the gliding club attended the funeral. So did his two ex-wives, Patsy and Joan, and his first girl-friend, Beryl. Overweight and unsteady on her feet, Beryl had been a beauty in her youth, so Pat had told me. His daughter, Pauline, now calling herself Polly, and divorced from a bullying husband, travelled down from Cumbria with Joan and gave a splendid reading at the funeral service.

Betty and my old friend, Wendy, were there too, giving me much help and support that difficult day.

Amanda came with her husband, Ian and my new little granddaughter, Rachel, a plump little bundle of six months, fussed over by everyone, and angelically quiet during the service. I was glad they could come.

It is odd that, not only was I dry-eyed that day, but I seemed to acquire a boundless supply of energy which stayed with me for many months afterwards. I don't know where it came from or why. I only know that I was able to stay up from dawn to midnight, sorting papers, writing, emptying the garage and the loft, parcelling mementos for the children. This went on for months. And I never got tired. I sometimes even felt I had more energy than I could cope with.

I sold Pat's grand piano and many of his books. The car went too, the proceeds going to his son, Nick. A year later I sold the house and moved from Chipperfield. It wasn't the ideal place for a non-driver. The nearest tube station was five miles away while buses were few and far between. And much as I loved the garden, it was more than I could manage without the help of a full time gardener.

I'll move to London, I decided. More to do. Better still, free travel for the elderly.

Moving from a good sized house in the country to a small flat in London took up much of the energy I had acquired. I also had surplus furniture to store. My plan was to buy a larger property eventually and move there.

But here I am, still in my small flat at Park Crescent. I've wasted much time looking at larger apartments, but I've become attached to this place and hate the thought of leaving it.

I shan't ever forget Patrick and our time together. He brought stability to my life as well as love and companionship. The first thing I did once I'd unpacked my furniture and licked my new flat into shape was to frame my favourite photographs of the two of us together. Later, I framed photos of my two favourite cats, Tigger and Lulu, and added friends and family to my collection.

I didn't give up on life. I got in touch with old friends such as Peter Bauer, joined the U3A, and started writing short stories soon afterwards. Several got published. Others won prizes in writing competitions. These little successes cheered me up and gave my confidence a boost.

I also travelled. I visited Spain for the first time, and later joined a cruise to the Baltic, one of the most enjoyable holidays I've ever had. Part of the reason was that I met there my next and last love: Bill. He lived in Hampstead, and called himself a Jewish atheist. I warmed to him, initially, I suppose, because of his tragic background. He came over here from Vienna at the age of nine with the Kinder transport, missed his parents desperately, then lost them both in the Holocaust.

Bill was one of the nicest, most generous people I have ever met. Like me, he was an animal lover. We made friends with the foxes that visited his garden, feeding them each evening with Sainsbury's sausages. They are wary animals, and I felt over-the-moon when they finally let me watch them feed without running away in panic.

My friendship with Bill lasted seven years after which he too died. Suffering from Type 2 Diabetes, he needed much support during his last years. The condition can cause many problems. He developed a leg-ulcer which became gangrenous. The doctors gave him a choice: Have your leg off. Or die. He chose to die. His daughter, Jo and I did nothing to influence his choice. It was his life, his decision.

"I've had enough," he told us, "It's time to go."

He left hospital to celebrate his 80th birthday and moved a day or two later to a hospice in St John's Wood where he spent his last days. Jo and I visited every day. I read to him from his new book *Lady Godiva* – he loved historical fiction. He finally slipped into unconsciousness and died quietly on January 11th 2009.

Recalling our good times together, I wept silently the whole way through his funeral service.

EPILOGUE

COUNTING MY BLESSINGS

Another year has gone by. It's 2014 and by now I've got used to living alone. It's not so bad. I'm still able to go out and about, meet friends, and keep up my interests at the U3A.

I visit the Welsh valleys from time to time but not with the old enthusiasm. So much has changed, so many old friends and relatives passed away, including Cousin Joan. She died last year and, though almost a recluse towards the end of her life, had more than a hundred people attending her funeral.

Today, here in London, I have woken to a rain-washed April morning. But the rain has cleared now and a watery sunshine is feeling its way into my apartment, sending a shaft of light across the floor. If I sit on the sofa, on the right of my living-room, all I can see through the window is the back of Harley Street with its brick walls, windows and chimney-pots. If, however, I move to the other side, the view improves: walls and windows give way to the fresh green leaves of a mimosa tree standing below.

I'm so lucky to live in the middle of busy London yet only yards away from Regents Park, and with the view of a tree from my window.

Now I think about it, I'm lucky in many ways. At the most basic level I'm lucky to have been born in *this* age, and in *this* country. And I'm very lucky to have been born *human* rather than some less fortunate animal, a farmyard pig, say, or a laboratory rat. And although I haven't become super-rich and famous, I have a comfortable home, good friends and absorbing interests. I also have enough money to get by and to keep me healthy and happy. What more can one ask for?

As for my moans about lost opportunities and lack of achievement, perhaps I should do as my psychotherapist suggested: start reflecting on what I *have* achieved rather than always on what I haven't.

Okay. Let's be more positive:

Through working, saving and educating myself, I managed to climb out of poverty. I didn't progress from rags to riches. To be *rich* these days you need more than a million or so to qualify. But I've progressed from having nothing to having sufficient. Perhaps that's progress enough.

I got my degree in spite of failing the 11+. I got it late but so what? It was still an achievement.

And even though my early ambitions to act and write were reckoned unrealistic, I achieved them. True, I never became a household name in either field. But I've earned money acting, and had at least a dozen stories published and paid for. That makes me professional. Right?

Most important, I found love when I thought it had passed me by. It took a time to arrive. But arriving late doesn't mean it was less cherished. Cherished too has been the building of a relationship with the daughter I thought I'd lost but who came into my life again.

So, on this bumpy journey through time, I've had little successes as well as a variety of memorable experiences. I don't know that I've become a better, wiser character as a consequence. It would help perhaps if I could lose the feeling that unless you've got to the top of the tree, you've failed as a person.

Maybe a change of focus is in order: less on myself, more on the world outside. I used to work for charities: collecting for the RSPCA; selling stuff for the Red Cross; having coffee mornings. Perhaps I should do so again but play a bigger role.

But changing oneself isn't easy. Good intentions and the feelings that translate them into action don't always go hand in hand but in opposite directions.

And there are some things you can't change. They're too ingrained in your basic temperament.

Pondering on ideas of change makes me think of that wonderful prayer by Francis of Assisi. Though not religious, I love his words of wisdom:

> *Lord, grant me the strength to accept*
> *The things I cannot change,*
> *The courage to change the things I can*
> *And the wisdom to know the difference.*

Lightning Source UK Ltd.
Milton Keynes UK
UKOW02f1213160117
292170UK00001B/36/P